BLACK HIGHER EDUCATION IN THE UNITED STATES

BLACK HIGHER EDUCATION IN THE UNITED STATES

A Selected Bibliography on Negro Higher Education and Historically Black Colleges and Universities

COMPILED BY FREDRICK CHAMBERS

GREENWOOD PRESS
WESTPORT, CONNECTICUT • LONDON, ENGLAND

Library of Congress Cataloging in Publication Data

Chambers, Fredrick, 1928-
Black higher education in the United States.

Bibliography: p
Includes index.
1. Afro-Americans—Education (Higher)—Bibliography.
I. Title
Z5814.B44C45 [LC2781] 016.37873 77-91100
ISBN 0-313-20037-8

Library of Congress Catalog Card Number: 77-91100
ISBN: 0-313-20037-8

First published in 1978

Greenwood Press, Inc.
51 Riverside Avenue, Westport, Connecticut 06880

Printed in the United States of America

10 9 8 7 6 5 4 3 2 1

For Doris, Cecilia and Fredrick

CONTENTS

PREFACE

Bibliographical guides, both general and specific, devoted to literature and research on Black Americans are numerous and extensive. However, one of the neglected areas in both *historical* and *educational* historiography is Negro higher education and historically Black colleges and universities in the United States.

Compiling *Black Higher Education in the United States* was begun initially to document published sources on Negro colleges and universities in the United States. The present bibliography represents an effort to bring together in one volume extensive but not exhaustive references to sources of information on various phases of the literature and research on Negro higher education and historically black colleges and universities.

Black Higher Education is a selective bibliography. With few exceptions, this bibliography concentrates on citations in literature and research that are generally available. Primary sources, if not published, disseminated, or available in secondary sources, are not included. No attempt to annotate various citations was made.

This bibliography is composed of an introduction, six chapters, and an index. Entries in each chapter are arranged in alphabetical order by author. For citations in chapter two, alphabetical order of authors' surnames follows state and institutional names. Citations in chapter six are arranged in alphabetical order following each subtitle.

Chapter 1, "Doctoral Dissertations, 1918-1976," includes many general studies that are not well known, and dissertations that have become classics as published books. Chapter 2, "Institutional Histories, 1867-1976," includes many well-known works. However, many colleges and universities are not included in this chapter because of the lack of historical publications on these institutions. Chapter 3, "Periodical Literature, 1857-1976," is the most extensive section of the bibliography. Included are both major and minor citations on almost every phase of literature on black higher education. Chapter 4, "Masters' Theses, 1922-1974," although not well known in the literature, represents much of the early scholarly research work done in historically Black institutions concerning various phases of developments in Negro colleges and universities. Chapter 5, "Selected Books and General References," includes published volumes with particular emphasis on Black colleges and those providing general overviews on higher education. Chapter 6, "Miscellaneous," includes entries that did not readily fit into previous chapters.

This bibliography will be helpful to all of its users. Hopefully librarians, teachers, writers, and researchers in history, higher education, and the history of education will find this volume to be essential in their work. It is also hoped that the identification of the broad range of sources will not only assist persons in several areas but suggest other possible lines of investigation as well as identify the omissions in our knowledge of higher education in the United States.

This bibliography is not without its errors and omissions. The compiler welcomes from readers and users identification of errors, omissions, and suggestions for future editions.

ACKNOWLEDGMENTS

For support, encouragement, and assistance from friends and colleagues in the completion of this volume, I am deeply grateful. Sincere appreciation is extended to John F. Ohles for his interest, enthusiasm, and assistance in the publication of this bibliography; to James P. Louis, who greatly enriched the focus of this volume by contributing an excellent Introduction; to the research librarians and staff members of historically Black colleges and universities, who completed survey forms in 1969, providing many of the citations that are included in this volume; to the librarians of the Reference and Inter-Library Loan Departments of Kent State University Libraries, who provided this compiler with outstanding assistance.

Special appreciation is extended to Vicky Householder, undergraduate student at Kent State University, who cheerfully translated my writing and typed drafts of this bibliography, and to Nancy Flinn, for her expert advice and skill in typing this volume.

INTRODUCTION

In compiling *Black Higher Education in the United States,* Fredrick Chambers has performed a welcome service. Hopefully it also is one that will be put to immediate use by historians, educators, historians of American education, sociologists, and those outside the formal "groves of academe" who concern themselves with matters of "public policy" of significant societal implications. Chambers's work also calls attention to a rather curious paradox abour contemporary American scholarship and the treatment (or virtual absence of analytical treatment) of his subject and provides an indispensable tool for the first step toward its resolution.

The paradox is simply this. Almost inevitably, the selection of subject matter or topic for study, exploration, and analysis by the academic and nonacademic practitioners alluded to above is influenced by the concerns of contemporary society; yet there is a virtual void in scholarly analytical works that dispassionately identify and assess the implications, nature, and roles of the "historically Black" colleges and universities in both the past and the present. Instead, there appear to proliferate dispute about basic "fact"; sharp disagreement in conclusions or assumptions about significance, effectiveness, and purpose; a boggling variance in taxonomical classification, definition, selection, presention, and interpretation of statistical and historical data related to these institutions; a virtual absence of anything approaching a consensus about the respective or collective pasts and presents—much less futures—of these institutions and the significance and effectiveness of their roles as social, socializing, and formally educational agencies of their and the American societies.

Among the issues that the current American generation has seen emerge as issues of vital societal concern and wide, often impassioned, discussion as matters of public policy, two seem especially pertinent. One is the question of the relationship of Black Americans to and within an at last officially integrated American society; the other is that of the validity and implications of America's educational institutions—most especially including those of higher education—as socializing and potentially politicizing agencies of the society. That the obvious connective between these two issues of public policy has not already engendered an exhaustive series of scholarly monographs and sophisticated analyses of the pasts and presents of the conjunction of these respective phenomena is perhaps as striking as is the fact that polemic, presumption, and superficial treatments of past and present to "prove" a predetermined point as to the desired or feared future have been substituted in their absence in the public "debate." That this appears to be no less true of Black social analysts, commentators, and historians than it is of those who have not emerged from or been shaped by the Black Experience only compounds the paradox.

I

As Chambers, among others, noted some time ago, with the exceptions of the Negro family and the Negro church, "Negro colleges and universities are the oldest and most influential institutions in the development of the so-called 'Black Experience' in American life."[1] From Hampton graduate and Tuskegee founder Booker T. Washington and Fisk undergraduate William E. B. Du Bois to the Morehouse-educated Martin Luther King, Jr., precisely these institutions provided the education and in most instances the training grounds and presumably significantly influenced the development and perspectives of virtually all of the race leaders and those viewed as spokespersons or symbols for Black Americans by the American society at large.

Also worthy of more attention from historians and social analysts of the apparently disrupted nature of contemporary America than apparently has been paid to date is the fact that it was from these colleges—including those generally regarded as being among the most prestigious and middle-class in the nature and orientation of their educations and their student bodies—that came the Black student generation that manned the sit-in demonstrations, established new organizations such as SNCC, revitalized and ultimately changed the social and political directions of older organizations such as CORE, and undertook summer projects and voter registration drives during their school recesses. As important as this so unanticipated and dynamic development was for the progress and direction of the Civil Rights Movement, it also constituted both a model and, at least in some instances, the initiation and inspiration for the variety of protest movements that were to follow and were characterized by an unwillingness to accept unquestioned American society and its institutions (including the schools and, most especially, the mores, folkways, traditions, and imposed expectations of the colleges and universities). In so doing, they also generated the response or backlash that has called into question, among other things, the effectiveness and viability of America's colleges and universities at least as social institutions.

Because of the circumstances that called them into existence, influenced their development, and imposed upon them their unique role within American society, these institutions also produced—and presumably significantly influenced—all but a very few of the more anonymous, rather small but nonetheless significantly influential "Black Bourgeoisie" of professionals and middle-class businessmen. (In the mid-1970s National Urban League sources continue to report that their studies indicate that Blacks constitute no more than 2 percent in virtually all of the professions.) The generalization also continues to be offered without significant challenge that the eighty-five historically Black four-year colleges, while encompassing approximately 42 percent of all blacks enrolled in college in the United States, grant 70 percent of the baccalaureate degrees earned by Black students and have educated (presumably, at least on the undergraduate level) virtually all Black dentists, 80 to 85 percent of all Black doctors, 75 percent of all Black military officers, 80 percent of all Black federal judges, 60 percent of all high-level Federal civil servants, and 75 percent of all Black Ph.D.s.[2]

The 1960s saw the imposition of federal law and policy: the forced opening of both public and private colleges to Blacks in compliance with the Civil Rights Act of 1964; the Higher Education Act of 1965 and the explicit conditions of subsequent programs of federal aid to higher education; the expected continuing pattern of Black exodus from the South, where with four exceptions the historically Black colleges are located; the proliferation in the South as elsewhere of public two-year institutions, in which Blacks are inclined to enroll in a significantly higher proportion (40 percent) than the general college population; and the expected continuation of the "boom" in higher education, which was expected to continue significantly to increase the size and number of institutions of higher education to which Blacks would now be compelled, even encouraged under later affirmative action guidelines, to be admitted. Despite these factors that seemed to call into question the future and perhaps even the necessity of the historically Black colleges and universities, these institutions have not shown any significant tendency to "wither away" in terms of either their existence or of their educational/social significance. Although less evenly and less susceptible to reliable projection than had been anticipated a decade ago, tendencies of Black college enrollments to increase and of the historically Black colleges and universities to share significantly in this increase continue to operate.

The estimated 700 to 800 Blacks enrolled in college in 1900 (which would have constituted 0.3 percent of all college enrollments for that year) has escalated at a rate that tends to double every decade to the present. According to the most recently available "Fact Book" of the American Council on Education, Black enrollment in America's colleges and universities in the fall semester or academic quarter of 1974 was 539,500 in the forty-eight states (excluding Alaska and Hawaii) and the District of Columbia, or 9 percent of total college enrollments. Despite uncertainties about their present and sharp division over the desired nature and purposes of their future, the historically Black colleges and universities appear to be continuing to secure slightly more than half of all Black enrollments in the United States and an absolute increase in numerical enrollments due to the continuing but not uniform tendency of college-age Blacks to enter college. (This impact and its implications for the future of the institution is felt unevenly, however, because Black students since the turn of the century continue to enroll in almost a 2:1 ratio in state-supported rather than private colleges and because the thirty-six oldest, largest, and most prestigious schools continue to account for approximately two-thirds of all enrollments in Black colleges.)

Of equal significance for American society, American educators, and social historians, and of the historical and continuing significance of the institutions to which Chambers directs our attention, is the disquieting fact that while Black *enrollments* in college may, at a slackening pace, be approaching the 11 percent proportion of the American population that American Blacks constitute, the ACE "Fact Book" for 1976 reports that Black "minority students" received only 5.3 percent of the baccalaureate degrees awarded from July 1973 to June 1974 by the 539 institutions it surveyed. This seems to parallel and confirm a somewhat earlier summary based on Carnegie Commission data[3] that in 1970 Black students constituted 8.3 percent of all college freshmen, 6.8 percent of sophomores, 5.4 percent of juniors, and slightly less than 5.0 percent of college seniors. Pifer also reported that Blacks comprised only 4.1 percent of all enrollments in graduate and professional schools in the United States. If one bears in mind the earlier statistic that no more than 2 percent of professionals are Black and that it is the historically Black institutions of higher education that continue to produce the overwhelming proportion of the baccalaureate and professional degrees awarded to Black Americans, these considerations would seem to underscore the necessity for a careful analysis of the pasts, presents, and projected or desirable futures of these institutions by educators, historians, and nonacademic analysts of American society.

With only occasional and usually intermittent exception, significant and sophisticated analysis of both the past and present of these institutions and their roles remains to be done. Chambers's bibliography, therefore, is both necessary and important. By detailing what does exist, it provides the means and encouragement by which the very large gaps of what does not currently exist can begin to be filled. Although, modestly, he professes to have attempted not to be exhaustive in the entries he has selected, included in his several sections is the grist for those who would study the history and development of the institutions (individually and collectively); for those who seek to identify and trace curricular and sociopolitical orientations, approaches, and changes over time; and for those who would explore and assess the implications of the influence of these historically Black institutions of higher education on individuals or on larger collective groupings and societies.

II

Chambers's current work, with its implicit notice of the volume and diversity of the work remaining to be done as well as of the resources presently available, is a product of a long-term concern and perception. More than five years ago in a presentation to the fifty-sixth annual meeting of the Association for the Study of Negro Life and History that was later published in the prestigious *Journal of Negro History,* he first called attention to the lack of adequate and sophisticated scholarly studies of the nature, roles, and histories of the historically Black colleges and universities and made the case for their necessity. If his call at that time for studies of the neglected individual institutions has broadened to embrace a parallel one for a sophisticated dispassionate synthesis of the collective aspects and their implications, consequences, and influences as well, and if the process of compilation of the bibliography reveals that more resources—primarily in the form of institutional histories, projects, or master's theses by students of those institutions—existed for these studies than he and others had anticipated at the time, both the need and the opportunity for its satisfaction continue to exist.

Chambers, of course, is neither unique nor even a pioneer in the orientation of his research interests and in his advocacy. For almost half a century that role was played by the venerable Horace Mann Bond (1904-1972). Yet at least two aspects of the significance of Bond's efforts and contributions point up the continuing significance of Chambers's bibliography.

When the American Education Research Association decided to publish *Encyclopedia of Educational Research* (1941) to report on and stimulate research on all phases of education by providing essays and bibliographies summarizing recent scholarship on a wide variety of topics and indicating fields or topics for needed research, the editors inevitably turned to Bond for a section on Negro education. Bond's extensive essays in this and the second edition (1950) called particular attention to the institutions and history of Black higher education as a field for needed research. That charge largely unresponded to, both Bond as a contributor and the section on Negro education rather strikingly were omitted from the subsequent third (1960) and fourth (1969) editions, although both the contributor and the subject remained alive, active, and vital.

In addition to the string of significant scholarly articles, his doctoral thesis on *Negro Education in Alabama* (1939) and his posthumously published

Education for Freedom: A History of Lincoln University, Pennsylvania (1976), all of which are cited in Chambers's bibliography, and his role as an educational administrator—including a twelve-year term as Lincoln's first Black president followed by a term as dean of the Atlanta University College of Education—Bond's major contribution to the study of Black higher education was the publication of *The Education of the Negro in the American Social Order* (1934, with a new introduction in 1966). In conjunction with Dwight Oliver Wendell Holmes's *The Evolution of the Negro College* (1934), it was considered the best general history of Black higher education to that date. More than forty years after its publication its significance continues to be not merely an early classic but an indispensable source.

Bond, in turn, had had his forerunners in the advocacy of the significance of the Black colleges and of the need for their study. As in all other matters, William E. B. Du Bois played the seminal role in providing the first scholarly and objective analysis of the American Negro and his institutions: *The College Bred Negro* (1900), which was prepared as the working paper basis for the Fifth Conference for the Study of the Negro Problem at Atlanta University (May 1900). Indeed, it was the relative handful of college-educated Blacks (probably no more than 2,500 in 1900) whom Du Bois envisioned as constituting the nucleus (and the teachers of the remainder) of the "Talented Tenth" who were to provide race leadership. Although Du Bois's perspective of the ongoing significance of the Black colleges and of the role they should play shifted radically with his growing disillusion in subsequent decades, Du Bois (and the *Crisis* under his editorship) remained consistent in his insistence upon the significance of the Black colleges as institutions of the Black society and of the need for careful and dispassionate assessments of the nature and effectiveness of their role(s).

So, too, Carter Woodson, the "father" of Black History and founder of the *Journal of Negro History,* also consistently stressed the need for study of the institutions of Black higher education and contributed to the literature of the field cited in the *Bibliography.* On a course parallel to those of Bond and Woodson, between 1933 and 1960 Charles H. Thompson made the *Journal of Negro Education* a vehicle for publications, studies, and reports on education by and for American Blacks. In addition to the string of his own contributions cited in Chambers's bibliography, Thompson periodically would issue editorial statements calling attention to the special need for studies of the nature, purposes, and institutions of Black higher education.

For all this advocacy and attention calling, however, the fact remains that the Bond and Holmes studies of 1934 have not effectively been superceded or updated, although valuable institutional, state, regional, and special-topic studies have emerged that touched upon the phenomenon. With World War II, the first gradual relaxation of the legal bonds of segregation as they affected higher education in the South, and relative improvement in economic mobility in the North, studies and concerns of the education of Black Americans, including those at the post-secondary level, increasingly came to focus on the prospects and implications of the long-deferred integration of the Black into American society.

This recent concern with historically Black higher education and its institutions, dating from the mid-1960s, has come to focus essentially on the future of these institutions in an age of integration given teeth at last by explicit federal law and by withholding from noncompliant institutions the federal funds upon which higher education has come to depend. Analyses of the past and of the circumstances and conditions that have shaped the contemporary institutions and the attitudes and expectations of the current students, however, have remained for the most part matters of superficial generalization and glib stereotype, characterized by a heavy reliance on assumption, presumption, and reasoning or the arrival at conclusions by a process of analogy and comparison with the institutions and systems of "mainstream" (read "historically predominantly white") American higher education and society.

A good portion of this debate as to the role and future of Black colleges and of subsequent studies, arguments, and contentions has been framed in response to the disdainful treatment of the Black colleges in Christopher Jencks and David Riesman's *The Academic Revolution* (1968) and the rather superficial conclusions of the Carnegie Commission Report *From Isolation to Mainstream* (1971), which could be summarized as acknowledging that the colleges would continue to exist; that they should anticipate a doubling of enrollments by the year 2000, if not 1980; that they should strive to become more like "real" colleges in curricular offerings, student-teacher ratios, faculty salaries, and equipment; and that all this would require an enormous increase in currently available funding.

A third nexus for this discussion and reflection of the orientation of the debate was the Summer 1971 issue of *Daedalus* (American Academy of Arts and Sciences), which was devoted to the future of the Black colleges. While containing a series of individually very valuable articles (although somewhat dated by subsequent social and economic developments), what seems characteristic of this issue are: the wide variety of perspectives displayed; the absence of anything approaching a "consensus" as to what the future role of the historically Black colleges *should* be beyond the fact that, for good or ill, they undoubtedly would continue to exist (if only for reasons of the then-current economic and demographic projections pertaining to the perceived "boom" in higher education); and the rather transparent desire of a number of the contributors to talk about something else that they considered more important than the Black colleges, paying only enough attention to the subject to constitute a peg upon which to hang the larger argument (and justify inclusion in the volume) and ultimately projecting as the future for the Black colleges a role consistent with the *a priori* presumption of the desired role of the Black in American society. This same period from 1968 to 1971 also produced —in a raft of published colloquia and anthologies on Black America and "public issues" series by publishers such as Frederick Praeger—the opportunity for publications of surveys, reports, or arguments on attitudes of contemporary Black students and institutions, but again with a central focus on attitude, aspiration, and implications for the future.

The impact of this orientation has distracted attention from the past, leaving a gap between the studies of the 1930s and current analyses, and shaped the concern with the present condition and status of the institutions and of the educations they offer and social roles they play toward projections and recommendations for future policy. This has left imperfectly explored the conditions of the current state of these institutions and has generally ignored the influences and implications of the past. The one common denominator, however, is the conclusion or assumption that these institutions—in whatever modified form or for whatever reshaped purpose—will of necessity continue to exist. Therefore, the series research opportunities into the pasts and presents, individually or collectively, of the historically Black institutions of higher education that Chambers's bibliography makes accessible remains pertinent and essential.

III

Any attempt to offer a brief summary, no matter how generalized, of the history and role of these historically Black colleges and universities within the context of Negro higher education to which Chambers's bibliography is devoted immediately runs into a series of vagaries of data and disputes among sources as to fact or implication. These derive for the most part from uncertainties and alternations in defining or identifying a Black student as far as institutional or governmental records and statistics are concerned and in agreeing upon the constellation of institutions that are to be regarded as historically Black and as higher education. Compounding these variables are variations and uncertainties in establishing effective dates when an institution became a college in some generally accepted definition of this status; the proportion of enrolled students who were doing work of a college level; whether junior colleges, other two-year institutions, and the relatively few but significant professional schools should be included; whether the four Northern but historically Black colleges should be included; whether both publicly and privately supported institutions are encompassed; and whether the study deals only with "accredited" (however defined) institutions. Certainly the project promised by Howard University in 1975 (cited in Chapter 3) to provide such a common set of definitions and data base will be welcome and an enormous encouragement to the sorts of studies Chambers advocates.

An eighteenth-century slave named John Chavis was enrolled in Princeton as an experiment, succeeded, and ultimately on his return to North Carolina was assigned to teach a school open only to white students. The distinction of the "first Black college graduate in America," however, is usually divided between two other individuals, Edward Jones and John Russwurm, who were graduated within two weeks of one another (in which order is unclear) from Amherst and Bowdoin, respectively. By 1900 the usual estimate is that probably no more than 200 (some estimates go as high as 250) Blacks had received degrees from white colleges, predominantly from Oberlin. Yet, Du Bois's data for *The College Bred Negro* estimated that there were approximately 2,500 Black college graduates at that date. The bulk, therefore, had received their degrees, which were not recognized by any formal accreditation agency at that time, from the historically Black colleges, which circumstances had compelled to be developed in the latter half of the nineteenth century.

The first institutions developed expressly for the education of American Blacks that were founded as or became college-level institutions were established in the North as an outgrowth of the Abolition Movement and as reflections of the values, purposes, and social commitments of their respective founding groups. Although chartered by the states in which they were located to give academic degrees, the bulk of their early curriculum and the programs followed by their students were basically of a secondary education level at best. Lincoln University (originally Ashmun Institute) was established by the Presbyterian Church in Pennsylvania in 1854. Wilberforce University was founded in 1855 by the Methodists in Ohio, who transferred control to the African Methodist Episcopal Church in 1862. Wilberforce claims primacy as the first Black college, however, on the basis of its 1853 first instruction date and the fact that its first baccalaureate award in 1857 predated by eleven years Lincoln's first college degree.

An even earlier northern institution, although clearly noncollegiate in its origins, is reflective of the evolution of the Black colleges. In Philadelphia in 1837 (the date often is given as 1839), the Quakers established a school that was incorporated as the Institute for Colored Youth in 1842. Following a move from Philadelphia to Cheyney in 1902, the name of the institution was changed to the Cheyney Training School for Teachers in 1914. Ultimately taken over by the state as the State Normal School in 1920 and undergoing a series of further name changes to its current designation as Cheyney State College, it awarded its first baccalaureate degree only in 1932.

A fourth northern institution that underwent a somewhat similar evolution in a shorter period of time and also became state-supported is the current Central State University in Ohio, which originally was chartered in 1887 as the Combined Normal and Industrial Department of Wilberforce and, in effect seceding from its parent institution, became a four-year college in its own right in 1941 and a state college (later, university) ten years later. These four northern black institutions continue to exist, while others that were established in the post-Civil War period do not.

As significant as these four northern institutions have been and continue to be within the framework of intentionally Black higher education, the significant developments took place in the South. There, of course, events had to await and were significantly shaped by the consequences of the Civil War and the abortive effort at Reconstruction. Given the respective natures of the war, the South, and the circumstances of the freedmen, inevitably the direction of education for the overwhelming majority of American Blacks was shaped by individuals, agencies, and purposes largely outside the South and outside the race. With temporary assistance and encouragement from the federal government in the form of the Freedmen's Bureau, the work in establishing institutions of education, including those of higher education, for the Southern Blacks was undertaken and shaped initially by the purposes of church-related organizations and, somewhat later, by Northern philanthropy, which sustained the approximately one hundred private colleges that survived into the twentieth century.

Thus, in association with the Congregationalist American Missionary Association, the Freedmen's Bureau played a significant role in the establishments in 1868 of Howard University and of Hampton Institute. Even earlier than this, in 1865 the American Baptist Mission Society established Atlanta University and the AMA, Fisk. Through the 1870s and 1880s, even after Reconstruction, white and Black religious groups established denominational colleges—perhaps as many as two hundred in number, no more than half of which were still in existence by 1900.

Despite the missionary, teacher-training, and/or classical models established for these early schools as they emerged to post-secondary education status, it was the industrial/agricultural training orientation instituted from the outset at Hampton and apothesized at Tuskegee from its founding by Booker T. Washington in 1881 that was to prove the more attractive purpose to the Northern philanthropists who permitted these institutions to endure, no matter how precariously, following the economic convolutions of the mid-1870s. To what extent the wishes of its founders or financial angels seriously and significantly altered the orientation of these institutions from the desires of their administrators, faculty, and students or may merely have constituted an image pleasing to and accepted by the North is one of the questions of scholarship that critical analyses of these institutions and their respective curricula could help resolve.

The great stimulus to the proliferation of Black institutions clearly identified as collegiate again came from the outside with the passage of the second Morrill Land-Grant College Act of 1890. Offered as a compromise to the abandoned Blair Bill, which would have insisted upon the admission of Blacks to the colleges supported under the original Morrill Act of 1863, the second Morrill Act offered as an alternative to integration additional funds on the condition that separate land-grant colleges for Negroes be established and the monies divided proportionately among these new institutions and the already established ones, which, except for Alcorn A. & M., which was established by the Reconstruction government in Mississippi, were all restricted to whites. By 1900 such state-supported Black colleges had been established in all of the states of the Old South and the border states.

With the hardening of race relations into a legal caste system in the half-century following the combined impacts of the second Morrill Act, the Depression of the 1890s, and the Disenfranchisement campaigns of 1890 to 1907 in all of these states, there was no prospect of Black entry into the white institutions of the South and little prospect of more than the legal minimal support from the state governments. With 90 percent of the American Black population continuing to be resident in the South until World War I, these institutions—public and private—became the only means of higher education for the vast majority of Black Americans. As Chambers has noted in his own publications, the Black college thereby became a major shaping institution of the Black experience—second only, perhaps, to the family and the church.

IV

Depending on how one treats recent mergers and affiliations and counts the constituent units of the more comprehensive universities such as Atlanta, Howard, and Texas Southern, the most consistent taxonomy of historically Black institutions of higher education includes a cluster of 105 to 115 quite disparate institutions that have survived to the present, all but four of which are located in the historic South. If one uses the lesser figure, this would subdivide into 85 four-year institutions and 20 two-year junior colleges. The 85 four-year institutions would further subdivide into 35 that are classified as public and 50 as private. They also subdivide by size and therefore by potential significance. As noted earlier, the 36 oldest and largest of the four-year colleges enroll approximately two-thirds of the collective student bodies. Even with the acceleration in numerical enrollments in recent years, at least half (and virtually all of the junior colleges) would have enrollments of less than 1,000. These institutions also vary greatly from one another in the educational and social purposes that they seek or are perceived to serve.

To assess their past, current, and potentially future influences on the Black Experience, American education, and American society would require a more extensive and sophisticated study of the institutions other than the most prominent than currently exists and then a series of more general analyses and syntheses of their collective impacts. To begin these efforts, Chambers's accompanying bibliography should be an indispensable tool and, hopefully, a positive encouragement.

V

Chapter 1, recording pertinent doctoral dissertations produced between 1918 and 1976, will be indispensable in light of the fact that the Ann Arbor Microfilm series of doctoral dissertations does not extend back that far in time and, even currently, does not include all graduate institutions in the United States. Similarly, Chapter 2 provides a larger bulk of institutional histories (no matter how self-serving and generally uncritical such documents usually are) than had been believed to exist at the time Chambers first made his appeal for the writing of institutional histories. The number and variety of entries (well in excess of 1,500) speaks for the comprehensiveness of the periodical literature contained in Chapter 3. Of special significance—and almost unique in this bibliography—is the inclusion of the listing of pertinent master's theses in Chapter 4 since such works, directed by established scholars of established graduate institutions, are far less likely to be cited in bibliographies and reference works than are doctoral dissertations. Similar to Chapter 3, Chapter 5 is certainly comprehensive even if, as Chambers professes, it is not intended to be exhaustive. Given the uncertainties on basic data, bemoaned at length in this introduction, Chapter 6 includes a compelling variety of proceedings, reports, and government publications as well as the biographical references to individuals who figure prominently in the history of Black higher education and its institutions.

James P. Louis
Associate Professor of History
Kent State University

NOTES

1. Fredrick Chambers, "Black Colleges and Universities—Are Histories Needed?" *Journal of Negro History* 57:3 (July 1972), p. 270.

2. See, for instance, Vernon E. Jordan, Jr., "Blacks and Higher Education—Some Reflections," *Daedalus* 104:1 (Winter 1975), pp. 164-165.

3. See Alan Pifer, "The Higher Education of Blacks in the United States," pp. 29-30.

BLACK HIGHER EDUCATION IN THE UNITED STATES

DOCTORAL DISSERTATIONS 1
1918–1976

Abbott, Martin Linton. "The Freedmen's Bureau in South Carolina, 1865-1872." Emory University, 1954.

Abel, James W. "A Study of the Speech of Six Freshmen From Southern University." Louisiana State University, 1949.

Abraham, Ansley A. "An Investigation of the Interaction of Freshmen With Their Curriculum in the School of Education at Florida A. & M. University." Indiana University, 1956.

Abramowitz, Jack. "Accommodation and Militancy in Negro Life, 1876-1916." Columbia University, 1950.

Adams, Alfred Hugh. "A History of Public Higher Education in Florida, 1821-1961." Florida State University, 1962.

Adams, Dale T. "An Evaluation of Summer Business Orientation Program for Selected Black Business Majors." University of Cincinnati, 1972.

Adams, Rosemary F. "A Study of Community Services as Professional Laboratory Experiences in the Preservice Preparation of Teachers of Music at Knoxville College, Tennessee." New York University, 1961.

Alexander, Herbert Clarke. "An Analysis of Selected Attitudes of Seniors in Predominantly Negro Colleges and Universities." University of Tennessee, 1969.

Alexander, Lydia Lewis. "A Study of the Real and Ideal College Environment as Perceived by Black Students in Racially Contrasting Junior Colleges in Alabama." Auburn University, 1972.

Allen, Anita Ford. "New Careers in Senior Black Private Colleges as a Strategy for Institutional Survival in the 1980's." University of Massachusetts, 1976.

Allen, Robert William. "The Relationship of Self-Perceptions to Realism of Vocational Preferences Among Male Freshmen in a Small Black Liberal Arts College." Atlanta University, 1973.

Alston, Littleton A. "Providing Creative Activities and Participation in the Arts at the Agricultural and Technical College of North Carolina." Teachers College, Columbia University, 1950.

Amprey, Joseph Leonard, Jr. "An Evaluation of Student Personnel Services as Viewed by Black and White College Students on Both Predominantly Black and Predominantly White Student Populated Campuses." American University, 1973.

Anderson, Edison H., Sr. "The Historical Development of Music in the Negro Secondary Schools of Oklahoma and at Langston University." State University of Iowa, 1957.

Anderson, Tommie Marie. "The Achievement in Mathematics and Science of Students in the Negro Schools and Colleges in Mississippi." Indiana University, 1958.

Armstrong, Bryon K. "Factors in the Formulation of Collegiate Programs for Negroes." University of Michigan, 1938.

Asgill, Amanda. "Accreditation and Its Importance as Perceived by Selected Chief Administrators of Traditionally Black Colleges and Traditionally White Colleges in the Southern Association of Colleges and Schools." The University of Toledo, 1972.

Badger, William V. "A Systematic Analysis of the U. S. Supreme Court Cases Dealing With Education; 1790-1951." Florida State University, 1953.

Bailey, Rubelia J. "The Relationship of Educational Background, Socio-Economic Status, Level of Aspiration and Intelligence to Success in Business Education." Temple University, 1965.

Baker, Robert Andrew. "The American Baptist Home Mission Society and the South, 1832-1894." Yale University, 1947.

Banning, Magnolia. "The Contribution of the Julius Rosenwald Fund to Negro Education and Better Race Relations." University of Arizona, 1947.

Barrow, G. L. "The Louisiana Plan of Rural Teacher Education." Columbia University, 1942.

Beasley, Leon Odum. "A History of Education in Louisiana During the Reconstruction Period, 1862-1877." Louisiana State University, 1957.

Beck, James Dennis. "Functions and Responsibilities of Deans of Students in Selected Negro Institutions of Higher Learning." Indiana University, 1959.

Bell, Charles McDonald. "A Study of Career Orientations and Rewarded Activity as Perceived by Teachers in Predominantly Negro Senior Colleges." University of Georgia, 1969.

Bell, James. "An Appraisal of Undergraduate Teacher Education in Physical Education in Selected Land-Grant Colleges and Universities for Negroes: With Special Reference to Southern University." Teachers College, Columbia University, 1960.

Bennett, Rolla James. "History of the Founding of Educational Institutions by the Disciples of Christ in Virginia and West Virginia." University of Pennsylvania, 1932.

Bentley, George R. "A History of the Freedmen's Bureau." University of Wisconsin, 1949.

Berry, Charles A., Jr. "Student Part-Time Employment Policies and Practices in Negro Land-Grant Colleges." Indiana University, 1954.

Bishop, Harold Lucius. "A Process Model for the Improvement of Graduate Programs in Business Administration at Black Institutions." University of Alabama, 1974.

Blackwell, Velma Levern. "A Black Institution Pioneering Adult Education: Tuskegee Institute Past and Present (1881-1973)." The Florida State University, 1973.

Boclair, Nathaniel A. "The Indentification of a Mathematics Program for Capable But Poorly Prepared College Freshmen." Rutgers University The State University of New Jersey, 1972.

Boger, Dellie L. "The Problems of Morehouse College Students." Teachers College Columbia University, 1956.

Boggs, Grace B. "Laboratory Experiences in Music Education Prior to Student Teaching at Morris Brown College, Atlanta, Georgia." Teachers College, Columbia University, 1956.

Boggs, Wade Hamilton, III. "State Supported Higher Education in North Carolina, 1877-1945." Duke University, 1972.

Bolton, Ina A. "The Problem of Negro College Women." University of Southern California, 1969.

Bond, Horace Mann. "Social and Economic Influences on Public Education of the Negro in Alabama, 1865-1930." University of Chicago, 1936.

Bonner, Leon W. "Factors Associated With the Academic Achievement of Freshmen Students at a Southern Agricultural College." Pennsylvania State University, 1956.

Bowen, Hilliard A. "Student Personnel Services in the Negro Land-Grant Colleges." Ohio State University, 1947.

Boyer, Joe Louis. "Knowledge and Perceptions of Knowledge Related to Teaching and Learning in Disadvantaged Areas: A Comparative Study of Pre-Service Teachers in Predominantly Black and Predominantly White Universities." The Ohio State University, 1971.

Bracy, Randolph, Jr. "The Black Private College--Strategies for Its Survival." University of Florida, 1974.

Bradley, Dorothy Phillips. "Student Participation in the Governance of Predominantly Negro Colleges and Universities: A Comparison of Views Held by Administrators and Students." University of Mississippi, 1968.

Branch, London Grigsby. "Jazz Education in Predominantly Black Colleges." Southern Illinois University, 1975.

Braxton, Harold Edwin. "A History of the General Education Program at Virginia State College Since 1950." University of Virginia, 1973.

Brett, T. Ruth. "A Student Personnel Program for the Negro College." Teachers College, Columbia University, 1945.

Brewer, June H. "An Ecological Study of the Psychological Environment of a Negro College and the Personality Needs of Its Students." University of Texas, at Austin, 1963.

Brice, Edward W. "A Study of the Status of Junior Colleges for Negroes in the United States." University of Pennsylvania, 1950.

Brigham, Robert Irving. "The Education of the Negro in Missouri." University of Missouri, 1946.

Broderick, Francis Lyons. "W. E. B. Du Bois: The Trail of His Ideas." Harvard University, 1955.

Brody, Richard Samuel. "W. E. B. Du Bois Educational Ideas." Rutgers University The State University of New Jersey, 1972.

Brooks, Layman Beecher. "A Socio-Economic and Educational Study of Negro High-School and Junior College Training." University of Michigan, 1943.

Brooks, Thomas Edward. "The Inception and Development of Student Personnel Services at Tuskegee Institute." Indiana University, 1955.

Broom, Kathleen W. "The Julius Rosenwald's Aid to Education in the South." University of Chicago, 1950.

Brown, Emma Wesley. "A Study of the Influence of the Philosophies of Accommodation and Protest on Five Colleges Established in Virginia for Negroes, 1865-1940." Teachers College, Columbia University, 1967.

Brown, Herman. "Origin Development and Contributions of Negro Colleges and Universities as Institutions of Higher Education in the United States, 1776-1890." The Catholic University of America, 1972.

Brown, Jessie L. "Writing Opportunities at Hampton Institute in the Student Activities Program." Teachers College, Columbia University, 1954.

Brown, Jonel L. "A Critical Appraisal of the Philosophy Organization, and Educational Program of a Land-Grant College for Negroes." University of Wisconsin, 1946.

Brown, Nina Woody. "An Investigation of Personality Characteristics of Negroes Attending a Predominantly White University and Negroes Attending a Black College." The College of William and Mary in Virginia, 1973.

Brown, Theresa Kennedy. "A Study of Home Economics Graduates at Morgan State College, Baltimore, Maryland, From 1944 to 1953: An Investigation for Curriculum Development." New York University, 1958.

Brown, William Crawford. "An Evaluation of the Course Offerings and Requirements in the Secretarial Science Curriculum at Hampton Institute." New York University, 1960.

Brown, William Crews. "An Evaluation of the Present Status of Health Services in Negro Land-Grant Colleges." New York University, 1960.

Buck, James R., Jr. "Some Identifiable Characteristics of Students Entering Negro Senior Colleges in Mississippi." George Peabody College for Teachers, 1964.

Buckles, Eddie. "A History of Physical Education and Athletics at Alcorn Agricultural and Mechanical College." Ohio State University, 1972.

Buckner, Beatrice Dilla and Burkhead, Iely G. "Reforms in Basic English in Black Mississippi Colleges, 1960-70." (Both Authors Received Degrees at Rutgers University) Rutgers University The State University of New Jersey, 1973.

Buckner, Donald Raymond. "A Survey of Allied Health Curricular Capabilities of Selected Traditional Black Institutions of Higher Education." University of Massachusetts, 1973.

Buckner, William Pat., Jr. "The Prevalence of Sex Misconceptions Among Freshmen Students Enrolled in State Supported Predominantly Negro Colleges in Louisiana." Indiana University, 1969.

Burlingame, Martin. "The N. A. A. C. P. and Equal Educational Opportunities for Negroes, 1909-1954." University of Chicago, 1969.

Butler, Addie Louise Joyner. "The Distinctive Black College: Talladega, Tuskegee, and Morehouse." Columbia University, Teachers College, 1976.

Butler, John H. "An Historical Account of the John F. Slater Fund and the Anna T. Jeanes Foundation." University of California, 1931.

Butler, Ralph Backstrom. "Aptitude Test Performance of Negro College Students as Affected by Item Difficulty Sequence, Anxiety Reaction Type, and Sex Differences." The University of Oklahoma, 1971.

Caldwell, Marion Milford. "An Evaluation of the Undergraduate Curriculum in Agricultural Education at South Carolina State College." Ohio State University, 1959.

Caliver, Ambrose. "A Personnel Study of Negro College Students: A Study of the Relations Between Certain Background Factors of Negro College Students and Their Subsequent Career in College." Teachers College, Columbia University, 1931.

Campbell, Clarice T. "History of Tougaloo College." University of Mississippi, 1970.

Capers, Joseph Wilbert. "A Comparison of Biological Science in General Education Programs Among Black Institutions of Higher Learning in 1967 and 1973." North Texas State University, 1975.

Capers, Norris Russell. "A Descriptive Study of the Relationship of Certain Variables to College R. O. T. C. Success of Army Cadets at Predominantly Black Institutions of Higher Education." The George Washington University, 1974.

Capps, Marian P. "The Virginia Out-of-State Graduate Aid Program 1936-1950." Teachers College, Columbia University, 1954.

Cardozo, Joseph Anthony. "The Development of the Art Program in Negro Land-Grant Colleges." Indiana University, 1970.

Carpenter, Henry D., Jr. "A Proposal for Developing Procedures for the Community Program of Grambling College of Louisiana." Teachers College, Columbia University, 1961.

Carson, Suzanne C. "Samuel Chapman Armstrong: Missionary

to the South." Johns Hopkins University, 1952.

Chait, Richard Paul. "The Desegregation of Higher Education: A Legal History." University of Wisconsin, 1972.

Chambers, Fredrick. "Historical Study of Arkansas Agricultural, Mechanical, and Normal College, 1873-1943." Ball State University, 1970.

Chang, Edward C. F. "Norms and Correlates of the _Watson-Glaser Critical Thinking Appraisal_ and Selected Variables for Negro Students." University of Oklahoma, 1969.

Chapman, Oscar James. "An Historical Study of Negro Land-Grant Colleges in Relationship With Their Social, Economic, Political, and Educational Backgrounds and a Program for Their Improvement." The Ohio State University, 1940.

Cheatham, Harold E. "The Status of Counseling in Traditionally Black Colleges and Universities of the South." Case Western Reserve University, 1973.

Cheek, William Francis, III. "Forgotten Prophet: The Life of John Mercer Langston." University of Virginia, 1961.

Christian, Edwin C. "A Plan for Improving the Music Curriculum for Educating Music Teachers at Morris Brown College, Atlanta, Georgia." Teachers College, Columbia University, 1960.

Christophe, LeRoy M., Sr. "A Study of the Provisions for the Pre-Service and In-Service Education of Secondary School Principals in Arkansas Negro Colleges With Recommendations for Improvement." New York University, 1954.

Citro, Joseph F. "Booker T. Washington's Tuskegee Institute: Black School Community, 1900-1915." University of Rochester, 1972.

Clark, Felton G. "The Control of State Supported Teacher-Training Programs for Negroes." Teachers College, Columbia University, 1934.

Clark, Geraldine L. "A Comparative Study of Fictional Reading of Negro College Freshmen and Seniors." University of Chicago, 1956.

Clayborne, William Murry. "A History of the Teacher Education Programs in Five Negro Colleges of Virginia from 1876 to 1954." The George Washington University, 1971.

Clary, George Esmond. "The Founding of Paine College--A Unique Venture in Interracial Cooperation in the New South, 1882-1903." University of Georgia, 1965.

Clem, William W. "Administrative Practices in Laboratory Schools Connected With Land-Grant and State Teachers Colleges for Negroes." University of Wisconsin, 1950.

Clement, Rufus E. "A History of Negro Education in North Carolina, 1865-1928." Northwestern University, 1930.

Clift, Virgil A. "An Appraisal of Curricular Offerings in Four Negro Teacher Education Institutions in North Carolina." The Ohio State University, 1944.

Coaxum, Callie Butler. "Career Patterns of Selected Graduates of United Negro College Fund Institutions." Southern Illinois University, 1976.

Cobbins, Sam, Jr. "Industrial Education for Black Americans in Mississippi--1862-1865." Mississippi State University, 1975.

Cohen, Arthur M. "Miami-Dade Junior College: A Study in Racial Integration." Florida State University, 1964.

Cole, Earl L. "A Study of the Follow-Up Program of Grambling College With Specific Recommendations for Further Development and Improvement." Teachers College, Columbia University, 1958.

Cole, Tommie Joe. "The Historical Development of Junior Colleges in Arkansas." University of Arkansas, 1955.

Colen, Joseph Weiss. "Goals of Departments of Mathematics at Predominantly Black Colleges as Related to Success of Their Graduates in Graduate Study." Indiana University, 1975.

Collins, William Milton. "A Study to Determine Practices in Secondary Student Teaching Programs in Nine Negro Colleges and Universities in Texas and the Improvements that are Needed." Cornell University, 1957.

Colson, Cortlandt Matthews. "Appraisal of Cadet Teaching at Virginia State College." Ohio State University, 1951.

Colson, Edna M. "An Analysis of the Specific References to Negroes in Selected Curricula for the Education of Teachers." Columbia University, 1941.

Colson, Elsie C. "A Co-ordinated Plan of Organization and Administration of Certain Phases of Teacher Education for all Departments of Virginia State College Concerned With the Preparation of Teachers." Pennsylvania University, 1960.

Colston, James Allen. "Higher Education in Georgia From 1932 to 1949, With Specific Reference to Higher Education for the Negro." New York University, 1950.

Connor, Miles W. "A Study of the Facilities and Practices of Laboratory-School Departments of Tax-Supported Normal Schools and Colleges for the Preparation of Negro Teachers of Elementary Schools." New York University, 1936.

Conyers, Charline Fay Howard. "A History of Cheyney State Teachers College, 1837-1951." New York University, 1960.

Cope, William, Jr. "A Study of Selected Characteristics of the Drop-Out at Dillard University." Indiana University, 1958.

Cooper, Charles Logan. "Major Factors Involved in the Vocational Choices of Negro College Students." Cornell University, 1936.

Cooper, Matthew N. "To Determine the Nature and Significance, if any, of Certain Differences in the Social and Personal Adjustment of Fifty-One Successful and Fifty-One Non-Successful College Students at Texas Southern University." New York University, 1955.

Cordery, Sara B. "The Training of Business Teachers in Degree-Granting Institutions Attended Predominantly by Negroes." Teachers College, Columbia University, 1957.

Cotton, George R. "Collegiate Technical Education for Negroes in Missouri With Proposed Plans for Development." The Ohio State University, 1944.

Cowser, James Thomas. "Administrative Perceptions of Goals in Selected Public and Church-Related Historically Black Institutions of Higher Education." Kent State University, 1976.

Coyner, Anna S. "Factors Involved in the Holding Power of Central State College From September 1, 1947 to June 30, 1950." University of Oklahoma, 1951.

Craig, William Lafayette, Jr. "A Model for the Administration of a Department of Industrial Education With Special Reference to Norfolk State College." Wayne State University, 1970.

Crawford, Harold Wakeling. "Organizational Patterns for Industrial Education Programs in Selected Land Grant Colleges." Wayne State University, 1960.

Crofts, Daniel Wallace. "The Blair Bill and the Election Bill: The Congressional Aftermath to Reconstruction." Yale University, 1968.

Currie, Edward MacGregor. "Raising Achievement Levels of Negro-College Students in the Subject Field of Accounting." University of Minnesota, 1967.

Cuthbert, Marion Vera. "Education and Marginality; A Study of the Negro Woman College Graduate." Teachers College, Columbia University, 1942.

Dabney, Lillian G. "The History of Schools for Negroes in the District of Columbia, 1807-1947." Catholic University of America, 1943.

Daniel, Walter Green. "The Reading Interest and Needs of Negro College Freshmen Regarding Social Science Materials." Teachers College, Columbia University, 1942.

Daniel, William Andrew. "Negro Theological Seminary Survey." University of Chicago, 1925.

David, Arthur La Curtiss. "The Involvement of the Black Man in the Teaching of Western Civilization: A Study of Black Colleges and Universities." Middle Tennessee State University, 1973.

Davis, Alonzo J. "Status Factors in Personality Characteristics of Negro College Students." University of Minnesota, 1948.

Davis, Elmyra Richardson. "A Comparative Study of Langston University Freshmen Who Graduated From Integrated High Schools and Those From Predominantly Negro Schools." The University of Oklahoma, 1970.

Davis, Everett Frederick Samuel. "A Plan for Increasing the Effectiveness of Religion in Virginia State College." Columbia University, 1946.

Davis, Howard. "A Comparison of Academic Achievement and Success on the National Teacher Examinations of Physical Education Majors and Non-Majors in Selected Predominantly Negro Colleges and Universities." Oklahoma State University, 1971.

Davis, Lawrence A. "A Comparison of the Philosophies, Purposes and Functions of the Negro Land-Grant Colleges and Universities With Emphasis Upon the Program of Agricultural, Mechanical and Normal College, Pine Bluff, Arkansas." University of Arkansas, 1960.

Davis, Malcom Adkins. "A Study of the Personalities and Social Interests of a Group of Negro College Freshmen as Revealed in Their Compositions." New York University, 1953.

Davis, Richmond Cowan. "A Proposal for Strengthening the Program of Agricultural, Mechanical and Normal College of Arkansas." Michigan State University, 1957.

Davis, Wiley Mason. "A Follow-Up Study of Graduates of Saint Augustine's College, 1964, 1966, and 1970." Brigham Young University, 1974.

Davis, William R. "The Development and Present Status of Negro Education in East Texas." Teachers College, Columbia University, 1934.

Dawson, Edgar Earl. "Theory and Practice in Negro Colleges Underlying the Preparation of Teachers of the Social Studies for Secondary Schools." University of Kansas, 1942.

Dawson, Leonard Ervin. "The Effects of a Program of Counseling and Tutoring on Academic Achievement of Black College Freshmen." The George Washington University, 1974.

Decker, Paul M. "A Study of Job Opportunities in the State of Florida for Negro College Graduates, With Special Reference to Students of Bethune-Cookman College." University of Northern Colorado, 1958.

Derbyshire, Robert L. "Personal Identity: An Attitude Study of American Negro College Students." University of Maryland, 1964.

Dickerson, Milton O., Jr. "The External Administration of Negro Land-Grant Colleges and Universities From 1890-1920." The Catholic University of America, 1975.

Donaldson, Leon Matthew. "The Influence of Federal Grants on Research and Instruction in the Sciences as Perceived by Selected Predominantly Black Private Institutions." Rutgers University The State University of New Jersey, 1973.

Dorsett, Herman Willington. "Social, Economic, and Emotional Problems Anticipated by Graduate School-Bound Negro College Students." Columbia University, 1969.

Dorsey, James Elmo. "Music and Music Education in the Negro College." Teachers College, Columbia University, 1945.

Dove, Pearlie Croft. "A Study of the Relationship of Certain Selected Criteria and Success in the Student Teaching Program at Clark College, Atlanta, Georgia." University of Colorado, 1959.

Dowdy, Lewis C. "A Critical Analysis of the Purpose, Philosophy and Objectives of Agricultural and Technical College of North Carolina With Implications for Change." Indiana University, 1965.

Drake, Joseph F. "Occupational Interests and Opportunities as Determinants in the Construction of Curricula for a Negro Land Grant College in Alabama." Cornell University, 1938.

Drake, Richard Bryant. "The American Missionary Association and the Southern Negro, 1861-1868." Emory University, 1957.

Drew, Jesse M. "A Study of the Student Personnel Services of the Negro Land-Grant Colleges of the United States." Harvard University, 1950.

Duncan, Catherine W. "Pre-Service Teacher Education for Negroes in Georgia." The Ohio State University, 1949.

DuValle, Sylvester Howard. "An Evaluation of the Standards of Chemistry Teaching in the Universities and Colleges for Negroes in the United States." New York University, 1943.

Easton, William D. "Survey of the Characteristics of the Successful Black Deans in Predominantly Black Four-Year Colleges and Universities in the Southeastern United States." University of Montana, 1973.

Echols, Jack W. "Criteria for Evaluating Teacher Education in the Negro Colleges of Texas." University of Denver, 1956.

Eddy, Edward D., Jr. "The Development of the Land-Grant College: Their Programs and Philosophy." Cornell University, 1956.

Edmonds, William S. "A Study of the Technological Curricula of the Separate Southern Land-Grant Colleges, 1941-1951." Teachers College, Columbia University, 1954.

Ellois, Edward R., Jr. "Teacher Employment Services in Negro Colleges and Universities." University of Oklahoma, 1967.

Enck, Henry S. "The Burden Borne: Northern White Philanthrophy and Southern Black Industrial Education, 1900-1915." University of Cincinnati, 1970.

Ennis, Ronald Frederick. "A Typology for the Development of the Achievement Syndrome in Black College Students." Vanderbilt University, 1971.

Epps, Willie James. "Factors in Employment Migration of Black Doctorate Holders From Predominantly Black Colleges to Predominantly White Colleges: 1965-1972." Kansas State University, 1974.

Espy, James A. "Factors Influencing Choice of College Teaching as a Career: A Study of Faculties in Predominantly Negro Institutions." University of Minnesota, 1963.

Farley, Lester Martin. "A Comparison of the General Athletic Ability of White and Negro Men of College Age." George Peabody College for Teachers, 1939.

Fingal, William Adolphus. "The Role of the Director of Planning and Development as Perceived by Trustees, Presidents and Directors of Planning and Development in Traditionally

Black State Supported Institutions of Higher Learning." Southern Illinois University, 1974.

Forbes, Frank Lafayette. "A Four-Year Undergraduate Professional Physical Education Curriculum for Men at the Atlanta University Center." New York University, 1953.

Forbes, John Melville. "The Music Program of Berea College (Kentucky) and the Folk-Music Heritage of Appalachia." University of Michigan, 1974.

Ford, Joseph Allen. "Evaluation of Vocational-Industrial Teacher Education at Norfolk State College: A Comparative Analysis." The Pennsylvania State University, 1974.

Franklin, George W. "An Evaluation of Counseling and Employment Activities of Disabled Negro Veterans." Purdue University, 1955.

Freeman, Ludwig Felix. "Federal Agency Support to Black Colleges and Universities: Patterns and Problems." University of Pittsburgh, 1973.

Gallager, Buell G. "American Caste and the Negro College." Columbia University, 1938.

Galloway, Oscar Fitzgerald. "Higher Education for Negroes in Kentucky." University of Kentucky, 1931.

Gamblin, Hance. "The Relative Importance of Selected Factors Indicative of Teacher Effectiveness Among Graduates in Elementary Education at Jackson State College." University of Oklahoma, 1962.

Garth, Arlyce James. "Teacher Education Programs in Selected Predominantly Black Institutions: Opinions of the Departmental Leaders Utilizing the Delphi Technique." George Peabody College for Teachers, 1975.

Gatlin, F. Nathaniel. "A Plan for Housing the Department of Music at Virginia State College Involving Alterations to an Existing Structure and Recommendations for Equipment." Teachers College, Columbia University, 1960.

Gayles, Anne R. "Proposed Program for the Improvement of College Instruction at Florida Agricultural and Mechanical University." Indiana University, 1961.

George, Arthur Allen. "The History of Johnson C. Smith University, 1867 to the Present: To Present and Analyze the Growth and Development of the Administrative and the Curricula Aims and Practices of Johnson C. Smith University 1867 to the Present." New York University, 1954.

Gibson, De Lois. "A Historical Study of Philander Smith College, 1877-1969." University of Arkansas, 1972.

Gist, Annie Lou. "Health Misconceptions Subscribed to by Freshmen in Selected Negro Colleges: A Study of the Relative Prevalence of Health Misconceptions Subscribed to by Freshmen in Selected Negro Colleges." New York University, 1956.

Goines, Leonard. "Music and Music Education in Predominantly Negro Colleges and Universities Offering a Four-Year Program of Music Study Terminating in a Degree." Columbia University, 1963.

Goins, William F. "An Evaluation of Science Courses Offered for General Education in Selected Negro Colleges." Ohio State University, 1951.

Goodwin, Louis Charles. "A Historical Study of Accreditation in Negro Public and Private Colleges, 1927-1952, With Special Reference to Colleges in the Southern Association." New York University, 1956.

Gore, Blinzy L. "An Analysis of the Use of Selected Sit-In Demonstrations by Negro College Students in the South as Part of and Organized and Continuing Social Protest Movement Among American Negroes." New York University, 1967.

Gould, Mary Holloman. "Career Choice Process of Black College Students: An Analysis of Social Factors Affecting Career Choice Based on Perceptions of Black and White College Students." University of Massachusetts, 1976.

Goulding, Robert L. "The Development of Teacher Training in Florida." George Peabody University, 1933.

Graham, James Larmour. "A Quantitative Comparison of Rational Responses of Negro and White College Students." George Peabody College for Teachers, 1928.

Graham, William L. "Patterns of Intergroup Relations in the Cooperative Establishment, Control, and Administration of Paine College (Georgia) by Southern Negro and White People: A Study of Intergroup Process." New York University, 1955.

Grant, Earnest Aiken. "A Proposed Program for the Improvement of Pre-Employment Teacher Training in Agriculture for Negroes in Alabama Based Upon an Analysis and Evaluation of What Teachers of Agriculture Do." Cornell University, 1941.

Graves, Linwood D. "Proposals for Improving Teacher Education at Morris Brown College." Teachers College, Columbia University, 1954.

Gray, William H. "A Study of Needs of Negro High School Graduates in Louisiana and the Recognition Accorded Them in College." University of Pennsylvania, 1942.

Green, Dan S. "The Truth Shall Make Ye Free: The Sociology of W. E. B. Du Bois." University of Massachusetts, 1973.

Griffith, Albert Roger. "The Perceived Effects of Race on the Careers of Black College Graduates." Columbia University, 1975.

Grimes, Lloyd E. "The Development of Constitutional and Statutory Provisions for Education in Missouri Since 1874." University of Missouri, 1944.

Groomes, Benjamin Herbert. "Study of the Academic Performance of Students Enrolled in and Experimental Curriculum as Compared With Students Enrolled in Regular Curriculum in the Freshmen and Sophomore Years of College at Florida Agricultural and Mechanical University, 1967 to 1969." The Florida State University, 1971.

Grossley, Richard S. "The Public Relations Program of the Negro Land-Grant College. Determination of Factors and Trends in the Recent Development of the Public Relations Program of the Negro Land-Grant Colleges." New York University, 1943.

Guines, James T. "Professional Laboratory Experience Provided Elementary Majors in Negro Teacher Education Programs." University of Tennessee, 1961.

Hale, Morris Smith, Jr. "A History of Florida Junior Colleges." George Peabody University, 1966.

Hall, Clyde Woodrow. "A Survey of Industrial Education for Negroes in the United States Up to 1917." Bradley University, 1953.

Hall, Frederick D. "A Revised Program of Music Education for Alabama State College at Montgomery." Teachers College, Columbia University, 1952.

Hamlett, Hunter Douglass. "A Evaluation of Biological Science Courses Offered for General Education in Selected Predominantly Negro Colleges." The Ohio State University, 1967.

Hancock, Allen C. "A Study of Programs for the Professional Preparation of Secondary School Teachers in the Negro Publicly Supported Colleges." University of Colorado, 1952.

Hardy, Blanch B. "A Follow-Up Study of Stillman College Graduates." Michigan State University, 1960.

Harris, Benjamin Watkins. "Status of the General Extension Function at the Sixteen Negro Land-Grant Colleges and Universities." North Carolina State University at Raleigh, 1973.

Harris, Nelson H. "An Analysis and Appraisal of North Carolina Provisions for Furnishing Teachers for Her Negro Secondary Schools." University of Michigan, 1938.

Harrison, General Lamar. "A Program of Teacher Training by Prairie View State College for the Improvement of the Rural Negro Schools of Texas." Ohio State University, 1937.

Haymon, Francene Elenor. "Counselors' and Students' Perceptions of Black Colleges." University of Pittsburgh, 1974.

Haynes, Leonard L., III. "An Analysis of the Effects of Desegregation Upon Public Black Colleges." The Ohio State University, 1975.

Haynes, Roland E. "The Place of Religiosity in the Self-Reports of Negro Students in a Church-Related College." Boston University Graduate School, 1961.

Headd, Peral Walker. "An Evaluation of the Effectiveness of Tuskegee Institute's Basic Course in Audio-Visual Education With Recommendations for Improvement." Indiana University, 1960.

Heckman, Oliver S. "Northern Church Penetration of the South." Duke University, 1939.

Hempstead, Berry. "Student Participation in Administrative Processes in a Selected Group of Predominantly Negro Colleges." University of Kansas, 1971.

Henderson, Romeo C. "The Academic Adaptability of Negro Junior College Graduates to Senior College." Pennsylvania State University, 1950.

Heningburg, Alphonse. "The Teacher in the Negro College." New York University, 1939.

Hicks, Odess Edward. "A Plan for Improving the Teaching of First Year French in the General Education Program at Fort Valley State College, Fort Valley, Georgia." Teachers College Columbia University, 1958.

Hill, Johnny Ray. "A Study of the Public-Assisted Black College Presidency." Miami University, 1972.

Hoig, Stanley W. "A History of the Development of Institutions of Higher Education in Oklahoma." University of Oklahoma, 1971.

Holley, James Melvin. "An Evaluation of the Pre-Service Teacher Education Curriculum in Agricultural Education at the Virginia State College." The Ohio State University, 1958.

Holman, Forest H. C., Jr. "A History of Selected Critical Factors and Barriers in the Development of Black Higher Education." Michigan State University, 1975.

Holmes, Dwight Oliver Wendell. "The Evolution of the Negro College." Teachers College, Columbia University, 1934.

Holtzclaw, Katharine. "Some Factors Related to Curriculum Development for a Minority Segregated Group as Revealed by a Study of Home Economics Education in North Carolina." University of North Carolina, 1945.

Hope, Edward S. "Statues for Non-Teaching Employees at Howard University." Columbia University, 1942.

Hopson, Raymond Wilbur. "An Evaluation of the General Service Programs of Physical Education of Several Negro Institutions of Higher Education as Determined by Criteria Evolved From an Examination of the Purposes of Higher Education and Physical Education." Ohio State University, 1952.

Horton, Allison N. "Origin and Development of the State College Movement in Tennessee." George Peabody College for Teachers, 1954.

Howard, Boyd Davis. "The Origin of Higher Education in the State of Kentucky." University of Cincinnati, 1940.

Howard, Willie Thomas, Jr. "An Analysis of the Effect of Differentiation in Method of Presenting Educational Techniques in Preparing Students in a Predominantly Negro College to Take the National Teacher Examination: Common Examinations." American University, 1969.

Hrabowski, Freeman Alphonsa. "A Comparison of the Graduate Academic Performance of Black Students Who Graduated From Predominantly Black Colleges and From Predominantly White Colleges." University of Illinois at Urbana-Champaign, 1975.

Hubert, Gadua J. "An Examination of the Music Programs of Four Selected Negro Colleges in the Atlanta University Center With Recommendations for Morris Brown College." Teachers College, Columbia University, 1961.

Huggins, Willis N. "The Contribution of the Catholic Church to the Progress of the Negro in the United States." Fordham University, 1932.

Humphreys, Cecil C. "State Financial Support to Higher Education in Tennessee From 1930-1952." New York University, 1958.

Hunter, Robert W. "An Analysis and Critique of the Administrative Organization and Faculty Personnel Policies and Practices at Alcorn A. & M. College." Teachers College,

Columbia University, 1954.

Irvine, Freeman Raymond, Jr. "An Analysis of Black Studies Programs in Black Colleges Within the Southeastern United States With Recommendations for a Masters Degree Program." The University of Tennessee, 1972.

Irving, James Lee. "Some Evidence of Democratic Procedures With Reference to Five Phases of Teacher Education at Langston University." Ohio State University, 1947.

Jackameit, William Preston. "The Political, Social, and Economic Factors in the Shaping of the Structure of Public Higher Education in West Virginia: A History, 1863-1969." The College of William and Mary in Virginia, 1973.

Jackson, Julia. "A Plan for Improving the Beginning Course in French at Morris Brown College, Atlanta, Georgia." Teachers College, Columbia University, 1955.

Jackson, Kara V. "A Plan for the Advance Professional Education of Jeanes Teachers Through Direct Community Participation as an Intergral Part of the Grambling-Tuskegee Study Plan." Teachers College, Columbia University, 1948.

Jackson, Maxine Sherard. "Selected Institutional Characteristics and Special Implications for Science Teacher Education in Predominantly Black Colleges." The University of Iowa, 1972.

Jackson, Norman Allen. "Role Perceptions of the Members of the Southern Association of Black Administrative Personnel Who are Employed by Institutions That Hold Membership in the Southern Association of Colleges and Schools." The Florida State University, 1972.

Jackson, Prince Albert. "The Negro Land-Grant College in the United States: A Study of Developments in Administration, Faculty and Curriculum From 1940 to 1965." Boston College, 1966.

Jackson, Reid E. "A Critical Analysis of Curricula for Educating Secondary School Teachers in Negro Colleges of Alabama." Ohio State University, 1938.

Jacobs, Mary G. "An Evaluation of the Physical Education Service Program for Women in Certain Selected Colleges." New York University, 1957.

Jenkins, Clara Barnes. "A Historical Study of Shaw University, 1865-1963." University of Pittsburgh, 1965.

Joesting, Joan Axtell. "A Comparative Study of Activists and Non-Activists at a Southern Black College." University of Georgia, 1970.

Johnson, Alandus Cordella. "The Growth of Paine College, A Successful Interracial Venture, 1903-1946." University of Georgia, 1970.

Johnson, David Clay. "Decision-Making Characteristics of Administrators in Predominantly Black Institutions of Higher Education." Miami University, 1972.

Johnson, David Horace. "Student Influence in Selected Administrative Policies: An Empirical Study of Three Predominantly Negro Colleges in East Texas." Texas A. & M. University, 1972.

Johnson, Frank Louis. "A Report of a Training Program in Humanistic Teaching Techniques for Prospective Student Teachers at Bowie State College." Columbia University, 1974.

Johnson, George Albert. "A Study of the Relative Academic Success of Negro Junior College Graduates Who Transferred to Negro Senior Colleges in Mississippi in 1964." Mississippi State University, 1970.

Johnson, Harry A. "A Proposed Plan for a Communication Materials Center at Virginia State College, Petersburg, Virginia." Teachers College, Columbia University, 1953.

Johnson, Helen E. W. "The Relationship of the Self-Concepts of Negro and White College Freshmen to the Nature of Their Written Work." North Texas State University, 1970.

Johnson, Henry Morrison. "The Methodist Episcopal Church and the Education of Southern Negroes, 1862-1900." Yale University, 1939.

Johnson, Johnny Bernard. "The Relationship Between the Type of Residence and Scholarship of Students at Arkansas Agricultural, Mechanical and Normal College." University of Arkansas, 1963.

Johnson, Joseph Benjamin. "The Black College and University President: A Description and Analysis of His Profile." University of Colorado, 1973.

Johnson, Lester B., Jr. "A Comparative Study of Three Engineering Technology at Savannah State College as Perceived by Graduates and Supervisors." University of Missouri--Columbia, 1973.

Johnson, Norman Jack. "A Comparative Study of the Interest Patterns of Students Enrolled in Selected Curricula at Prairie View Agricultural, and Mechanical College, Texas, 1956-1958." University of Michigan, 1961.

Johnson, Ras O. "A Plan for Studying the Needs of Students as a Means of Continuing the Program of Curriculum Improvement and Evaluation at Morris Brown College." Columbia University, 1944.

Johnson, Ruth B. "Factors Affecting the Financing of Private Negro Colleges and Universities in the United States." Fordham University, 1961.

Johnson, Rufus C., Jr. "A Study of the Selection and Guidance Procedures for Students in the Program of Industrial Arts Teachers Education at the State Teachers College, Cheyney, Pennsylvania." Pennsylvania State College, 1950.

Johnston, William E., Jr. "A Study of the Registrar in State Supported Colleges for Negroes." University of Oregon, 1952.

Jones, Eugene W. "An Investigation into the Growth and Development of the American Teachers Association With Particular Reference to Its Function and Contribution to Negro Education." Temple University, 1954.

Jones, James B. "An Interpretation and Appraisal of Personnel Services in Negro Colleges." Washington (Seattle) University, 1949.

Jones, Wendall Primus. "The Negro Press and the Higher Education of Negroes 1933-1952: A Study of News and Opinion on Higher Education in the Three Leading Negro Newspapers." University of Chicago, 1954.

Jordan, Clarence Richard. "The Effects of Federal Financial Assistance on Quality Characteristics of Black Colleges as Perceived by College Presidents." University of Minnesota, 1975.

Kennedy, James Scott. "A Study of the Teacher Education Aspects of Speech in Negro Colleges of America: Including the Relationship Between Training Received and the Teaching Activities of Teachers of Speech to Speech Programs in Negro Colleges." New York University, 1961.

Kennedy, Joseph Calvin. "A Study of Ethnic Stereotypes of Negro College Students." Columbia University, 1958.

Kidd, Richard Demosthenes. "Problems Encountered by the Faculty of Central State College, Wilberforce, Ohio." Indiana University, 1959.

Killian, Charles Denmore. "Bishop Daniel A. Payne: Black Spokesman for Reform." Indiana University, 1971.

Kimbrough, Fred Howard. "Analytical and Philosophical Study of Black Educators' Viewpoints on Higher Education in the United States for Black Students in Majority-White Institutions: 1961-1971." Saint Louis University, 1973.

Kimmons, Willie J. "An Analysis of Self-Perceived Roles and Status of Black Administrators in Selected Public Community Colleges." Northern Illinois University, 1974.

Kirby, Joe Earl. "Informal Rules and Institutional Goals at West Virginia State College." West Virginia University, 1974.

Kirkland, Madeline W. "A Plan to Secure a Functional Relationship Between the Special Methods Course in Home Economics and the Supervised Student Teaching Course at Howard University." Teachers College, Columbia University, 1940.

Kleinpeter, Eva Bonnet. "An Investigation of Black Female College Faculty in the Twenty Largest Private Predominantly Black Colleges and Universities." Kansas State University, 1975.

Knight, Charles Lavella. "An Evaluation of Student Personnel Programs in Negro Colleges Accredited by the Southern Association." University of Denver, 1951.

Koonts, Jones Clavin. "Development, Organization, and Administration of Student Teaching in South Carolina." George Peabody College for Teachers, 1958.

Lane, Ulysses Simpson. "The History of Southern University: 1879-1960." Utah State University, 1970.

Lanier, Raphael O'Hara. "The History of Higher Education of Negroes in Texas 1930-1955, With Particular Reference to Texas Southern University." New York University, 1957.

Lao, Rosina Chih-hung Chia. "A Study of the Relationship of Expectancy Patterns to Competent and Innovative Behavior of Male Negro College Students." University of Michigan, 1969.

Lawless, Harrison Duncan, Jr. "The Professional, Social, Economic Status of the Four-Year Teacher Education Graduates of Southern University." Indiana University, 1953.

Leavell, Ullin W. "Philanthropy in Negro Education." George Peabody College for Teachers, 1930.

LeBeau, Oscar R. "Factors Affecting the Need Among Negroes for Graduate Courses in Agriculture." Cornell University, 1937.

LeBlanc, Helen Goff. "An Exploratory Study on the Responses to Students' Needs in Foreign Language Instruction in College and Universities Predominantly Attended by Afro-American Students." University of Minnesota, 1972.

Lee, Lurline M. "The Origin, Development, and Present Status of Arkansas' Program of Higher Education for Negroes." Michigan State University, 1955.

Leif, Thomas Parrish. "The Decision to Migrate: Black College Graduates and Their Tendency to Leave New Orleans."

Tulane University, 1970.

Lewinson, Barbara Sue Kaplan. "Three Conceptions of Black Education: A Study of the Educational Ideas of Benjamin Elijah Mays, Booker T. Washington, and Nathan Wright, Jr." Rutgers University the State University of New Jersey, 1973.

Lewis, Alba Myers. "Comparisons of Student-Faculty Perceptions of Real and Ideal Environments at Five Negro Colleges, 1957-1968." University of North Carolina at Chapel Hill, 1968.

Lewis, Elmer Clifford. "A History of Secondary and Higher Education in Negro Schools Related to the Disciples of Christ." University of Pittsburgh, 1957.

Lewis, William J. "The Educational Speaking of Jabez L. M. Curry." University of Florida, 1955.

Long, John C. "The Disciples of Christ and Negro Education." University of Southern California, 1960.

Lowry, Carmen E. "The Prediction of Academic Success in a Private Liberal Arts College for Negroes." University of Texas, 1957.

Lucas, Aubrey Keith. "The Mississippi Legislature and Mississippi Public Higher Education: 1890-1960." Florida State University, 1966.

Lyons, James Earl. "The Admission of Non-Black Students as an Indicator of a Potential Shift in the Traditional Role of the Black Publicly Supported Colleges and Universities." University of Connecticut, 1974.

Mac Kenna, David Warren. "Developmental Recommendations for a Selected Texas Black College." North Texas State University, 1972.

McAdoo, Douglas Decator. "America's Black Colleges-Survival or Demise: Do They Still Have a Place in our Present Society?" University of Massachusetts, 1974.

McAffee, Sandra Ruth Wray. "Organizational Variables and Educational Innovation in Selected Black Colleges and Universities: A Comparative Study." University of Michigan, 1974.

McAllister, Jane Ellen. "The Training of Negro Teachers in Louisiana." Teachers College, Columbia University, 1929.

McClellan, James F. "Seminary Training in Pastoral Counseling at Howard University." Teachers College, Columbia University, 1956.

McCoy, Clarence Edward. "The Relationship of Black and White Students' Expectations Contrasted With Faculty Perceptions of College Environments." East Texas State University, 1973.

McCoy, Walter Jennings. "The Black College: An Analysis of Recurring Themes in the Literature on the Black College." University of Pittsburgh, 1973.

McCuiston, Fred. "Graduate Instruction for Negroes in the United States." George Peabody College for Teachers, 1939.

McDaniel, Vernon. "Administering and Supervising a Program for Preparing Secondary Teachers at Tuskegee Institute." New York University, 1962.

McFee, Dalton Hays. "The Role of Adult Education in Traditionally Black Public Colleges and Universities." The Ohio State University, 1975.

McGinnis, Frederick Alphonso. "A History of Wilberforce University." University of Cincinnati, 1940.

McKinney, Frederick J. D. "The Guidance Program in Selected Negro Institutions for Higher Education." Indiana University, 1953.

McKinney, Charles Wesley. "A Study of Selected Variables Related to the Movement of Educators From Predominantly Black Colleges and the Effects of This Phenomenon on Predominantly Black Institutions." University of Missouri--Columbia, 1974.

McKinney, Richard Ishmael. "Religion in Higher Education Among Negroes." Yale University, 1942.

McManus, Harold L. "The American Baptist Home Mission Society and Freedmen Education in the South, With Special Reference to Georgia 1862-1897." Yale University, 1953.

McManus, Luther Mitchelle, Jr. "Fayetteville State University Governance: A Descriptive Analysis of the Problems and Changes in Its Development From a State Teachers College." The George Washington University, 1973.

McMillan, William Asbury. "The Evolution of Curriculum Patterns in Six Senior Negro Colleges of the Methodist Church From 1900 to 1950." University of Michigan, 1957.

McPheeters, Alphonso A. "The Origin and Development of Clark University and Gammon Theological Seminary, 1869-1944." University of Cincinnati, 1944.

McQueen, Finley Taylor. "An Evaluation of the Pre-Service Professional Curriculum in Agricultural Education at Tuskegee Institute." The Ohio State University, 1957.

Madden, Samuel A. "A Plan for a Conference Service Bureau at Virginia State College, Petersburg, Virginia." Teachers College, Columbia University, 1953.

Mann, Harold W. "The Life and Times of Atticus Greene Haygood." Duke University, 1962.

Manning, Ivory Cleon. "Job Motivations and Satisfactions of Science Teachers in Predominantly Negro Colleges." University of Minnesota, 1973.

Marion, Claud C. "A Qualitative and Quantitative Study of the Effectiveness of Instructional Programs in Technical Agriculture in Negro Land-Grant Colleges." Cornell University, 1948.

Marshall, David Coughlin. "A History of the Higher Education of Negroes in the State of Louisiana." Louisiana State University, 1956.

Marshall, Jesse E., Jr. "A Study in the Adjustment of Undergraduates in Selected Colleges for Negroes." Indiana University, 1953.

May, Annie Florence. "A Study of Speech Education in Four-Year Negro Colleges and Universities in the United States." Northwestern University, 1951.

Mayo, Judy Jean. "Constituency Group Preceptions of the Institutional Effectiveness of a Black, Urban, Community College." Kent State University, 1973.

Meier, August. "Negro Racial Thought in the Age of Booker T. Washington, Circa 1880-1915." Columbia University, 1957.

Menchan, William M. "An Evaluation of the Cheyney Training School for Teachers." University of Pennsylvania, 1950.

Mileham, Hazel B. "The Junior College Movement in Missouri." University of Missouri, 1934.

Miller, Kenneth Carson. "The Teaching and Learning of Modern Foreign Languages in Colleges and Universities for Negroes." The Ohio State University, 1953.

Miller, Stephen S. "The Emergence of Comprehensive Public Higher Education in the District of Columbia: The Establishment of Federal City College." Catholic University of America, 1970.

Miller, Tyree Jones. "A Quantitative Study of the "Free Modifiers" in Narrative-Descriptive Compositions Written by Black College Freshmen After Leaving the Influence of the Christensen Rhetoric Program and a Study of Their Attitudes Toward Written Composition." Ball State University, 1972.

Minor, Edward Orville. "An Analytical Study of Audio-Visual Programs in Four-Year Accredited Negro Colleges." Indiana University, 1954.

Mitchell, Fred Tom. "Proposed Plan For Training Negro Teachers of Vocational Agriculture." Cornell University, 1931.

Mohr, Paul B., Sr. "A Study of Mathematics Faculties in Predominantly Negro Institutions." Oklahoma State University, 1969.

Moore, Bradley G., Jr. "Implications For the Teacher Education Programs of Two Florida Negro Colleges Found in Problems of Recent Graduates Who Taught and of Senior Students." Ohio State University, 1959.

Moore, Lawrence Henry. "The Relationship of the State Board of Control to the State-Supported Institutions of Higher Education in Texas." University of Texas, 1930.

Moore, Nancy Lazar. "The Socio-Cultural and Historical Foundations of Afro-American Education." University of Massachusetts, 1972.

Moore, Ross H. "Social and Economic Conditions in Mississippi During Reconstruction." Duke University, 1937.

Mooring, Kittye Dale Samuels. "A Study of the Graduates, Department of Business Administration, Prairie View Agricultural and Mechanical College May, 1946-January, 1968." University of Houston, 1969.

Morgan, John William. "The Origin and Distribution of the Graduates of Negro Colleges in Georgia." Teachers College, Columbia University, 1940.

Morgan, Warren Woodrow. "An Assessment of the Goals of a Selected Number of Predominantly Black Institutions of Higher Education." Oklahoma State University, 1970.

Morrison, Richard D. "Occupational Opportunities in Agriculture and Related Fields and Their Implications for Agricultural Education of Negro Students." Michigan State University, 1954.

Morrow, Ralph Ernst. "The Methodist Episcopal Church, the South and Reconstruction, 1865-1880." Indiana University, 1954.

Mose, Ashriel Ira. "To What Extent Do Certain Factors Influence the Academic Success of Freshmen Students in Social Science Courses at South Carolina State College." New York University, 1957.

Murphy, Ella Louise. "Origin and Development of Fayetteville State Teachers College, 1867-1959: A Chapter in the History of the Education of Negroes in North Carolina." New York University, 1960.

Murry, Thelma T. "An Appraisal of Reading Programs in Negro Colleges." Northwestern University, 1951.

Nealy, William Lloyd. "A Survey of Selected Personnel and Their Research Efforts in the Predominantly Black Four-Year Public Institutions." The Ohio State University, 1975.

Neilson, Herman N. "The Development of a Professional Curriculum in Physical Education for Hampton Institute in Its Reorganized Program of Teacher Preparation." New York University, 1956.

Neverdon, Cynthia A. C. "The Articulation and Implementation of Educational Goals for Blacks in the South 1895-1925." Howard University, 1974.

Nicholas, Freddie W. "The Black Land-Grant Colleges: An Assessment of the Major Changes Between 1965-1966 and 1970-1971." University of Virginia, 1973.

Nicholas, James F. "Professional Laboratory Experiences Provided in Teacher Education Programs by Negro Colleges in Virginia and Nearby Areas." Pennsylvania State College, 1950.

Nicholson, Joseph W. "Occupational Study of the Christian Ministry Among Negroes." Northwestern University, 1932.

Noble, Jeanne L. "The Negro Woman Looks at Her College Education." Columbia University, 1955.

Noble, Stuart Grayson. "Forty Years of the Public Schools in Mississippi, With Special Reference to the Education of the Negro." Teachers College, Columbia University, 1918.

Norris, Clarence Windzell, Jr. "St. Phillip's College: A Case Study of a Historically Black Two-Year College." University of Southern California, 1975.

Nyabongo, Virginia S. "Achievement in Modern Foreign Language in Negro Colleges of America." University of Wisconsin, 1944.

Oak, Vishnu V. "Commercial Education in Negro Colleges." Clark University, 1937.

O'Brien, Kenneth B., Jr. "The Supreme Court and Education." Stanford University, 1956.

Oppenheimer, Martin. "The Genesis of Southern Negro Student Movement (Sit-In Movement): A Study of Contemporary Negro Protest." University of Pennsylvania, 1963.

Orbell, John McLeod. "Social Protest and Social Structure: Southern Negro College Student Participation in the Protest Movement." University of North Carolina, 1962.

Orr, Charles W. "Admission Policies and Practices in Negro Land-Grant Colleges." Teachers College, Columbia University, 1954.

Orr, Clyde Lynn. "An Analytical Study of the Conference of Presidents of Negro Land-Grant Colleges." University of Kentucky, 1959.

Orr, Oliver Hamilton, Jr. "Charles Brantley Aycock: A Biography." University of North Carolina, 1958.

Owens, Robert Leon, III. "Financial Assistance for Negro College Students in America: A Social Historical Interpretation of the Philosophy of Negro Higher Education." State University of Iowa, 1953.

Pacter, Paul Allan. "A Program for Improvement of Information Systems at Small, Private, Predominantly Negro Colleges." Michigan State University of Agriculture and Applied Science, 1967.

Paige, Joseph C. "Administrator Faculty and Student Evaluations of Science Programs in Nine Negro Colleges Associated With the African Methodist Episcopal Church." American University, 1965.

Parker, Franklin. "George Peabody Founder of Modern Philanthropy." Georgetown University, 1956.

Parker, Marjorie H. "The Educational Activities of the Freedman's Bureau." University of Chicago, 1951.

Parker, Sellers J. "The Implications of Selected Problems in Teaching Vocational Agriculture for Placing Emphasis on the Content of the Teacher-Training Program at the Agricultural, Mechanical and Normal College in Arkansas." Cornell University, 1949.

Partridge, Deborah Cannon. "A Plan for Redesigning the Curriculum of the Rural Laboratory Schools of Tuskegee Institute." Teachers College, Columbia University, 1945.

Patterson, Joseph Norenzo. "A Study of the History of the Contribution of the American Missionary Association to the Higher Education of the Negro--With Special Reference to Five Selected Colleges Founded by the Association 1865-1900." Cornell University, 1956.

Payne, Joseph Arthur, Jr. "An Analysis of the Role of The Association of Colleges and Secondary Schools for Negroes from 1934-1954." Indiana University, 1957.

Payne, N. Joyce. "The Status of Black Women in Education Administration." Atlanta University, 1975.

Payne, William Vincent. "A Proposed Program for the Development and Use of Instructional Media in Industrial Teacher Education at Tuskegee Institute." Ohio State University, 1965.

Payton, Carolyn Robertson. "Negro College Students." Teachers College, Columbia University, 1962.

Perry, James Olden. "A Study of a Selective Set of Criteria for Determining Success in Secondary Student Teaching at Texas Southern University." University of Texas, 1962.

Pfanner, Daniel J. "The Thought of Negro Educators on Negro Higher Education, 1900-1950." Teachers College, Columbia University, 1957.

Phelps, Ralph A., Jr. "The Struggle for Public Higher Education for Negroes in Texas." Southwestern Baptist Theological Seminary, 1949.

Phillips, Augustus C. "Industrial Education for Negroes in the South Atlantic Region-- Development of a Program Based on the Population and Occupational Changes." Ohio State University, 1942.

Pierce, Juantia G. "The Organization and Administration of Health, Physical Education and Recreation in the Atlanta University Center." New York University, 1945.

Pierro, Armstead A. "A History of Professional Preparation for Physical Education in Some Selected Negro Colleges and Universities, 1924-1958." University of Michigan, 1962.

Pirkle, William B. "A Study of the State Scholarship Aid Program for Negroes in Georgia, 1944-1955." Alabama Polytechnic Institute, 1956.

Pitts, Willis N., Jr. "A Critical Study of Booker T. Washington as a Speech-Maker With an Analysis of Seven Selected Speeches." University of Michigan, 1952.

Player, Willa. "Improving College Education for Women at Bennett College." Teachers College, Columbia University, 1948.

Price, Joseph St. Clair. "Predicting Freshman Achievement: A Follow-Up Study." Harvard University, 1940.

Pruitt, William Nelson. "A Comparison of the Developmental Differences Between Black Students Attending a Predominantly Black Institution and Black Students Attending a Predominantly White Institution." University of Michigan, 1974.

Puckett, John R. "An Evaluation of Certain Areas of Physical Education Service Programs of Selected White and Negro Colleges in Tennessee." University of Tennessee, 1959.

Pugh, Griffith Thompson. "George Washington Cable: A Critical Biography." Vanderbilt University, 1945.

Pullum, Fred Douglas. "Professional Preparation in Physical Education at Historically Black Institutions in Georgia." University of Georgia, 1974.

Rackley, Larney G. "The Influence of the National Defense Education Act of 1958 on the Seventeen Original Negro Land-Grant Colleges With Emphasis on Audio-Visual Education." University of Oklahoma, 1963.

Ramsey, Berkley Carlyle. "The Public Black College in Georgia: A History of Albany State College, 1903-1965." The Florida State University, 1973.

Rand, Earl W. "An Analysis of the Boards of Control of a Group of Selected Negro Protestant Church-Related Colleges." Indiana University, 1952.

Rea, Katharine. "A Follow-Up Study of the Women Graduates From the State Colleges of Mississippi, Class of 1956." The Ohio State University, 1958.

Redd, George N. "A Suggested Plan for the Education of Rural Teachers in a Small Liberal Arts College." Teachers College, Columbia University, 1940.

Reed, William T. "A Partial Selection of Curriculum Content for the Improvement of Industrial Teacher Education in Colleges for Negroes." University of Pittsburgh, 1947.

Reedy, Sidney Joseph. "English Composition in Representative Negro Teacher-Education Institutions." Colorado State College of Education, 1939.

Reeves, Elizabeth W. "A Program in Speech for the College of Liberal Arts at Howard University." Teachers College, Columbia University, 1956.

Rhodes, Francis A. "The Legal Development of State Supported Higher Education in Florida." University of Florida, 1949.

Rice, Jessie P. "J. L. M. Curry, Southerner, Statesman and Educator." Columbia University, 1950.

Richard, Alvin Joseph. "Patterns of Student Participation in Policy-Making in Southern Four-Year Black Colleges and Universities." University of Illinois at Urbana-Champaign, 1972.

Richards, Violet K. "A Study of Teacher Education Programs in Selected Liberal Arts Colleges for Negroes." Northwestern University, 1952.

Richardson, John Francis. "A Comparison of Certain Characteristics of a Group of Negro Education and Non-Education College Students: An Investigation to Determine the Nature and Significance of the Differences in Various Characteristics Between Negro College Students Who Select Teaching and Those Who Choose Other Vocational Goals." New York University, 1963.

Ridley, Walter Nathaniel. "Prognostic Values of Freshmen Tests Used at Virginia State College." University of Virginia, 1953.

Roberts, Edward B. "The Administration of the Peabody Education Fund From 1880 to 1905." George Peabody College for Teachers, 1936.

Robinson, James Christopher. "South Carolina's Black Colleges: A Strategy for Survival." University of Massachusetts, 1973.

Robinson, Walter Julius. "Origin and Development of Industrial Education in Louisiana." University of Missouri, 1950.

Robinson, William Hannibal. "The History of Hampton Institute, 1868-1949." New York University, 1954.

Roche, Richard J. "Catholic Colleges and the Negro Students." Catholic University of America, 1948.

Rochelle, Charles Edward. "Graduate and Professional Education for Negroes." University of California (Berkeley), 1943.

Roundtree, Thelma Louise Johnson. "The Place of Humanities in Sixteen Negro Colleges." Emory University, 1968.

Rouse, Michael Francis. "A Study of the Development of Negro Education Under Catholic Auspices in Maryland and the District of Columbia." John Hopkins University, 1933.

Rudwick, Elliott M. "W. E. B. Du Bois: A Study in Minority Group Leadership." University of Pennsylvania, 1956.

Ryder, William Henderson. "Music at Virginia State College, 1883-1966." University of Michigan, 1970.

Sadberry, Lonnie. "A Study of the Attitudes of Negro Faculty Members Toward White Faculty Members in Selected Predominantly Negro Colleges." University of Houston, 1974.

Saine, Matilda L. "Relationship of Selected Factors to the Reading Interests of Negro College Freshmen." University of Chicago, 1951.

Sanders, Charles Douglas. "Student Personnel Services in Negro Colleges of the South Atlantic States." Oregon State University, 1963.

Sandle, Floyd L. "A History of the Development of the Educational Theater in Negro Colleges and Universities From 1911 to 1959." Louisiana State University, 1959.

Sanford, Paul Lawrence. "The Origins and Development of Higher Education for Negroes in South Carolina to 1920." University of New Mexico, 1965.

Satneck, Walter Joseph. "The History of the Origins and Development of Delaware State College and Its Role in Higher Education for Negroes in Delaware." New York University, 1962.

Satterwhite, Mildred M. "The Vocational Interests of Negro Teachers' College Students." University of California (Berkeley), 1949.

Sawyer, Robert McLaran. "The Gaines Case: Its Background and Influence on the University of Missouri and Lincoln University, 1936-1950." University of Missouri, 1966.

Saylor, Lucile Phillips. "Students' Expectations and Perceptions of the University Environment at Florida Agricultural and Mechanical University." Florida State University, 1973.

Schein, Leon Arthur. "Attitudes of a Sample of Freshmen and Senior College Students From Several Roman Catholic, Military and Negro Institutions." Pennsylvania State University, 1969.

Schroeder, Betty Lou Foster. "An Examination of the Characteristics of Students and Faculty in a Small, Black, Denominational College." The University of Texas at Austin, 1970.

Scrafford, Elmer Joseph. "The Utilization of Collegiate Enrollment Projections in West Virginia as Applied to Bluefield State College." The Ohio State University, 1964.

Senger, Kenyon B. "A History of the Community College Movement in North Carolina, 1927-1963." University of North Carolina, 1966.

Settle, Joseph Curtis. "A Study of Alternative Roles and Patterns for Two Small Private Black Church-Related Colleges in North Carolina." Duke University, 1974.

Shannon, Irwin V. "Negro Education and the Development of a Group Tradition." Vanderbilt University, 1934.

Shaw, Willie George. "A Description of General Education Requirements in Physical Education for Selected Private, Predominantly Black Four-Year Colleges and Universities in Tennessee, Alabama, and Georgia." Middle Tennessee State University, 1975.

Shepard, Cynthia Norton. "The Black College as a Contributor to the Intellectual Common Market: Readiness of Faculty and Students of the Black College for International Involvement." University of Massachusetts, 1972.

Shepherd, Robert E. "A Study of National Teaching Fellows in Predominantly Black Public Colleges, 1968-1972." Southern Illinois University, 1975.

Sherer, Robert Glenn. "Let Us Make Man: Negro Education in Nineteenth Century Alabama." University of North Carolina, 1969.

Shipman, F. George. "An Evaluative Study of the Southern Education Foundation's Regional Research and Leadership Development Program." George Peabody College for Teachers, 1961.

Shipman, Meada Gibbs. "A Study of the Graduates Who Earned Bachelor Degrees in Business in 1964, 1965, 1969 and 1970 From Four Predominantly Black Universities." The University of Wisconsin, 1973.

Shoots, Queen Esther. "Gainful Employment of Negro Home Economics Graduates With Implications for Education Programs." University of Wisconsin, 1965.

Silas, Samuel Louis. "Role Expectations of Presidents in Predominantly Black State and Privately Supported Colleges and Universities as Perceived by Trustees, Presidents and Deans." Southern Illinois University, 1974.

Silverman, Pincus. "Characteristics of a Negro College Environment and Its Relationship to Student Value Systems." North Texas State University, 1964.

Simpson, James C. "A Study of Recent Litigation Arising From the "Separate But Equal" Doctrine as it Applies to Higher Education of the Negro in the South." Cornell University, 1953.

Smith, Bernard Shelton. "Evaluation of the Carnegie Exchange Program's Cross Cultural Experience Component: An Appraisal of the Experiences of Eighteen White Students on a Predominantly Black University Campus." The Florida State University, 1972.

Smith, John Thomas. "Programs of Preparation for School Administration in Negro Graduate School." University of Kentucky, 1961.

Smith, Walter Lee. "A Study of the Black Public Junior Colleges in Florida: 1957-1966." The Florida State University, 1974.

Smith, William N. "An Investigation of Certain Factors in Test of Mental Ability and Achievement to Determine Their Influence on Scores Obtained by Southern Negro Students." Indiana University, 1952.

Smith, William P., Jr. "A Follow-Up of Selected Graduates of Alabama State College." Rutgers the State University of New Jersey, 1959.

Spann, Annabelle E. "A Follow-Up Study of Alabama Agricultural Mechanical College Home Economic Graduates With Implications for Curriculum Improvement." University of Wisconsin, 1958.

Speigner, Theodore Roosevelt. "An Analysis of the Resource-Use Education Program of North Carolina College at Durham." University of Michigan, 1961.

Stallings, Charles W. "Some Aspects of the Evolution of Negro Colleges in America as Depicted by the Execution of a Mural." Pennsylvania State University, 1954.

Stark, Grace W. "Beginnings of Teacher Training in Mississippi." George Peabody University, 1946.

Stenhouse, Richard Eugene. "Current Status of Chief Student Personnel Administrators in United Negro College Fund Member Institutions." University of Denver, 1968.

Stewart, William W. "Activities and Training of Louisiana Negro High School Teachers." University of Nebraska, 1946.

Stinnett, Tim Moore. "The Accreditation of Institutions for Teacher Preparation." University of Texas, 1951.

Stone, Raymond P. "Separate But Equal"; The Evolution and Demise of a Constitutional Doctrine." Princeton University, 1964.

Strider, Rutherford H. "Music in the General College Program: A Plan for Morgan State College." New York University, 1955.

Stukes, Bernice B. Wells. "Special Education Teacher Preparation in South Carolina State College: Future Directions." Columbia University, 1973.

Styles, Marvalene Hughes. "Personality Characteristics, Self-Concept, Vocational Aspiration and Academic Performance of Negro Freshmen at a Predominantly White University as Compared With Negro Freshmen at a Predominantly Negro University." The Florida State University, 1969.

Sullivan, John Edward. "A Historical Investigation of the Negro Land-Grant College From 1890-1964." Loyola University of Chicago, 1969.

Summersette, John Fred. "The Structure of the Atlanta University Center." Stanford University, 1952.

Swain, Myrtle Thompson. "Selection and Retention of Faculty in the Private Predominantly Negro Colleges in North Carolina." Duke University, 1970.

Swint, Henry Lee. "The Northern Teacher in the South, 1862-1870." Vanderbilt University, 1939.

Talbot, David Arlington. "The Predictive Value of Selected Variables in Determining Achievement of the Doctorate by Graduates of Arkansas Agricultural, Mechanical and Normal College." University of Arkansas, 1966.

Taylor, Alrutheus Ambush. "The Negro in the Reconstruction of Virginia." Harvard University, 1936.

Taylor, Cyrus B. "Mechanic Arts Program in Land-Grant Colleges Established for Negroes: A Study of the Types and Status of the Programs Operating and an Analysis of These Programs." University of Minnesota, 1955.

Taylor, Hoy. "An Interpretation of the Early Administration of the Peabody Fund." George Peabody College for Teachers, 1933.

Taylor, Joseph Thomas. "An Analysis of Some Factors Involved in the Changing Function and Objectives of the Negro College." Indiana University, 1952.

Taylor, Paul L. "An Analysis of Religious Counseling Practices of Nine Selected Negro Colleges." Indiana University, 1958.

Taylor, Prince Albert, Jr. "A History of Gammon Theological Seminary." New York University, 1948.

Taylor, Ralph Lee. "A Comparison of the Self-Concept of Negro Students at the University of Alabama and Negro Students at Stillman College." The University of Alabama, 1970.

Teele, Arthur E. "Education of the Negro in North Carolina, 1862-1872." Cornell University, 1954.

Terry, William E. "Origin and Development of Texas Southern University, Houston, Texas." University of Houston, 1968.

Thomas, Emma Joahanne. "Career Patterns of Black Women Administrators in Historically Negro Senior Colleges and Universities." Washington State University, 1976.

Thomas, Gregory. "Historical Survey of Black Education as a Means of Black Liberation: 1875-1969." The Ohio State University, 1971.

Thomas, William Henry. "An Assessment of Booker Taliaferro Washington's Educational Influence in the United States and West Africa Between the Years 1880 and 1925." Michigan State University, 1972.

Thompkins, Robert E. "A History of Religious Education Among Negroes in the Presbyterian Church of the United States of America." University of Pittsburgh, 1951.

Thompson, Cleopatra Davenport. "The Jackson State College Graduate in American Society: A Follow-Up Study of 306 Graduates, 1944-1953." Cornell University, 1960.

Thompson, Daniel C. "Teachers in Negro Colleges. (A Sociological Analysis)." Columbia University, 1955.

Thompson, Ray. "Counselor Training in State Supported Negro Colleges and Universities in States With Dual Educational Systems." Michigan State College, 1953.

Thornton, Peter Benedict. "Analysis of the Counselor-Training Program at Texas Southern University." Colorado State College, 1963.

Threatt, Robert. "A Study of Selected Characteristics and College Success of High and Low Achieving Negro Students on the CEEB Scholastic Aptitude Test in Georgia." University of Oklahoma, 1963.

Tilford, Michael Phillip. "Factors Related to the Choice of Science as a Major Among Negro College Students." Oklahoma State University, 1971.

Tindall, George B. "The Negro in South Carolina After Reconstruction, 1877-1900." University of North Carolina, 1951.

Tinsley, Sammy Jay. "A History of Mississippi Valley State College." University of Mississippi, 1972.

Tobin, Mc Lean. "A Profile of Black Women Doctorate Holders in Black Public Colleges and Universities: 1973-1974." Kansas State University, 1975.

Toles, Caesar F. "Regionalism in Southern Higher Education." University of Michigan, 1953.

Townes, Ross E. "A Study of Professional Education in Physical Education in Selected Negro Colleges." Indiana University, 1951.

Troup, Cornelius V. "A Study of the Student Personnel Services Offered by the Negro Colleges of Georgia." Ohio State University, 1948.

Turner, Bridges Alfred. "Objectives and Problems of Industrial Education in Negro Colleges." Pennsylvania State University, 1941.

Van Wright, Aaron, Jr. "Factors Relative to Job Selection in Music Faculties of the Original Negro Land-Grant Colleges Since the 1954 Supreme Court Decision." University of Oklahoma, 1965.

Venable, Tom C. "A History of Negro Education in Kentucky." George Peabody College for Teachers, 1953.

Voorhees, Lillian. "A Program of Speech Education for Talladega College." Columbia University, 1944.

Wade, Charles. "A Survey of Student Personnel Services in the Thirty-Three Private Predominantly Negro Colleges of the United Negro College Fund." University of Montana, 1968.

Walker, George Henry, Jr. "A Coordinated Plan for a Communication Center at the Norfolk Division of Virginia State College." New York University, 1949.

Walker, Paul. "Court Decisions Dealing With Legal Relationships Between American Colleges and Universities and Their Students." University of Southern California, 1961.

Ward, Arthur W. "Characteristics of Instructional Personnel of Industrial Teacher Education Programs in Traditionally Black Institutions." Indiana University, 1974.

Ward, John H. "The Status of Psychology in the Seven Negro Colleges of Alabama." New York University, 1955.

Ward, Richard H. "The Development of Baptist Higher Education in Tennessee." George Peabody College for Teachers, 1954.

Washington, Walter. "Utica Junior College, 1903-1957: A Half Century of Education for Negroes." University of Southern Mississippi, 1970.

Watkins, Clifford Edward I. "The Works of Three Selected Band Directors in Predominantly Black American Colleges and Universities." Southern Illinois University, 1975.

Weatherford, Allen Ericson, II. "Professional Health Education, Physical Education, and Recreation in Negro Colleges and Universities in the United States--A Study of Negro Institutions Offering the Four-Year Teacher Education in Health, Physical Education, and Recreation, 1945-1946." Pennsylvania State College, 1948.

Weaver, Ollie Garfield. "The Educational Philosophy of Booker T. Washington." Temple University, 1948.

Welch, Lucille S. "A Critical Analysis of Negro College Catalogs to Determine the Course Offering in Elementary Education, Particularly in the Field of Teacher Training." Indiana University, 1950.

West, Earl H. "The Life and Educational Contributions of Barnas Sears." George Peabody College for Teachers, 1961.

West, Gordon L. "An Appraisal of Selected Aspects of a Teacher Education Program at Saint Augustine's College Based Upon a Follow-Up of Beginning Secondary School Teachers." Indiana University, 1959.

West, Sam Carrol. "A Comparative and Historical Study of the Educational Programs for Negroes of the Methodist Episcopal Church, South 1844-1910." Teachers College, Columbia University, 1946.

Wharton, Vernon L. "The Negro in Mississippi, 1865-1890." University of North Carolina, 1940.

Wheaton, Louis Augustus. "The Black Subculture and the Traditional Black College: The Ideology of Future Black Educators." Columbia University Teachers College, 1973.

White, Frank H. "The Economic and Social Development of Negroes in South Carolina Since 1900." New York University, 1960.

White, Howard A. "The Freedmen's Bureau in Louisiana." Tulane University, 1956.

White, Robert H. "The Tallahasse Sit-Ins and Core: A Non-Violent Revolutionary Sub-Movement." Florida State University, 1964.

Whitehead, Matthew Jackson. "Negro Liberal Arts College Deans." New York University, 1944.

Wiggins, Elnora. "An Analysis of Teaching Strengths and Weaknesses of Black Business Teachers in the Southeastern United States." University of Mississippi, 1975.

Wilder, Mary Roberts. "An Evaluation of the Pre-Service and In-Service Academic Preparation in English for Teachers of Disadvantaged Students in Selected Colleges in the State of Georgia." The Florida State University, 1970.

Wiley, Grace Delois. "A Proposed In-Service Education Program in Music for Agricultural, Mechanical, and Normal College at Pine Bluff, Arkansas." University of Oklahoma, 1969.

Wiley, Walter Eugene. "The Influence of the State and the United States Supreme Court Decisions on the Education of the Negro." Ohio State University, 1951.

Wilkinson, Rachel Elizabeth Diggs. "A Determination of Goals for Alumni Relations in the Colleges for Negroes in North Carolina." New York University, 1952.

Williams, Audrey Yvonne. "An Analysis of the Relationship of Connecticut State Community College Central Administrators' Leadership Styles to Their Opinions of the Black Tradition in Higher Education." The University of Connecticut, 1973.

Williams, Elson Kearney. "The Status of College-Teacher Preparation in North Carolina State Colleges for Negroes." New York University, 1948.

Williams, Joshua L. "A Plan for Making More Meaningful the Course in Freshmen College Algebra at State Agricultural and Mechanical College, Orangeburg, South Carolina." Teachers College, Columbia University, 1955.

Williams, Willie Coye. "The Efficacy of Group Counseling on the Academic Performance of Black College Freshmen With Low-Predicted Grade Point Averages." University of Georgia, 1971.

Wilson, Anaise Victorianne. "A Study of the Relationship of Selected Factors to the Academic Achievement of College Freshmen in the School of Education of Tuskegee Institute." New York University, 1968.

Wilson, George Dewey. "Developments in Negro Colleges During the 20 Year Period, 1914-1915 to 1933-1934." The Ohio State University, 1935.

Wilson, Herbert A. "An Analysis of the Views of Alcorn A. & M. College Held by Its Students, Faculty and Non-Academic Staff." Teachers College, Columbia University, 1958.

Wilson, Johnnie Harrison. "A Comparative Study of the Music Curriculum of the Negro and White Colleges and Universities in Sixteen States of the United States." University of Kansas, 1951.

Winder, Thelma V. "Financial Experiences of Families: Family Financial Experiences of Selected Graduates of Morgan State College and the Implications of These Experiences for Teaching Family Finance." New York University, 1957.

Windom, John Henry. "Comparison of the Duties of Deans of Men and Women in Four-Year Colleges for Negroes Throughout the United States." Indiana University, 1950.

Witherington, Henry C. "History of State Higher Education in Tennessee." University of Chicago, 1931.

Wittaker, Jeweleane Wilma Parker. "Effects of the Application of Linguistics on Reading Comprehension of Black Freshmen Students at Texas Southern University." University of Houston, 1974.

Woodbury, Willie, Jr. "A Comparative Study of the Educational Attitudes of Student Teachers, Their Cooperating Teachers and Principals From Two Predominantly Black Colleges; and Final Evaluation of the Student Teachers." University of Colorado, 1974.

Woodson, Grace I. "The Implications of Purpose for the Definition of a College Program, With Special Reference to the Separate Negro College." The Ohio State University, 1940.

Wright, Stephen J. "A Study of Certain Attitudes Towards the Education of Negroes Since 1865." New York University, 1943.

Wright, Wilbert. "A Comparative Study Between Socio-Economic Status, Race, Sex, Classification and Student Opinions Related to Personnel Services of Selected Texas Colleges." University of Houston, 1969.

Wright, William Henry. "A Study of Professional Preparation in Physical Education for Men at Predominantly Negro State-Supported Institutions of Higher Education." Columbia University, 1971.

Yancey, Maude Josephine. "A Study of Some Health Misconceptions of Prospective Teachers in Negro Colleges of North Carolina." University of Michigan, 1952.

Young, Herman Andre. "An Educational and Professional Profile of Black American Doctorates in the Natural Sciences." Indiana University, 1973.

Young, Percy. "Guidance in Negro Land-Grant Colleges." Harvard University, 1946.

Younge, James Wells. "A Study High School Preparation and Freshmen Failures at North Carolina College at Durham." Temple University, 1967.

Zion, Carol L. "The Desegregation of a Public Junior College: A Case Study of Its Negro Faculty." Florida State University, 1965.

INSTITUTIONAL HISTORIES 1867-1976 2

ALABAMA

Alabama Agricultural and Mechanical University
Normal, Alabama

Orr, Charles Walter. "The Educational Philosophy of William H. Councill." Master's Thesis, Fisk University, 1939.

Talladega College
Talladega, Alabama

Beard, Augustus Field. _Talladega College_. New York: American Missionary Association, 1907.

Tuskegee Institute
Tuskegee, Alabama

Bell, Sallie M. Brown. "A Study of the Development of Tuskegee Institute Under the Administration of Washington, Moton, and Patterson." Master's Thesis, Atlanta University, 1950.

Blackwell, Velma Lavern. "A Black Institution Pioneering Adult Education: Tuskegee Institute Past and Present (1881-1973)." Doctoral Dissertation, The Florida State University, 1973.

Brooks, Thomas Edward. "The Inception and Development of Student Personnel Services at Tuskegee Institute." Doctoral Dissertation, Indiana University, 1955.

Bruce, R. C. "Tuskegee Institute." Chapter 3 in American Unitarian Association. _From Servitude to Service_. American Unitarian Association, 1905.

Campbell, Thomas M. _The Movable School Goes to the Negro Farmer_. Tuskegee, Ala.: Tuskegee Institute Press, 1936.

Citro, Joseph F. "Booker T. Washington's Tuskegee Institute: Black School-Community, 1900-1915." Doctoral Dissertation, University of Rochester, 1972.

Deloney, Willie Louise. "A History of Tuskegee." Master's Thesis, University of Michigan, 1938. [Missing-not available at U. M.]

Dryer, Edmund Hext. *Origin of Tuskegee Normal and Industrial Institute*. Birmingham, Ala.: Roberts and Sons, 1938.

Ludlow, Helen Wilhemina. ed. *Tuskegee Normal and Industrial School for Training Colored Teachers. Its Story and Its Songs*. Hampton, Va.: Normal School Steam Press, 1884.

Stokes, Anson P. *Tuskegee Institute: The First 50 Years*. Tuskegee, Ala.: Tuskegee Institute Press, 1931.

Thrasher, Max B. *Tuskegee and Its Work*. Boston: Small and Maynard, 1900.

Stillman College
Tuscaloosa, Alabama

Bottoms, L. W. "The Policies and Rationale Underlying the Support of Negro College and Schools Maintained by the Presbyterian Church in the United States." *Journal of Negro Education*, 29 (Summer, 1960), 264-273.

Sikes, William Marion. "The Historical Development of Stillman Institute." Master's Thesis, University of Alabama, 1930.

Terry, Paul W. ed. *A Study of Stillman Institute-A Junior College for Negroes*. Research Studies Number 8. University of Alabama: Bureau of Educational Research, College of Education, University of Alabama, 1946.

ARKANSAS

Philander Smith College
Little Rock, Arkansas

Brawley, James P. "Historical Sketch of Philander Smith College." Chapter 21 in *Two Centuries of Methodist Concern: Bondage, Freedom, and Education of Black People*. New York: Vantage Press, Inc., 1974.

Gibson, De Lois. "Philander Smith College, 1877-1969." Doctoral Dissertation, University of Arkansas, 1972.

University of Arkansas at Pine Bluff
Pine Bluff, Arkansas

"Branch Normal," in Reynolds, John Hugh and Thomas, David Yancey. History of the University of Arkansas. Fayetteville, Arkansas: University of Arkansas, 1910. (pp. 299-311)

Chambers, Fredrick. "Historical Study of Arkansas Agricultural, Mechanical, and Normal College, 1873-1943." Doctoral Dissertation, Ball State University, 1970.

DELAWARE

Delaware State College
Dover, Delaware

Satneck, Walter Joseph. "The History of the Origins and Development of Delaware State College and Its Role in Higher Education for Negroes in Delaware." Doctoral Dissertation, New York University, 1962.

DISTRICT OF COLUMBIA

District of Columbia Teachers College
Washington, D. C.

Hatter, Henrietta Roberts. "History of Miner Teachers College." Master's Thesis, Howard University, 1939.

O'Connor, Ellen M. ed. Myrtilla Miner, A Memoir. Boston: Houghton Mifflin and Company, 1885.

Federal City College
Washington, D. C.

Miller, Stephen S. "The Emergence of Comprehensive Public Higher Education in the District of Columbia: The Establishment of Federal City College." Doctoral Dissertation, Catholic University of America, 1970.

Howard University
Washington, D. C.

Coles, Anna B. "The Howard University School of Nursing in Historical Perspective." Journal of the National Medical Association, 61 (March, 1969), 105-118.

Duncan, Anne McKay. "History of Howard University Library, 1867-1929." Master's Thesis, Catholic University of America, 1951.

Dyson, Walter. The Founding of Howard University. Washington, D. C.: Howard University Press, 1921.

_____. History of Federal Appropriations for Howard University 1867-1926. Washington, D. C.: Howard University Press, 1927.

_____. Founding the School of Medicine of Howard University 1868-1873. Washington, D. C.: Howard University Press, 1929.

_____. Howard University; The Capstone of Negro Education, A History: 1867-1940. Washington, D. C.: The Graduate School, Howard University, 1941.

Holmes, Dwight O. W. "50 Years of Howard University." Journal of Negro History, 3 : 2 (April and October, 1918), 128-138; 368-380.

Lamb, Daniel S., compiler. Howard University Medical Department, Washington, D. C. A Historical, Biographical and Statistical Souvenir. Washington, D.C.: [Howard University] 1900

Logan, Rayford W. Howard University: The First One Hundred Years, 1867-1967. New York: New York University Press, 1969.

Melchor, Beulah. "A History of the Title to the Campus of Howard University, 1851-1885." Master's Thesis, Howard University, 1943.

Miller, Kelly. "Howard University." Chapter 1 in American Missionary Association. From Servitude to Service. Boston: American Missionary Association, 1905.

"Origin and Development of Howard University, Washington, D. C." Barnard's American Journal of Education, 19 : 245.

Patton, William W. History of Howard University. Washington, D. C.: Howard University, 1896.

Twenty-Fifth Anniversary of the Organization of Howard University, March 2, 1892. Washington, D. C.: Howard University Press, 1895.

FLORIDA

Bethune-Cookman College
Daytona Beach, Florida

Brawley, James P. "A Brief Historical Account of Bethune-Cookman College." Chapter 12 in Two Centuries of Methodist Concern: Bondage, Freedom, and Education of Black People. New York: Vantage Press, Inc., 1974.

Peare, Catherine O. Mary McLeod Bethune. New York: Vanguard Press, 1951.

Florida Agricultural and Mechanical University
Tallahassee, Florida

Griffin, Robert P. "Historical Development of Athletics at Florida Agricultural and Mechanical College." Master's Thesis, Ohio State University, 1946.

Neyland, Leedell W., and Riley, John W. The History of Florida Agricultural and Mechanical University. Gainesville: University of Florida Press, 1963.

Paddyfote, C. J. Archer. "The Administration of J. R. E. Lee, President of Florida Agricultural and Mechanical College 1924 to 1944." Master's Thesis, Florida Agricultural and Mechanical University, 1957.

Spellman, Cecil L. Rough Steps on My Stairway: The Life History of a Negro Educator. New York: Exposition Press, 1953.

GEORGIA

Albany State College
Albany, Georgia

Harper, Hoyt Howard. "A History of Albany State College." Master's Thesis, Atlanta University, 1950. (In Atlanta University--Bell and Howell Black Culture Collection, see Microfilm Roll #560)

Holley, Joseph Winthrop. You Can't Build a Chimney From the Top: The South Through the Life of a Negro Educator. New York: William-Frederick Press, 1948.

Ramsey, Berkley Carlyle. "The Public Black College in Georgia: A History of Albany State College, 1903-1965." Doctoral Dissertation, The Florida State University, 1973.

Atlanta University Center
Atlanta, Georgia

Adams, Myron Winslow. A History of Atlanta University. Atlanta: Atlanta University Press, 1930.

Bacote, Clarence A. The Story of Atlanta University: A Century of Service, 1865-1965. Atlanta: Atlanta University, 1969.

Du Bois, W. E. B. "Atlanta University." Chapter 5 in American Unitarian Association. From Servitude to Service. Boston: American Unitarian Association, 1905.

Fernandez, Lilia Valentina. "History and Development of the Department of Sociology at Atlanta University, Atlanta, Georgia, From 1934 to 1965." Master's Thesis, Atlanta University, 1966.

Heyliger, Edna Ethel. "A Study of the Development of the Atlanta University School of Social Work, 1920-1942." Master's Thesis, Atlanta University, 1943.

Jones, Edward A. "History of the Transfer of Land and Buildings in Connection With Development of the Plan of Affiliation of Atlanta University, Morehouse College and Spelman College." Appendix "J" in A Candle in the Dark--A History of Morehouse College. Valley Forge: The Judson Press, 1967.

Summersette, John J. "The Structure of Atlanta University Center." Doctoral Dissertation, Stanford University, 1952.

Towns, George A. "The Sources of the Traditions of Atlanta University." Phylon, 3 : 2 (Second Quarter, 1942), 117-134.

Clark University
Atlanta, Georgia

Brawley, James P. "A Brief Sketch of Clark College." Chapter 14 in Two Centuries of Methodist Concern: Bondage, Freedom, and Education of Black People. New York: Vantage Press, Inc., 1974.

_____. "Brief Historical Sketch of Gammon Theological Seminary." Chapter 16 Ibid.

McPheeters, Alphonso A. "The Origin and Development of Clark University and Gammon Theological Seminary, 1869-1944." Doctoral Dissertation, University of Cincinnati, 1944.

_____. "Clark College: 90 Years of Progress." Central Christian Advocate, June 1, 1959.

Taylor, Prince Albert, Jr. "A History of Gammon Theological Seminary." Doctoral Dissertation, New York University, 1948.

Morehouse College
Atlanta, Georgia

Boger, Dellie L. "Problems of Morehouse College Students." Doctoral Dissertation, Teachers College, Columbia University, 1956.

Brawley, Benjamin G. History of Morehouse College. Atlanta: Morehouse College, 1917.

Jones, Edward Allen. A Candle in the Dark--A History of Morehouse College. Valley Forge: The Judson Press, 1968.

_____. "Morehouse College in Business Ninety Years--Building Men." Phylon, 18 : 3 (3rd Quarter, 1957), 231-245.

Sisk, Glenn. "Morehouse College." Journal of Negro Education, 27 (Winter, 1958), 201-208.

Morris Brown College
Atlanta, Georgia

Ponton, Mungo Melanchthon. Life and Times of Henry M. Turner. Atlanta: A. B. Caldwell, 1917.

Thomas, Anna B. Morris Brown College, 1885-1932. Atlanta: Morris Brown College, 1932.

Paine College
Augusta, Georgia

Brawley, James P. "A Brief Historical Sketch of Paine College." Chapter 20 in Two Centuries of Methodist Concern: Bondage, Freedom, and Education of Black People. New York: Vantage Press Inc., 1974.

Clary, George E. "The Founding of Paine College--A Unique Venture in Interracial Cooperation in the New South, 1882-1903." Doctoral Dissertation, University of Georgia, 1965.

_____. "Southern Methodism's Unique Adventure in Race Relations: Paine College, 1882-1903." Methodist History, 9 : 2 (1971), 22-33.

Dempsey, Elain Franklin. Atticus G. Haygood. Nashville: Parthenon Press, Methodist Publishing House, 1940.

Graham, William L. "Patterns of Intergroup Relations in the Cooperative Establishment, Control, and Administration of Paine College (Georgia) by Southern Negro and White People: A Study of Intergroup Process." Doctoral Dissertation, New York University, 1955.

Johnson, Alandus Cordella. "The Growth of Paine College, A Successful Interracial Venture, 1903-1946." Doctoral Dissertation, University of Georgia, 1970.

Spelman College
Atlanta, Georgia

Jones, Edward A. "A History of the Transfer of Land and Buildings in Connection With Development of the Plan of Affiliation of Atlanta University, Morehouse College, and Spelman College." Appendix "J" in A Candle in the Dark--A History of Morehouse College. Valley Forge: The Judson Press, 1967.

Read, Florence Matilda. The Story of Spelman College. Princeton: Princeton University Press, 1961.

Tapley, Lucy Hale. "Spelman College." Atlanta Historical Bulletin, 1 : 3 (May, 1930), 38-56.

KANSAS

Western University
Kansas City, Kansas

Murry, Orrin McKinley, Sr. The Rise and Fall of Western University. Kansas City: Privately Printed, The Author, 3070 33rd Street, Kansas City, Kansas.

KENTUCKY

Berea College*
Berea, Kentucky

[Berea College]. Historical Sketch of Berea College, Together With Addresses in Its Behalf. New York: D. D. Nicholson Printer, 1869.

Black, Isabella. "Berea College." Phylon, 18 : 3 (3rd Quarter, 1957), 267-276.

Fairchild, E. H. Berea College Kentucky: An Interesting History. Cincinnati: Elm Street Printing Company, 1883.

Forbes, John Melville. "The Music Program of Berea College (Kentucky) and the Folk-Music Heritage of Appalachia." Doctoral Dissertation, University of Michigan, 1974.

Frost, William Goodell. "Berea College." Chapter 2 in American Unitarian Association. From Servitude to Service. Boston: American Unitarian Association, 1905.

Hall, Betty Jean, and Heckman, Richard Allen. "Berea's First Decade." Filson Club History Quarterly, 42 (October, 1968), 323-339.

Hutchins, Francis S. "Berea College in Its Centennial Year." Filson Club History Quarterly, 29 (January, 1955), 104-117.

Morgan, Charles Thomas. The Fruit of This Tree: The Story of a Great American College and Its Contribution to the Education of a Changing World. Kingspoint, Tenn.: Kingspoint Press, Inc., 1946.

Peck, Elizabeth (Sinclair) Berea's First Century, 1855-1955. Lexington, Ky.: University of Kentucky Press, 1955.

Rogers, John Almanza Rowley. Birth of Berea College A Story of Providence. Philadelphia: Henry T. Coates and Company, 1903. [Reprinted, Berea College Press, 1933]

---

*Not a Black College in the historical tradition of other institutions cited. Included because of the importance of its role in the higher education of Blacks.

Titus, A. W. President Frost's Betrayal of the Colored People in His Administration of Berea College. Danville, Ky.: Kentucky State Teachers Association, 1907. [Source: Levi Jenkins Coppin Collection, Carnegie Library, Wilberforce University, Wilberforce, Ohio]

Wright, George C. "The Founding of Lincoln Institute." [Kentucky] Filson Club History Quarterly, 49 (January, 1975), 57-70.

Kentucky State College
Frankfort, Kentucky

Coleman, Lena Mae. "A History of Kentucky State College for Negroes." Master's Thesis, Indiana University, 1938.

Edwards, Austin, Jr. "A History Kentucky State Industrial College for Negroes." Master's Thesis, Indiana State Teachers College, 1936.

Louisville Municipal College
Louisville, Kentucky

Abell, Irvin. "The Medical School of the University of Louisville Its History and Its Contribution," in [University of Louisville]. A Century of Municipal Higher Education: A Collection of Addresses Delivered During the Centennial Observances of the University of Louisville, America's Oldest Municipal University, March 31 to June 8, 1937. Chicago: Lincoln Printing Company, 1937.

Kent, R. A. "A Municipal College of Liberal Arts." Opportunity, 20 (February, 1942), 42-43.

LOUISIANA

Dillard University
New Orleans, Louisiana

Brawley, James P. "Dillard University." Chapter 4 in Two Centuries of Methodist Concern: Bondage, Freedom, and Education, of Black People. New York: Vantage Press Inc., 1974.

_____. "A Brief Sketch of New Orleans University, Later Dillard University." Chapter 15 Ibid.

Brownlee, Fred L. "Dillard University Up to 1945." The Dillard Bulletin, 10 : 1, October, 1945.

Kriege, O. E., and Faculty of New Orleans University. Seventy Years of Service. New Orleans: Faculty of New Orleans University, 1935.

Grambling College
Grambling, Louisiana

Maxie, Earl. "The Development of Grambling College." Master's Thesis, Tuskegee Institute, 1950.

Southern University
Baton Rouge, Louisiana

Lane, Ulysses Simpson. "The History of Southern University, 1879-1960." Doctoral Dissertation, Utah State University, 1970.

Xavier University
New Orleans, Louisiana

Agatha, Mother M. "A New Educational Force in the South-Xavier University." Opportunity, 10 (October, 1936), 299-301, 313.

"Negro Catholic College: Xavier College, New Orleans." Commonweal, 17 (November 30, 1932), 116.

MARYLAND

Bowie State College
Bowie, Maryland

Chapman, Oscar James. "A Brief History of Bowie Normal School for Colored Students." Master's Thesis, University of Michigan, 1936.

Morgan State College
Baltimore, Maryland

Low, W. A. "Methodism and Morgan State College, 1866-1900." Negro History Bulletin, 21 (November, 1957), 33-37, 39.

Owings, Vivian B. "A History of the Library of Morgan State College From 1867 to 1939." Master's Thesis, Catholic University of America, 1952.

Williams, R. D. "Historical Sketch of Morgan College." Morgan College Bulletin, October, 1913.

Wilson, Edward N. "Morgan State College, A Century of Purpose in Action, 1867-1967." MS., Morgan State College, 1967.

University of Maryland-Eastern Shore
Princess Anne, Maryland

Low, W. A. "The Establishment of Maryland State College." Chapter 33, Reprinted from The Eastern Shore of Maryland and

Virginia. Charles B. Clark, editor. New York: Lewis Historical Publishing Company, 1950.

MISSISSIPPI

Alcorn A. & M. College
Lorman, Mississippi

Buckles, Eddie. "A History of Physical Education and Athletics at Alcorn Agricultural and Mechanical College." Doctoral Dissertation, Ohio State University, 1972.

Davis, Walker Milan. *Pushing Forward; A History of Alcorn A. & M. College and Portraits of Some of Its Successful Graduates*. Okolona, Mississippi: Okolona Industrial School, 1938.

Sewell, George A. "A Hundred Years of History: Alcorn A. & M. College Observes Centennial, 1871-1971." *Negro History Bulletin*, 34 (April, 1971), 78-80.

Jackson State College
Jackson, Mississippi

Dansby, B. Baldwin. *A Brief History of Jackson College*. New York: American Book, Stratford Press, Inc., 1953.

Mississippi Valley State College
Itta Bena, Mississippi

Tinsley, Sammy Jay. "A History of Mississippi Valley State College." Doctoral Dissertation, University of Mississippi, 1972.

Rust College
Holly Springs, Mississippi

Baker, Webster B. *A History of Rust College*. Greensboro, N. C.: Berrnett, 1924.

Brawley, James P. "A Brief Historical Sketch of Rust College (Founded as Shaw University Later Became Rust University and Then Rust College)." Chapter 22 in *Two Centuries of Methodist Concern: Bondage, Freedom, and Education of Black People*. New York: Vantage Press, Inc., 1974.

Houghton, Frederick. "History of Rust College," in *Rust College Centennial Yearbook-1966*. Holly Springs: Rust College, 1966.

Kirk, W. Astor. *The Rust College Story*. Holly Springs, Mississippi: Rust College, 1967.

Underwood, Kenneth. "McCoy of Rust College." Chapter 5 in *Christianity Where You Live*. New York: Friendship Press, 1945.

Tougaloo College
Tougaloo, Mississippi

Campbell, Clarice T. "The Founding of Tougaloo College." Master's Thesis, University of Mississippi, 1967.

_____. "History of Tougaloo College." Doctoral Dissertation, University of Mississippi, 1970.

Utica Junior College
Utica, Mississippi

Holtzclaw, William Henry. The Black Man's Burden. New York: Neale Publishing Company, 1915.

Washington, Walter. "Utica Junior College, 1903-1957; A Half Century of Education for Negroes." Doctoral Dissertation, University of Southern Mississippi, 1970.

MISSOURI

Lincoln University
Jefferson City, Missouri

Foster, R. B. Historical Sketch of Lincoln Institute. Jefferson City, Mo.: n. p., 1871.

Peters, Dustin A. "Lincoln University in the Nineteenth Century: The Founding and Development of a Laboratory of Leadership and Race Relations." Negro History Bulletin, 34 (April, 1971), 80-83.

Savage, William Sherman. The History of Lincoln University. Jefferson City: Lincoln University, New Day Printers, 1939.

Savage, William Sherman. "Lincoln University," in History of Jefferson City. Jefferson City, Mo.: New Day Press, 1938. pp. 274-277.

Stowe Teachers College
St. Louis, Missouri

Harris, Ruth M. Stowe Teachers College and Her Predecessors. North Quincy, Mass.: Christopher Publishing House, 1967.

NORTH CAROLINA

Bennett College
Greensboro, North Carolina

Brawley, James P. "A Brief Historical Account of the Founding and Development of Bennett College." Chapter 11 in

Two Centuries of Methodist Concern: Bondage, Freedom, and Education of Black People. New York: Vantage Press, Inc., 1974.

Simmons, Virginia. "Bennett History." MS., June, 1939, Addendum 1958. Bennett College Library, c 1939.

Fayetteville State University
Fayetteville, North Carolina

Murphy, Ella L. "Origin and Development of Fayetteville State Teachers College, 1867-1959: A Chapter in the History of the Education of Negroes in North Carolina." Doctoral Dissertation, New York University, 1960.

Johnson C. Smith University
Charlotte, North Carolina

George, Arthur Allen. "The History of Johnson C. Smith University, 1867 to the Present: To Present and Analyze the Growth and Development of the Administrative and the Curricula Aims and Practices of Johnson C. Smith University 1867 to the Present." Doctoral Dissertation, New York University, 1954.

_____. 100 Years 1867-1967: Salient Factors in the Growth and Development of Johnson C. Smith University. Charlotte: Dowd Press, Inc., 1968.

McCrory, Henry Lawrence. "A Brief History of Johnson C. Smith University." Quarterly Review of Higher Education Among Negroes, 1 (April, 1933), 29-36.

_____. "A Brief History of Johnson C. Smith University." Johnson C. Smith University Bulletin, 1 : 4, May 30, 1935.

Livingstone College
Salisbury, North Carolina

Campbell, William J. "Origin and Development of Livingstone College and Hood Theological Seminary of the A. M. E. Zion Church and the Progressive Administration of President William Johnson Trent." Master's Thesis, Hood Theological Seminary, Livingstone College, 1950.

Johnson, B. A. "History of Livingstone College." A. M. E. Zion Quarterly Review, 5 (April, 1895), 8-15.

North Carolina A. & T. State University
Greensboro, North Carolina

Gibbs, Warmoth T. History of North Carolina Agricultural and Technical College, Greensboro, North Carolina. Dubuque, Iowa: W. C. Brown Company, 1966.

North Carolina Central University
Durham, North Carolina

Seay, Elizabeth. "A History of North Carolina College for Negroes." Master's Thesis, Duke University, 1941.

Saint Augustine's College
Raleigh, North Carolina

Chitty, Arthur Ben. "St. Augustine's College, Raleigh, North Carolina." Historical Magazine of the Protestant Episcopal Church, 35 (September, 1966), 207-218.

Halliburton, Cecil Durelle. A History of Saint Augustine's College, 1867-1937. Raleigh, N. C.: St. Augustine's College, 1937.

[St. Augustine's School] A Record of Fifty Years, 1867-1917, St. Augustine's School. Raleigh: Edwards and Broughton, 1917.

Shaw University
Raleigh, North Carolina

Carter, Wilmoth A. Shaw's Universe. Washington, D. C.: National Publishing, Inc., 1973.

Jenkins, Clara Barnes. "A Historical Study of Shaw University, 1865-1963." Doctoral Dissertation, University of Pittsburgh, 1965.

Jones, C. A. "The History of Shaw University." MS., Shaw University, c 1940.

OHIO

Central State University
Wilberforce, Ohio

Wesley, Charles H. Central State College: Its Birth and Growth. Ann Arbor: Edwards Brothers, 1953.

Wilberforce University
Wilberforce, Ohio

Arnett, B. W., Underwood, J. P. and Payne, Daniel A. Laws and Historical Sketches of Wilberforce University, Cincinnati: Robert Clarke and Company, 1876.

Brown, Hallie Queen. ed. Pen Pictures of Pioneers of Wilberforce. Xenia, Ohio: Aldine Publishing Company, 1937.

Coan, J. R. Daniel Alexander Payne, Christian Educator. Philadelphia: A. M. E. Book Concern, 1935.

Jackson, Reid E. "The 'New' Wilberforce." Crisis, 55 (March, 1948), 74-77, 92.

Killiam, Charles. "Wilberforce University: The Reality of Bishop Payne's Dream." _Negro History Bulletin_, 34 (April, 1971), 83-86.

McGinnis, Frederick Alphonso. "A History of Wilberforce University." Doctoral Dissertation, University of Cincinnati, 1940.

_____. _History and Interpretation of Wilberforce University_. Blanchester, Ohio: Brown Publishing Company, 1941.

Mitchell, S. T. _Wilberforce University: Its Inception, Growth and Present Status_. Indianapolis: Freeman Publishing Company, 1895.

Payne, D. A. _Annual Report and Retrospection of the First Decade of Wilberforce University_. Cincinnati: [Wilberforce University], 1878.

_____. _Recollections of Seventy Years_. Nashville, Tenn.: Publishing House of the A. M. E. Sunday School Union, 1888.

Ranson, Reverdy C. _School Days at Wilberforce_. Springfield, Ohio: New Era Printing Company, 1894.

Scarborough, W. W. and Talbert, Horace. _Wilberforce University, A School for Colored Youth_. Xenia, Ohio: Smith Advertising Company, 1910.

Smith, Charles S. _The Life of Daniel Alexander Payne_. Nashville: The Publishing House of the A. M. E. Sunday School Union, 1894.

Smith, David. _Biography of Rev. David Smith, of the A. M. E., Church: Being a Complete History Embracing Over Sixty Years' Labor in the Advancement of the Redeemer's Kingdom on Earth. Including "The History of the Origin and Development of Wilberforce University."_ Xenia, Ohio: Printed at the Xenia Gazette Office, 1881.

Talbert, Horace. _The Sons of Allen. Together With a Sketch of the Rise and Progress of Wilberforce University, Wilberforce, Ohio_. Xenia, Ohio: The Aldine Press, 1906.

PENNSYLVANIA

Cheyney State College
Cheyney, Pennsylvania

Conyers, Charline Fay Howard. "A History of the Cheyney State Teachers College, 1837-1951." Doctoral Dissertation, New York University, 1960.

Hill, Leslie Pinckney. "State Teachers College, Cheyney, Pennsylvania." Teacher Educational Journal, 2 : 2 (September, 1940), 91-94.

"Humphreys, Richard, Founder of Institute for Colored Youth." Barnard's American Journal of Education, 19 : 379.

James, Milton Morris. "The Institute for Colored Youth." Negro History Bulletin, 21 : 4 (1958), 83-85.

Johnson, William H. "Institute for Colored Youth." Pennsylvania School Journal, 5 (1857), 387.

Lincoln University
Lincoln, Pennsylvania

Bond, Horace Mann. Education for Freedom: A History of Lincoln University, Pennsylvania. Lincoln University, Pa.: Lincoln University, 1976.

Carr, George B. John Miller Dickey: His Life and Times. Philadelphia: Westminster Press, 1929.

Carter, James. A Century of Service: In Memoriam to President Isaac Norton Rendall, D. D., and President John Ballard Rendall, D. D., LL., D. Philadelphia: Allen, Lane, and Scott, 1924.

Johnson, William D. Lincoln University; or the Nation's First Pledge of Emancipation. Philadelphia: Alfred Martien Printer, 1867.

[Lincoln University]. College and Theological Seminary Biographical Catalogue. Lancaster, Pa.: New Era Printing Company, 1918.

Lunt, Paul S. Coordinator. Lincoln University Today: Final Report The Lincoln University Self-Study. Lincoln University, Pennsylvania, January, 1959.

Paynter, John H. Fifty Years After. New York: Magent, 1940.

Rendall, John B. A Historical Sketch of Lincoln University. Philadelphia: Wood Printing Company, 1904.

Wright, George C. "The Founding of Lincoln Institute." Filson Club Historical Quarterly, 49 (January, 1975), 57-70.

SOUTH CAROLINA

Claflin College
Orangeburg, South Carolina

Brawley, James P. "A Brief Historical Sketch of Claflin University, Now Claflin College." Chapter 13 in *Two Centuries of Methodist Concern: Bondage, Freedom, and Education of Black People*. New York: Vantage Press, Inc., 1974.

Fitchett, E. Horace. "The Role of Claflin College in Negro Life in South Carolina." *Journal of Negro Education*, 12 (Winter, 1943), 46-49.

TENNESSEE

Fisk University
Nashville, Tennessee

Bennett, H. S. "Fisk University." Chapter 7 in G. W. Hubbard, Compiler. *A History of the Colored Schools of Nashville, Tennessee*. Nashville: Wheeler, Marshall and Bruce, Printers and Stationers, 1874.

Jones, Thomas E. *Progress at Fisk University: A Summary of Recent Years, 1914-1930*. Nashville: Fisk University Press, 1930.

Merrill, James G. "Fisk University." Chapter 6 in American Unitarian Association. *From Servitude to Service*. Boston: American Unitarian Association, 1905.

_____. *Fisk University After Thirty-Nine Years*. New York: American Missionary Association, 1907.

Richardson, Joe M. "Fisk University, The First Critical Years." *Tennessee Historical Quarterly*, 29 (1970), 24-41.

Taylor, Alrutheus A. "Fisk University and the Nashville Community, 1866-1900." *Journal of Negro History*, 39 (April, 1954), 111-126.

Lane College
Jackson, Tennessee

Savage, Horace C. *Life and Times of Bishop Isaac Lane*. Nashville: National Publishing Company, 1958.

LeMoyne-Owen College
Memphis, Tennessee

McCullock, Margaret C. *Fearless Advocate of the Right: The Life of Francis Julius LeMoyne, M.D., 1798-1879*. Boston: The Christopher Publishing House, 1941.

Meharry Medical College
Nashville, Tennessee

Brawley, James P. "A Brief Historical Sketch of Meharry Medical College." Chapter 18 in *Two Centuries of Methodist*

Concern: Bondage, Freedom, and Education of Black People. New York: Vantage Press, Inc., 1974.

Harrison, Grace. "Hubbard Hospital and Meharry Medical College for Negroes." Master's Thesis University of Chicago, 1945.

Mullowney, John J. America Gives A Chance. Tampa: Tribune Press of Tampa, 1940.

Roman, Charles Victor. Meharry Medical College: A History. Nashville: Sunday School Publishing Board of the National Baptist Convention, Inc., 1934. [Reprinted Freeport, N. Y.: Books for Libraries, 1972]

Morristown Junior College
Morristown, Tennessee

Brawley, James P. "A Brief Historical Sketch of Morristown Normal and Industrial College." Chapter 19 in Two Centuries of Methodist Concern: Bondage, Freedom, and Education of Black People. New York: Vantage Press, Inc., 1974.

Tennessee State University
Nashville, Tennessee

Lamon, Lester C. "The Tennessee Agricultural and Industrial Normal School: Public Higher Education for Black Tennesseans." Tennessee Historical Quarterly, 32 (Spring, 1973), 42-58.

Lloyd, R. Grann. Tennessee Agricultural and State University, 1912-1962. Nashville: n. p. 1962.

TEXAS

Bishop College
Dallas, Texas

Rhoads, Joseph J. "Historical Sketch of Bishop College." MS., Archives of Bishop College, Dallas, Texas. n. d. 44 pages.

Toles, Caesar F. "The History of Bishop College." Master's Thesis, University of Michigan, 1947.

Huston-Tilloston College
Austin, Texas

Brawley, James P. "Historical Sketch of the Founding and Development of Samuel Huston College: Subsequently Huston-Tilloston College." Chapter 17 in Two Centuries of Methodist Concern: Bondage, Freedom and Education of Black People. New York: Vantage Press, Inc., 1974.

Jones, William Henry. Tilloston College From 1930-1940. A Decade of Progress. Austin: Tilloston College, 1940.

Richardson, George A., and Richardson, Emma. Early Days of Samuel Huston College. Austin: Private Publication, 1938.

Shackles, Chrystine I. Reminiscences: The Story of Tilloston College and Samuel Huston, 1928-1968. Austin: Best Publishing Company, 1973.

Prairie View Agricultural and Mechanical College
Prairie View, Texas

Gee, Ruth Ella. "The History and Development of the Prairie View Training School, 1916-1946." Master's Thesis, Prairie View University, 1946.

Prairie View Agricultural and Mechanical College. The First Seventy-Five Years: A History of Prairie View Agricultural and Mechanical College. Issued as a Souvenir Bulletin. Prairie View: The College, 1951.

Sims, Van E. "The Willette Rutherford Banks Administration: A Study in the Historical Development of Prairie View Agricultural and Mechanical College." Master's Thesis, Prairie View College, 1950.

White, Annie May Vaught. "The Development of the Program of Studies of the Prairie View State Normal and Industrial College." Master's Thesis, University of Texas, 1938.

Woolfolk, George Ruble. Prairie View: A Study in Public Conscience, 1878-1946. New York: Pageant Press, 1962.

St. Phillips College
San Antonio, Texas

Buxton, Alfred G. "A Study of St. Phillip's College, San Antonio, Texas." Master's Thesis, Trinity University, 1955.

Norris, Clarence Windzell, Jr. "St. Phillip's College: A Case Study of a Historically Black Two-Year College." University of Southern California, 1975.

Texas Southern University
Houston, Texas

Lanier, Raphael O'Hara. "The History of Higher Education for Negroes in Texas 1930-1955, With Particular Reference to Texas Southern University." Doctoral Dissertation, New York University, 1957.

Terry, William Edward. "Origin and Development of Texas Southern University, Houston, Texas." Doctoral Dissertation, University of Houston, 1968.

Wiley College
Marshall, Texas

Allen, Jewel. "The History of Negro Education at Wiley College." Master's Thesis, East Texas State Teachers College, 1940.

Brawley, James P. "A Brief Historical Sketch of Wiley University Now Wiley College." Chapter 23 in Two Centuries of Methodist Concern: Bondage, Freedom, and Education of Black People. New York: Vantage Press, Inc., 1974.

Gibbs, Warmoth T. President Matthew W. Dogan of Wiley College, A Biography. Marshall, Texas: Wiley College, 1940.

McNeely, Lois Towles. "A History of the Music Education of Wiley College." Master's Thesis, University of Iowa, 1942.

Totten, Herman L. "The Wiley College Library the First Library for Negroes West of the Mississippi River." Negro History Bulletin, 32 (January, 1969), 6-10.

VIRGINIA

Hampton Institute
Hampton, Virginia

Armstrong, Mary Frances, and Ludlow, Helen W. Hampton and Its Students. New York: G. P. Putnam's Sons, 1875.

_____. Hampton Institute, 1868-1885: Its Work for Two Races. Hampton, Va.: Normal School Press, 1893.

Armstrong, Samuel Chapman. Twenty-Two Years' Work of the Hampton Normal and Agricultural Institute. Hampton, Va.: Normal School Press, 1893.

Carson, S. C. "Samuel Chapman Armstrong, Missionary to the South." Doctoral Dissertation, John Hopkins University, 1952.

Frissell, H. B. "Hampton Institute." From Servitude to Service. Boston: American Unitarian Association, 1905.

Graham, Edward K. "The Hampton Institute Strike of 1927: A Case Study in Student Protest." American Scholar, 38: 4 (Autumn, 1969), 668-681.

Hampton Institute. Hampton Normal and Agricultural Institute. A Brief History. Hampton, Va.: Normal School Press, 1883.

_____. The Hampton Normal and Agricultural Institute and Its Work for Negro and Indian Youth. Hampton, Va.: Normal School Press, 1896.

Jackson, L. P. "The Origin of Hampton Institute." _Journal of Negro History_, 10 (April, 1925), 131-149.

John, Walton Colcord. _Hampton Normal and Agricultural Institute: Its Evolution and Contribution to Education as a Land-Grant College_. U. S. Department of the Interior, Bureau of Education, Bulletin 1923 No. 27. Washington: U. S. Government Printing Office, 1923.

Peabody, Francis Greenwood. _Education for Life: The Story of Hampton Institute. Told in Connection With the Fiftieth Anniversary of the Founding of the School_. Garden City, N. Y.: Doubleday, Page and Company, 1918.

Phenix, George P. "Hampton Institute, 1868-1932." _Southern Workman_, 32 (December, 1923), 574.

Robinson, William Hannibal. "The History of Hampton Institute, 1868-1949." Doctoral Dissertation, New York University, 1955.

Smith, S. L. "The Passing of the Hampton Library School." _Journal of Negro Education_, 9 (January, 1940), 51-58.

St. Paul's College
Lawrenceville, Virginia

Jones, Thomas Hardy E. "An Historical Study of the Curricular Development of St. Pauls' Polytechnic Institute, Lawrenceville, Virginia." Master's Thesis, Atlanta University, 1950.

Russell, James Soloman. _Adventure in Faith: An Autobiographical Story of St. Paul Normal and Industrial School Lawrenceville, Virginia_. New York: Morehouse Publishing Company, 1936.

Virginia State College
Petersburg, Virginia

Braxton, Harold Edwin. "A History of the General Education Program at Virginia State College Since 1950." Doctoral Dissertation, University of Virginia, 1973.

Gandy, John M. "The Development of Virginia State College." _Virginia State College Gazette_, December, 1940.

Jackson, Luther P. "The History of Virginia Normal and Industrial Institute." _Virginia Normal and Industrial Institute Gazette_, 32 (September, 1928), 18-22.

Jeffreys, Richard Langston. "A History of Virginia State College for Negroes, Ettrick, Virginia." Master's Thesis, Iowa University, 1937.

Johnston, James Hugo, Jr. "A History of Virginia State College." MS., Office of the President, Virginia State College, Petersburg, Virginia, *Circa*, 1960.

Virginia Union University
Richmond, Virginia

Corey, Charles Henry. *A History of Richmond Theological Seminary, With Reminiscences of Thirty Years' Work Among the Colored People of the South*. Richmond, Va.: J. W. Randolph Company, 1895.

Fisher, Miles M. ed. *Virginia Union University and Some of Her Achievements: Twenty-Fifth Anniversary 1897-1924*. Richmond, Va.: Brown Print Shop, Inc., 1924.

Morgan, T. J. *Virginia Union University, What it Signifies*. New York: The American Baptist Home Mission Society, c 1900.

Virginia Union University. "A Century of Service to Education and Religion, 1865-1965." *Virginia Union University Bulletin--Centennial Issue*, 65 : 5 (June, 1965), Richmond.

WEST VIRGINIA

Storer College
Harpers Ferry, West Virginia

Gordon, Vivian Verdell. "A History of Storer College, Harpers Ferry, West Virginia." *Journal of Negro Education*, 30 (Fall, 1961), 445-449.

West Virginia State College
Institute, West Virginia

Drain, John Robert. "The History of West Virginia State College From 1892-1950." Master's Thesis, West Virginia State College, 1958.

_____. *Early Aeronautics Program at West Virginia State College*. Institute: West Virginia State College Bulletin, No. 1, February, 1945.

Ferrell, Harrison H. *Twenty-Five Years, West Virginia State College and Its President*. Institute: West Virginia State College Bulletin, No. 1, February, 1945.

Harlan, John C. *A History of West Virginia State College 1891-1965*. Dubuque: William C. Brown Company, 1968.

"Review of Fifty Years of Sports at State." *The West Virginia Digest*, May 10, 1941.

PERIODICAL LITERATURE 3
1857-1976

"A College Beset by Black Revolutionaries." U. S. News and World Report, May 12, 1969.

"A Conference on Colleges for Negro Youth." Journal of Negro Education, 3 (April, 1934), 313-314.

Abbott, E. A. "Our Livingstone." A. M. E. Zion Quarterly Review, 42 (July-September, 1932), 11.

Abbott, Layman. "Hampton Revisited." The Outlook, 103 (April 12, 1913), 802-805.

_____. "Hampton Revisited." The Outlook, 119 (May 15, 1918), 114-115.

Aber, Elaine. "A Reverse Pattern of Integration." Journal of Educational Sociology, 32 (February, 1958), 283-289.

Abramowitz, Jack. "Crossroads of Negro Thought, 1890-1895." Social Education, 18 (March, 1954), 117-120.

Aery, William Anthony. "The Booker T. Washington Monument." Southern Workman, 51 (May, 1922), 217.

_____. "College Education for Negroes: Integration of Liberal and Vocational Aims at Hampton Institute." Southern Workman, 63 (August, 1934), 227-237.

_____. "Colleges for Negro Youth." Southern Workman, 63 (February, 1934), 55-59.

_____. "Dr. Frissell's Twenty-Five Years at Hampton Institute, Training the Negroes and Indians." Mississippi Review, 41 (January, 1918), 48-49.

_____. "Howard University Semi-Centennial and Negro Education." School and Society, 5 (March 31, 1917), 371-378.

_____. "Negro Education and the University." Southern Workman, 60 (March, 1931), 137-139.

_____. "The School of Education at Hampton Institute." Southern Workman, 54 (March, 1925), 130-136.

_____. "Teaching Teachers at Hampton." Southern Workman, 43 (August, 1914), 430.

"Agencies in the Growth of Livingstone College." A. M. E. Zion Quarterly Review, 11 (July-September, 1901), 308.

Alderman, E. A. "Higher Education in the South." Education Review, 11 (1896), 29.

Alderson, William T. "The Freedmen's Bureau and Negro Education in Virginia." North Carolina Historical Review, 29 (January, 1952), 64-90.

Alexander, Florence O., and Whiteside, Mary G. "Negro Higher and Professional Education in Mississippi." Journal of Negro Education, 17 (Summer, 1948), 312-320.

Allen, LeRoy B. "The Possibilities of Integration for Public Colleges Founded for Negroes." Journal of Negro Education, 35 (Fall, 1966), 452-458.

_____. "Religious Attitudes of a Selected Group of Negro College Students." Journal of Negro Education, 16 (Spring, 1947), 142-147.

Allen, Robert. "Black Campuses Today." Guardian, March 9, 1968.

Allison, A. J. "Policies and Practices of Negro Colleges in Placing Graduates." Negro Schools, (March, 1940), 8-14.

Allman, Reva White. "A Study of Selected Competencies of Prospective Teachers in Alabama." Journal of Negro Education, 22 (Spring, 1953), 136-144.

_____. "An Evaluation of the Goals of Higher Education by 294 College Seniors of Alabama." Journal of Negro Education, 29 (Spring, 1960), 198-203.

_____. "A Study of General Education With Emphasis on Teacher Education in Negro Colleges." Journal of Negro Education, 18 (Fall, 1949), 582-588.

Alverson, Charles. "Howard University's 'Relevance Throes'." Wall Street Journal, June 17, 1968.

"The American Negro in College, 1933-1934." Crisis, 41 (August, 1934), 239-240.

"The American Negro in College, 1937-1938." Crisis, 45 (August, 1938), 258-261.

"The American Negro in College, 1938-1939." *Crisis*, 46 (August, 1939), 234-238.

"The American Negro in College, 1939-1940." *Crisis*, 47 (August, 1940), 233-237.

"The American Negro in College, 1940-1941." *Crisis*, 48 (August, 1941), 248-252.

"The American Negro in College, 1941-1942." *Crisis*, 49 (August, 1942), 249-252.

"The American Negro in College, 1942-1943." *Crisis*, 50 (August, 1943), 234-241.

"The American Negro in College, 1943-1944." *Crisis*, 51 (August, 1951), 252-261.

"The American Negro in College, 1944-1945." *Crisis*, 52 (August, 1945), 220-230.

"The American Negro in College, 1945-1946." *Crisis*, 53 (August, 1946), 237-248.

"The American Negro in College, 1946-1947." *Crisis*, 54 (August, 1947), 239-246.

"The American Negro in College, 1947-1948." *Crisis*, 55 (August, 1948), 237-243.

"The American Negro in College, 1948-1949." *Crisis*, 56 (August-September, 1949), 238-245.

"The American Negro in College, 1949-1950." *Crisis*, 57 (August-September, 1950), 488-501.

"The American Negro in College, 1950-1951." *Crisis*, 58 (August-September, 1951), 445-458.

"The American Negro in College, 1951-1952." *Crisis*, 59 (August-September, 1952), 428-441.

"The American Negro in College, 1952-1953." *Crisis*, 60 (August-September, 1953), 397-412.

"The American Negro in College, 1953-1954." *Crisis*, 61 (August-September, 1954), 405-420.

"The American Negro in College, 1954-1955." *Crisis*, 62 (August-September, 1955), 405-420.

"The American Negro in College, 1955-1956." *Crisis*, 63 (August-September, 1956), 389-404.

"The American Negro in College, 1956-1957." *Crisis*, 64 (August-September, 1957), 389-404.

"The American Negro in College, 1957-1958." Crisis, 65 (August, 1958), 237-243.

"The American Negro in College, 1958-1959." Crisis, 66 (August-September, 1959), 411-423.

"The American Negro in College, 1959-1960." Crisis, 67 (August-September, 1960), 424-436.

"The American Negro in College, 1960-1961." Crisis, 68 (August-September, 1961), 424-432.

"The American Negro in College, 1961-1962." Crisis, 69 (August-September, 1962), 402-411.

"The American Negro in College, 1962-1963." Crisis, 70 (August-September, 1963), 418-430.

"The American Negro in College, 1963-1964." Crisis, 71 (October, 1964), 537-545.

Anderson, C. S., and Himes, J. S. "Dating Values and Norms on a Negro College Campus." Marriage and Family Living, 21 (August, 1959), 227-229.

Anderson, W. E. "Negro Higher and Professional Education in Alabama." Journal of Negro Education, 17 (Summer, 1948), 249-254.

Angoff, Allan. "Negro Colleges and Scholarly Publishing." College Language Association Journal, 1 (March, 1958), 58-67.

Aptheker, Bettina. "Aspects of the Crisis in Higher Education." Political Affairs, 46 (October, 1967), 9-18.

Aptheker, Herbert. "The Washington-Du Bois Conference of 1904." Science and Society, 13 (Fall, 1949), 344-351.

_____. "The Negro College Student in the 1920's--Year of Preparation and Protest: An Introduction." Science and Society, 33 (Spring, 1969), 150-167.

Armstrong, O.K. "Booker T. Washington-Apostle of Good Will." Reader's Digest, 50 (February, 1947), 25-30.

Arnold, S. G. "Education Among the Freedmen." Methodist Quarterly Review, 60 (January, 1876), 43-57.

Asbury, Charles A. "The Methodology Used in the Jencks Report: A Critique." Journal of Negro Education, 42 (Fall, 1973), 530-536.

Asgill, Amanda. "The Importance of Accreditation: Perceptions of Black and White College Presidents." Journal of Negro Education, 45 (Summer, 1976), 284-294.

Ashby, Lyle W. "A College Close to the People." *National Education Association Journal*, 35 (December, 1946), 576-579.

Atkins, James A. "Negro Education Institutions and the Veterans' Educational Facilities Program." *Journal of Negro* Education, 17 (Summer, 1948), 249-254.

Atkins, Russell C. "Tuskegee's Vocational Program for Men." *Journal of Educational Sociology*, 7 (November, 1933), 175-183.

Atkinson, R. W. "Interracial Conference of Florida Colleges and Universities." *Southern Workman*, 60 (May, 1931), 229-231.

"Atlanta University Library." *School and Society*, 34 (July 18, 1931), 87-88.

"Atlanta University's New Buildings." *School and Society*, 34 (November 21, 1931),

Atwood, Rufus B. "The Public Negro College in a Racially Integrated System of Higher Education." *Journal of Negro Education*, 21 (Summer, 1952), 352-363.

_____. "Private and Public Colleges--Whither Bound." *Crisis*, 44 (March, 1937), 77-78.

_____. "A Functional Program for the Negro Land-Grant College." *Negro College Quarterly*, 2 (June, 1944), 50-53.

_____. "The Future of the Negro Land-Grant College." *Journal of Negro Education*, 27 (Summer, 1958), 381-391.

_____. "The Role of Negro Higher Education in Post War Reconstruction: The Negro Land-Grant College." *Journal of Negro Education*, 11 (July, 1942), 391-399.

_____. "The Origin and Development of the Negro Public College With Especial Reference to the Land-Grant College." *Journal of Negro Education*, 31 (Summer, 1962), 240-250.

"Award of the Roosevelt Medal to Dr. Dillard." *School and Society*, 45 (May 22, 1937), 712.

Axt, Richard G. "Educational Programs of Government: Significance to Higher Education." *Quarterly Review of Higher Education Among Negroes*, 24 (April, 1956), 57-61.

Bacote, Clarence A. "James Weldon Johnson and Atlanta University." *Phylon*, 33 (4th Quarter, Winter, 1971), 333-343.

Badger, Henry G. "Colleges That Did Not Survive." *Journal of Negro Education*, 35 (Fall, 1966), 306-312.

_____. "Negro Colleges and Universities: 1900-1950." Journal of Negro Education, 21 (Winter, 1952), 89-93.

_____. "Finances of Negro Colleges 1929-1930 to 1938-1939." Journal of Negro Education, 9 (April, 1940), 162-166.

Baker, O. J. "Senior College Libraries for Negroes in Texas." College and Research Libraries, 5 (December, 1943), 75-83.

_____. "The Improvement of the Negro College Library." Journal of Negro Education, 16 (Winter, 1947), 91-100.

Banks, Maggie Hood. "On the Founding of Livingstone College." The Star of Zion, September 8, 1931.

"Baptist Colleges for Negro Youth." Southern Workman, 56 (July, 1927), 306-307.

"Barber-Scotia Junior College." Crisis, 49 (August, 1942), 263.

Bardolph, Richard. "Negro Religious and Educational Leaders in Who's Who in America, 1936-1955." Journal of Negro Education, 26 (Spring, 1957), 182-192.

Barksdale, Norval Parker. "The Gaines Case and Its Effect on Negro Education in Missouri." School and Society, 51 (March 9, 1940), 309-313.

_____. "Spelling as a College Subject." Journal of Negro Education, 8 (January, 1939), 20-21.

Barnes, George E. "Commencement Address for 1926 at North Carolina College for Negroes." Durham Morning Herald, June 4, 1926.

Barros, Francis J. "Equal Opportunity in Higher Education." Journal of Negro Education, 37 (Summer, 1968), 31-315.

Bass, Jack, and Clancy, Paul. "The Militant Mood in Negro Colleges." Reporter, May 16, 1968.

Bayer, Alan E., and Boruch, Robert F. "Black and White Freshmen Entering Four-Year Colleges." Educational Record, 50 (Fall, 1969), 371-386.

Bayton, James A., et al. "Reflections and Suggestions for Further Study Concerning the Higher Education of Negroes." Journal of Negro Education, 36 (Summer, 1967), 286-294.

Beale, Howard K. "Needs of Negro Education in the United States." Journal of Negro Education, 3 (January, 1934), 8-19.

_____. "On Rewriting Reconstruction History." American Historical Review, 45 (July, 1940), 807-827.

Beckham, Edgar F. "What Do We Mean by the Black University?" College Board Review, Spring, 1969.

Belcher, Leon H. and Campbell, Joel T. "An Exploratory Study of Word Associations of Negro College Students." Psychological Reports, August, 1968.

Belles, A. Gilbert. "The College Faculty, the Negro Scholar, and the Julius Rosenwald Fund." Journal of Negro History, 54 : 4 (1969), 383-392.

Bennett, Sister M. "A Negro University and a Nun." Community, March, 1966.

Berman, Edward H. "Tuskegee-In-Africa." Journal of Negro Education, 41 (Spring, 1972), 99-112.

Berry, Charles A. and Jones, Arlynne L. "The Predictive Value of the Tests of the National Freshmen Testing Program for Grambling College Freshmen." The Negro Educational Review, 9 (January, 1958), 23-33.

Berry, Charles A., and Jones, Arlynne L. "Factors Involved in the Withdrawal of Students From Grambling College at or Before the End of Their Freshmen Year." Journal of Negro Education, 25 (Summer, 1956), 445-447.

_____. "A Further Note on the Predictive Value of the National Freshmen Testing Program." Negro Educational Review, 11 (July, 1960), 120-125.

Bethune, Mary M. "The Educational Values of the College Bred." Southern Workman, 63 (July, 1934), 200-204.

_____. "College Built in Faith." Reader's Digest, 39 (June, 1941), 47-50.

_____. "Faith That Moved a Dump Heap." Who, The Magazine About People, 1 : No. 3, June, 1941.

Bianchi, B. A. "Some Pertinent Problems Confronting Negro Colleges in North Carolina." Quarterly Review of Higher Education Among Negroes, 3 (October, 1938), 287-288.

Bigglestone, W. E. "Oberlin College and the Negro Student, 1865-1940." Journal of Negro History, 56 (July, 1971), 198-219.

Binnion, R. B. "Solving the Negro Problem Through Education." Current History, 30 (May, 1929), 213-236.

Birnie, C. W. "The Education of the Negro in Charleston, South Carolina, Before the Civil War." Journal of Negro History, 12 (January, 1927), 13-21.

"Black College Athletic Officials Hit NCAA Drive to Silence Young Athletes." Muhammad Speaks, January 31, 1969.

"Black Colleges to Get $2 Million to Upgrade Technical Resources." Chronicle of Higher Education, 5 : 26 (April 5, 1971), 2.

"'Black Faculty Research' Moton Institute Plans Advanced Study Center." Chronicle of Higher Education, 10 : 11 (May 5, 1975), 14.

"Black Beaux-Arts; Art Department of Atlanta University." Time, 40 (September 21, 1942), 74.

"Blacks in Higher Education--Howard University Aims to Resolve Conflict in Data." Chronicle of Higher Education, 9 : 19 (February 10, 1975), 2.

Black, Isabella. "Berea College." Phylon, 18 : 3 (3rd Quarter, 1957), 267-276.

"Black Presidents Assail Nixon Policies." Chronicle of Higher Education, 4 : 34 (June 1, 1970), 2.

Black, Watt L. "Education in the South From 1820 to 1860 With Emphasis on the Growth of Teacher Education." La Student, 12 (Winter, 1973), 617-629.

"Black Students Challenge the Order at Mississippi Valley State." New York Times, May 25, 1970.

Blake, Elias. "The Negro Public College in Georgia." Journal of Negro Education, 31 (Summer, 1962), 299-309.

_____. "The Future Leadership Roles for Predominantly Black Colleges and Universities in American Higher Education." Daldalus, 100 : 3 (Summer, 1971), 745-771.

_____. "Background Paper on the Traditionally Negro College." Congressional Record, May 11, 1970. E4091.

Blake, Herman J. "The Black University and Its Community." Negro Digest, March, 1968.

Blanchard, F. Q. "Quarter Century in the American Missionary Association." Journal of Negro Education, 6 (April, 1937), 152-156.

Blanton, Robert J. "The Future of Higher Education Among Negroes." Journal of Negro Education, 9 (April, 1940), 177-182.

Bloomfield, Maxwell. "John Mercer Langston and the Rise of Howard Law School." Records of the Columbia Historical Society, Washington, D. C. 1971-1972, 48 (1973), 421-438.

Blue, Cecil A. "Open Address--Reading, and Writing in the Negro College." Quarterly Review of Higher Education Among Negroes, 8 (July, 1940), 176-179.

Bluford, Lucile H. "The Lloyd Gaines Story." Journal of Educational Sociology, 32 (February, 1958), 242-246.

Blumenfeld, Warren S. "College Preferences of Able Negro Students: A Comparison of Those Naming Predominantly Negro Institutions." College and University, 43 (February, 1959), 330-341.

Bokelman, W. Robert, and D'Amico, Louis A. "Changes in Faculty Salaries and Basic Student Charges in Negro Colleges: 1960-1961 and 1961-1962." Journal of Negro Education, 31 (Fall, 1962), 507-511.

Bolling, Mary L. "Hampton Institute's First Twenty-Five Years." Southern Workman, 67 (October, 1938), 313-321.

Bond, Horace Mann. "Langston Plan: Curriculum for Negro Teacher Training School." School and Society, 20 (December 27, 1924), 820-821.

_____. "The Influence of Personalities on the Public Education of Negroes in Alabama, I." Journal of Negro Education, 6 (January, 1937), 17-29.

_____. "The Influence of Personalities on the Public Education of Negroes in Alabama, II." Journal of Negro Education, 6 (April, 1937), 172-187.

_____. "Human Nature and Its Study in Negro Colleges." Opportunity, 6 (February, 1928), 38-39, 58.

_____. "What Was the First Black Institution of Higher Education?" School and Society, 96 (November 23, 1968), 430-431.

_____. "The Origin and Development of the Negro Church-Related College." Journal of Negro Education, 29 (Summer, 1960), 217-226.

_____. "Negro Leadership Since Washington." South Atlantic Quarterly, 24 (April, 1925), 115-130.

_____. "The Evolution and Present Status of Negro Higher and Professional Education in the United States." Journal of Negro Education, 17 (Summer, 1948), 224-235.

Bond, J., Max. "Some Aspects of Graduate and Professional Education for Negroes." Phylon, 10 (4th Quarter, 1949), 392-396.

Bond, James A. "Bethune-Cookman College: Community Service Station." Crisis, 48 (March, 1941), 31, 94.

_____. "The Education of the Bond Family." Crisis, 34 (April, 1927), 41, 60.

Boone, Irving. "An Appraisal--Livingstone Occupies Unique Position Among Institutions of Higher Education." Church School Herald Journal, 34 (July, 1956), 8.

Borinski, Ernst. "The Social Science Laboratory at Tougaloo College." Journal of Educational Sociology, 22 (December, 1948), 276-286.

Bottoms, L. W. "The Policies and Rationale Underlying the Support of Negro Colleges and Schools Maintained by the Presbyterian Church in the United States." Journal of Negro Education, 29 (Summer, 1960), 264-273.

Bousefield, M. O. "An Account of Physicians of Color in the United States." Bulletin of the History of Medicine, 17 (1945), 61-84.

Bowen, H. A. "Financial Aid to Students in Negro Land-Grant Colleges." School and Society, 68 (September 4, 1948) 156-158.

_____. "Orientation Services in the Negro Land-Grant Colleges." Journal of Negro Education, 19 (Winter, 1950), 108-114.

Bowen, J. W. E. "An Apology for the Higher Education of the Negro." The Methodist Review, 79 (September-October, 1897), 723-742.

Bowen, William A. "Wilberforce's Mercurial Maiden." [Jean Betty Lane] Opportunity, 19 (June, 1941), 172-173, 187-188.

"Bowie State College: The Negro School That White Students Saved." Sepia, 13 (June, 1964), 22-26.

Bowles, Frank. "What's Ahead for Our Negro Colleges?" College Board Review, (Fall, 1965), 16-19.

Boyd, William M. "Problems Affecting Social Studies Teachers on the College Level, With Special Reference to Political Science." Quarterly Review of Higher Education Among Negroes, 14 (July, 1946), 117-120.

Boykin, Leander, and Brazziel, William F., Jr. "Occupational Interest of 1741 Teacher Education Students as Revealed on the Lee-Thorpe Inventory." Journal of Negro Education, 28 (Winter, 1959), 42-48.

Boykin, Leander L. "The Survival and Function of the Negro College in a Changing Social Order." Journal of Negro Education, 12 (Fall, 1943), 589-599.

_____. "The Adjustment of 2,078 Negro Students." Journal of Negro Education, 26 (Winter, 1957), 75-79.

_____. "Personality Aspects of Counseling Negro College Students." Quarterly Review of Higher Education Among Negroes, 27 (April, 1959), 64-73.

_____. "Negro Publicly-Supported Higher Institutions in Louisiana." Journal of Negro Education, 31 (Summer, 1962), 330-340.

_____. "The Adjustment of 729 Negro College Students as Revealed by the Bernreuter Personality Inventory." Negro Educational Review, 11 (January, 1960), 43-47.

_____. "The Reading Performance of Some Negro College Students." Journal of Negro Education, 24 (Fall, 1955), 435-441.

_____. "A Summary of Reading Investigations Among Negro College Students, 1940-1954." Quarterly Review of Higher Education Among Negroes, 25 (April, 1957), 94-101. Ibid., Journal of Educational Research, 51 (February, 1958), 471-475.

_____. "Role of Higher Education for Negroes in a Changing Social Order." Association of American College Bulletin, 43 (May, 1957), 315-319.

_____. "Trends in American Higher Education With Implications for the Higher Education of Negroes." Journal of Negro Education, 26 (Spring, 1957), 193-199.

Bracey, Helen Harris. "Negro Higher and Professional Education in Florida." Journal of Negro Education, 17 (Summer, 1948), 272-279.

Braddock, Clayton. "Atlanta University President Warns Against Separation in Black Studies, Call for Scholarly Approach." Chronicle of Higher Education, 3 : 14 (March 24, 1969), 5.

Bradford, David H. "Courses Concerning the Negro in Negro Colleges." Quarterly Review of Higher Education Among Negroes, 8 (July, 1940), 136-137.

Bradley, Gladyce Helen. "What Do College Students Like and Dislike About College Teachers and Their Teaching." Educational Administration and Supervision, 36 (February, 1950), 113-120.

_____. "Negro Higher and Professional Education in Maryland." Journal of Negro Education, 17 (Summer, 1948), 303-311.

Brady, Carrie E. "Some Aspects of College Club Work on College Level." Modern Language Journal, 39 (February, 1955), 69-71.

Brann, James W. "Negro Students are Organizing National Groups." Chronicle of Higher Education, 2 : 17 (May 6, 1968),

1, 3.

Branson, Herman R. "Interinstitutional Programs for Promoting Equal Higher Educational Opportunities for Negroes." Journal of Negro Education, 35 (Fall, 1966), 469-476.

_____. "Microfilm in the Negro College." Journal of Negro Education, 11 (January, 1942), 14-17.

_____. "The Role of the Negro College in the Preparation of Technical Personnel for the War Effort." Journal of Negro Education, 11 (July, 1942), 297-303.

Brawley, Benjamin G. "The Profession and the Teacher." Southern Workman, 57 (December, 1928), 481-486.

_____. "A New Survey of Colleges." The Home Mission College Review, 1 (1827), 54 Ibid., "United Campaign for Home Mission Colleges." 1 (1927), 5; "Affiliation of College." 2 (1928), 2; "The Greatest Problem in the Negro College." 2 (1928), 5; "Dillard University." 3 (1929), 45; "Grambling." 3 (1929), 4; "The Study of the Bible in Our Colleges." 3 (1929), 3.

_____. "Hamlet and Negro." Southern Workman, 61 (November, 1932), 442-448.

_____. "The Outlook in Negro Colleges." Southern Workman, 49 (May, 1920), 204.

Brawley, James P. "The Academic, Cultural, Social and Moral Qualities Needed in College Teachers." Journal of the National Association of Collegiate Deans and Registrars, March 18-21, 19 . 17.

_____. "Negro Colleges in a Period of Social Change." New Christian Advocate, February, 1968.

_____. "Are Negro Colleges Good Enough?" Church and Campus, January-February, 1956.

Brazziel, William F. "Curriculum Choice in the Negro College." Journal of Negro Education, 29 (Spring, 1960), 207-209.

_____. "Federal Aid and the Negro Colleges." Teachers College Record, 68 (January, 1967), 300-306.

_____. "Some Dynamics of Curriculum Choice in the Negro Colleges." Journal of Negro Education, 30 (Fall, 1961), 436-439.

_____. "Occupational Choice in the Negro College." Personnel and Guidance Journal, 39 (May, 1961), 739-742.

Breathett, George. "William Edward Burghardt Du Bois: An Address to the Black Academic Community." [Document]

Journal of Negro History, 60 (January, 1975), 45-52.

_____. "Democratic School Administration and Its Implications for Higher Education." Quarterly Review of Higher Education Among Negroes, 29 (January, 1961), 1-8.

Bressler, Marvin. "White Colleges and Negro Higher Education." Journal of Negro Education, 36 (Summer, 1967), 258-265.

Brewer, June H. "In Defense of the Black College." Journal of the National Association of Women Deans and Counselors, (Winter, 1969).

Brewster, E., and Martelle, D. Trigg. "Moral Values Among Negro College Students: A Study of Cultural and Racial Determinants." Phylon, 23 (Fall, 1962), 286-293.

Brice, Edward Warner. "Enrollment in Institutions of Higher Learning Attended Predominantly by Negroes During the Past Decade." Negro Educational Review, 10 (July, 1959), 108-120.

Brigham, R. I. "Price of Segregation, Gaines Case." Survey Graphic, 35 (May, 1946), 156-157.

_____. "High Cost of Segregated Graduate Schools for Negroes." School and Society, 63 (May 18, 1946), 358.

_____. "Negro Public Colleges in St. Louis and Kansas City, Missouri." Journal of Negro Education, 17 (Winter, 1948), 51-57.

_____. "Church Related Colleges for Negroes in Missouri to 1945." Negro History Bulletin, 14 (January, 1951), 82-85, 89.

Brimmer, Andrew F. "The Economic Outlook and the Future of the Negro College." Daedalus, 100 : 3 (Summer, 1971), 539-572.

Britts, Maurice. "Blacks on White College Campuses: 1823 - Present." Negro History Bulletin, 37 (June-July, 1974), 269-272.

Brokenburr, Robert Lee. "Hampton Men in Professions and Business." Southern Workman, 48 (June, 1919), 262.

Brooks, Layman B. "The Development of a Junior College in the Norfolk Area." Virginia Teachers Bulletin, 21 (May, 1944), 21-22.

Brooks. Lynn B. "The Norfolk State College Experiment in Training the Hard-Core Unemployed." Phi Delta Kappan, November, 1964.

Brooks, L. M., and Lynch, R. G. "Consumer Problems and the Cooperative Movement in the Curricula of Southern Negro Colleges." Social Forces, 22 (May, 1944), 429-436.

Brown, Aaron. "Negro Higher and Professional Education in Georgia." Journal of Negro Education, 17 (Summer, 1948), 280-287.

_____. "The Negro Graduate, 1950-1960." Negro Educational Review, 11 (April, 1960), 71-81.

_____. "Graduate and Professional Education in Negro Institutions." Journal of Negro Education, 27 (Summer, 1958), 233-242.

Brown, Charles I. "The Married Student at Bennett College." Journal of Negro Education, 32 (Spring, 1963), 183-187.

_____. "The Male Student at Barber-Scotia College." Quarterly Review of Higher Education Among Negroes, 25 (July, 1957), 170-171. Ibid., Negro Educational Review, 9 (January, 1958), 39-40.

Brown, Charles I., and Stein, Phyllis. "The White Student in Five Predominantly Black Universities." Negro Educational Review, 23 (October, 1972), 148-169.

Brown, Gertrude Parthenia. "The Countee Cullen Memorial Collection of Atlanta University." Negro History Bulletin, 17 (October, 1953), 11-13.

Brown, Ina C. "The National Survey of Negro Higher Education and Post-War Reconstruction: The Place of the Negro College in Negro Life." Journal of Negro Education, 11 (July, 1942), 375-381.

Brown, Juantia. "A Unique Southern College. Southern Workman, 60 (July, 1931), 291-297.

Brown Kenneth I. "The Role of the Small Liberal Arts College in Times of Crisis and Change. . ." Morehouse College Bulletin, 25 (March, 1957), 7-15.

_____. "The College and Its Need for Community." Quarterly Review of Higher Education Among Negroes, 26 (April, 1958), 54-60.

Brown, R. W. "The George Washington Carver Foundation." Opportunity, 24 (October-December, 1946), 171-174, 201.

Brown, Sterling A. "The Atlanta University Summer Theatre." Opportunity, 12 (October, 1934), 308-309.

Brown, Theressa Wilson. "The Inception of Remedial Reading Instruction at Miner Teachers College." The Journal of the Columbian Educational Association, 8 (May, 1946), 58-60.

Brown, W. L. "Booker T. Washington as a Philosopher." Negro History Bulletin, 20 (November, 1956), 34-37.

Browning, James B. "A Historical Sketch of the Association of Social Science Teachers in Negro Colleges." Quarterly Review of Higher Education Among Negroes, 12 (July, 1944), 143-144.

Brownlee, Frederick L. "Heritage and Opportunity: The Negro Church Related College-A Critical Summary." Journal of Negro Education, 29 (Summer, 1960), 401-407.

_____. "Education Unlimited." Phylon, 10 (4th Quarter 1949), 328-333.

_____. "Moving In and Out, the Story of the American Missionary Association." Phylon, 9 : 2 (1948), 146-150.

Brunschwig, Lily. "Psychological Misconceptions of A Group of Negro College Students." Journal of Social Psychology, 18 (August, 1943), 111-126.

Bryant, G. E. "Recent Trends in Racial Attitudes of Negro College Students." Journal of Negro Education, 10 (January, 1941), 43-50.

Bryant, Lawrence C. "Graduate Training in Negro Colleges." Journal of Negro Education, 30 (Winter, 1961), 69-71.

Bryant, Lawrence C. "A Study of Music Programs in Public Negro Colleges." Journal of Negro Education, 32 (Spring, 1963), 188-192.

_____. Graduate Degree Programs in Negro Colleges, 1927-1960." Negro Educational Review, 11 (October, 1960), 177-184.

Bryce, James. "General Armstrong and His Work: An Address in Hampton Institute, January 29, 1910." Southern Workman, 39 (March, 1910), 142-144.

Bryson, William C. "Texas Southern University: Born in Sin. A College Finally Makes Houston Listen." Harvard Crimson, May 22, 1967.

Buck, J. L. B. "Colored Normal Schools in North Carolina." Southern Workman, 52 (December, 1923), 594.

Bullock, Henry Allen. "The Black College and the New Black Awareness." Daedalus, 100 (Summer, 1971), 573-602.

_____. "Negro Higher and Professional Education in Texas." Journal of Negro Education, 17 (Summer, 1948), 373-381.

Bunche, Ralph J. "The Role of the University in the Political Orientation of Negro Youth." Journal of Negro Education, 9 (October, 1940), 571-579.

Burke, Arthur E. "Standards in Negro Colleges." Crisis, 56 (August-September, 1949), 234-236, 253.

Burr, Amelia Josephine. "The Spirit of Hampton." Bellman, June 24, 1916.

_____. "A Master Builder." Bellman, December 15, 1917.

Buszek, Beatrice R. "Differential Treatment of Test Scores." College and University, 43 (Spring, 1968), 294-307.

Butcher, Philip. "Creative Writing in the Negro College." Journal of Negro Education, 20 (Spring, 1951), 160-163.

_____. "George W. Cable: History and Politics." Phylon, 9 (2nd Quarter, 1948), 137-145.

_____. "George W. Cable and Booker T. Washington." Journal of Negro Education, 17 (Fall, 1948), 264-468.

Butler, Addie. "Some Functions of the Black College." Negro Educational Review, 26 (October, 1975), 167-180.

Butler, Mamie Ruth. "What the Negro College Should do for Me." Negro College Quarterly, 4 (June, 1946), 87-88, 120.

Buttrick, Wallace. "Enduring Qualities of Booker T. Washington." Southern Workman, 50 (December, 1922), 550.

"C. A. A. and Negro Colleges." Art Journal, 28 (Winter, 1968-1969), 228.

Cade, John B., and Herbert, Elsie L. "Negro Higher and Professional Education in Louisiana." Journal of Negro Education, 17 (Summer, 1948), 296-302.

Caldwell, B. C. "Work of the Jeanes and Slater Funds." Annals of the American Academy, 49 (September, 1913), 173-176.

Calista, Donald J. "Booker T. Washington: Another Look." Journal of Negro History, 49 (October, 1964), 240-263.

Caliver, Ambrose. "Certain Significant Developments in the Education of Negroes During the Last Generation." Journal of Negro History, 35 (April, 1950), 111-134.

_____. "The Role of the Federal Government in the Higher Education of Negroes." Phylon, 10 : 4 (4th Quarter, 1949), 370-380.

_____. "Deans and Registrars." Crisis, 36 (April, 1928), 304-322.

_____. "Negro College Students and the Need of Personnel Work." Journal of Negro Education, 2 (July, 1933), 359-378.

_____. "Higher Education of Negroes Survey." School Life, 25 (December, 1939), 83-86.

_____. "Collegiate Educators of Negroes." School Life, 26 (March, 1941), 183-185.

_____. "Some Problems in the Education and Placement of Negro Teachers." Journal of Negro Education, 4 (January, 1935), 99-112.

_____. "Personnel Study of Negro College Students." Journal of Educational Research, 27 (October, 1933), 131-134.

_____. "Some Tendencies in Higher Education and Their Application to the Negro College." Opportunity, 6 (January, 1928), 6-9.

Callis, H. A. "The Need and Training of Negro Physicians." Journal of Negro Education, 4 (January, 1935), 32-41.

Campbell, Anne L. "Perspectives on the Negro College Teacher's World." College Language Association Journal, 1 (March, 1958), 85-92.

Campbell, E. Fay. "The Policies and Rationale Governing Support of Negro Private Colleges Maintained by the United Presbyterian Church in the United States of America." Journal of Negro Education, 29 (Summer, 1960), 260-263.

Campbell, Robert and Siegel, Barry. "The Demand for Higher Education in the United States, 1919-1964." American Economic Review, June, 1967.

"Campus Closed, Black Power Group Banned." Chronicle of Higher Education, 2 : 6 (November 22, 1967), 5.

Canady, Herman G. "Intelligence of Negro College Students and Prental Occupation." American Journal of Sociology, 42 (November, 1936), 388-389.

_____. "Individual Differences Among Freshmen at West Virginia State College." Journal of Negro Education, 4 (April, 1935), 246-258.

_____. "Psychology in Negro Institutions." Journal of Negro Education, 7 (April, 1938), 165-171.

Canady, Herman G. "The Character and Extent of Civic Knowledge Possessed by West Virginia State College Students." Negro College Quarterly, 1 (March, 1944), 5-14.

_____. "Psychology in Negro Institutions." West Virginia State College Bulletin, Series 26 : No. 3, June, 1939.

_____. "Sex Differences in Intelligence Among Negro College Freshmen." Journal of Applied Psychology, 22 (August, 1938), 437-439.

_____. "College Graduates and the World Crisis." West Virginia State College Bulletin, Series 3, No. 3, (August-November, 1941), 20-21.

_____. "A Study of Sex Differences in Intelligence-Test Scores Among 1,306 Negro College Freshmen." Journal of Negro Education, 12 (Spring, 1943), 167-172.

Capps, Marian P. "The Virginia Out-of-State Graduate Aid Program, 1936-1950." Journal of Negro Education, 25 (Winter, 1956), 25-35.

"Careers of Negro College Graduates." Outlook, 65 (July, 1900), 710.

Carnegie, M. E. Lancaster. "Nurse Training Becomes Nursing Education at Florida A. & M. College." Journal of Negro Education, 17 (Spring, 1948), 200-204.

Carter, Marion Elizabeth. "Human Relations in the Course Offerings of the District of Columbia Teachers College." Journal of Negro Education, 27 (Winter, 1958), 69-78.

Cater, James T. "The New Talladega Plan." The Talladegan, 51 (November, 1933), 2-4.

_____. "Fifty Degree-Granting Commencements." The Talladegan, 62 (November, 1944), 7.

_____. "One Year Under the New Plan." The Talladegan, 52 (November, 1934), 2-3.

Caution, Tollie L. "The Protestant Episcopal Church: Policies and Rationale Upon Which Support of Its Negro Colleges is Predicated." Journal of Negro Education, 29 (Summer, 1960), 274-283.

Centra, John A., et al. "Academic Growth in Predominantly Negro and Predominantly White Colleges." American Educational Research Journal, 7 (January, 1970), 83-98.

Chandler, Elizabeth W., and Herrington, Dora M. "Training Teachers at Hampton Institute for Elementary-School Service." Southern Workman, 64 (August, 1935), 249-252.

Chandler, Gladstone Lewis. "Scholarship and the Teaching of English in the Negro College." Quarterly Review of Higher Education Among Negroes, 9 (July, 1941), 113-116.

Chandler, J. King, III. "Cardinal Opportunities of Service for Church Owned Colleges." Negro Educational Review, 3 : 3 (July, 1952), 111-114.

Chao, T. T., and Moore, Malvin, Jr. "Correlation Study on Grades Between High School and Fayetteville State Teachers College." Savannah State College Bulletin, 17 (December, 1963), 42-49.

Chase, Thomas N. "Atlanta University." American Missionary, 37 (August, 1883), 232-234.

_____. "The Atlanta Examination." American Missionary, 15 (August, 1871), 181-182.

_____. "An Economical Industrial Department." American Missionary, 33 (November, 1879), 337-338.

_____. "Religious Life at Atlanta University." American Missionary, 32 (July, 1878), 207-210.

"Cheyney State Teachers College." Negro History Bulletin, 21 (January, 1958), 85.

"Cheyney: Quaker Heritage." Crisis, 47 (August, 1940), 238-267.

Chisum, James. "At Miles College, A Mere Lack of Knowledge Is No Bar." Southern Education Report, May, 1967.

Chivers, Walter R. "A Functional Program for the Liberal Arts College." Negro College Quarterly, 2 (June, 1944), 40-49.

_____. "Religion in Negro Colleges." Journal of Negro Education, 9 (January, 1940), 5-12.

_____. "The Founding of Spelman College--A Challenge to Negro Women." Spelman Messenger, 59 (May, 1943), 7-10.

_____. "Teaching Social Anthropology in a Negro College." Phylon, 4 (4th Quarter, 1943), 353-361. Ibid., Quarterly Review of Higher Education Among Negroes, 14 (June, 1946), 134-141.

Clancy, Paul. "The Fight for Quality on Two Negro Campuses." Reporter, July 13, 1967.

Clark, Blake. "Common Sense College." Negro Digest, 6 (June, 1948), 75.

Clark, Edgar Rogie. "Music Education in Negro Schools and Colleges." Journal of Negro Education, 9 (October, 1940), 580-590.

Clark, Felton G. "Findings of the [Seventeenth] Conference of Presidents of Negro Land-Grant Colleges." School and Society, 52 (July 6, 1940), 13-14.

Clark, Felton G. "Report of the Findings Committee, Conference of Presidents of Negro Land-Grant Colleges, 1940." School and Society, 53 (April 19, 1941), 513-514.

_____. "Administrative Control of Public Negro Colleges." Journal of Negro Education, 3 (April, 1934), 245-256.

_____. "Negro Higher Education and Some Fundamental Issues Raised by World War II." Journal of Negro Education, 11 (July, 1942), 279-291.

_____. "The Development and Present Status of Publicly-Supported Higher Education for Negroes." Journal of Negro Education, 27 (Summer, 1958), 221-232.

Clark, Hilton. "The Black Ivy League: Some Personal Observations on an Apathetic Negro." The Black Student, Spring, 1966.

Clark, J. L. "Race Relations Course in a State College." Southern Workman, 59 (February, 1930), 55-57.

_____. "Students Answer the Professor." Crisis, 37 (October, 1930), 336-370.

Clark, Kenneth B. "Higher Education for Negroes: Challenges and Prospects." Journal of Negro Education, 36 (Summer, 1967), 196-215.

Clark, Vernon L. "The Case for Black College Sponsorship of Head Start Programs." Journal of Negro Education, 44 (Fall, 1975), 476-481.

Clark, W. A. "Does Negro Education Pay?" Educational Sociology, 7 (November, 1933), 163-169.

Clark, William J. "Our Colleges - Virginia Union University." Opportunity, 1 (March, 1923), 14-15.

Cleary, Robert E. "Gubernatorial Leadership and State Policy on Desegregation in Public Higher Education." Phylon, 27 (Summer, 1966), 165-170. Ibid., Journal of Negro Education, 35 (Fall, 1966), 439-444.

Clement, Rufus E. "Student in the College for Negroes." Journal of Educational Sociology, 19 (April, 1946), 503-511.

_____. "Negro Higher and Professional Education in the Several States." Journal of Negro Education, 17 (Summer, 1948), 249-399.

_____. "The Impact of the War Upon the Negro Graduate and Professional Schools." Journal of Negro Education, 11 (July, 1942), 365-374.

_____. "The Present and Future Role of Private Colleges for Negroes." Phylon, 10 : 4 (4th Quarter, 1949), 323-327.

_____. "Liberal Arts College Curriculum and the Vocational Needs of Students." Quarterly Review of Higher Education Among Negroes, 2 (April, 1934), 80-82.

_____. "The Church School as a Factor in Negro Life." *Journal of Negro History*, 12 (January, 1927), 5-12.

_____. "The Historical Development of Higher Education for Negro Americans." *Journal of Negro Education*, 35 (Summer, 1966), 299-305.

_____. "Legal Provisions for Graduate and Professional Instruction for Negroes in States Operating Separate School Systems." *Journal of Negro Education*, 8 (April, 1939), 142-150.

Clift, Virgil A. "Higher Education of Minority Groups in the United States." *Journal of Negro Education*, 38 (Summer, 1969), 291-302.

_____. "Criteria for Teacher Education in Negro Institutions." *Journal of Negro Education*, 15 (Spring, 1946), 140-145.

_____. "The Role of Higher Education in Transmitting Democratic Ideals into Behavior Patterns." *Journal of Negro Education*, 17 (Spring, 1948), 134-140.

_____. "The History of Racial Segregation in American Education." *School and Society*, 88 (May 7, 1960), 220-229.

Clinard, Marshall B., and Noel, Donald L. "Role Behavior of Students From Negro Colleges in a Non-Segregated University Situation." *Journal of Negro Education*, 27 (Spring, 1958), 182-188.

Clinton, G. W. "A. M. E. Zion Church History." *A. M. E. Zion Quarterly Review*, 5 (April, 1895), 25-36.

Cobb, Henry E. "Rank and Tenure Practices in Thirty-Six Negro Colleges." *Journal of Negro Education*, 20 (Fall, 1951), 535-546.

Cobb, W. Montague. "Howard, Meharry, and Separate Professional Education." *Bulletin of the Medico-Chirurgical Society of the District of Columbia, Inc.*, 4 (1947), 3-9.

Cochran, Anne Scarlet. "The Development of Teacher Education at Morris Brown College." *Journal of Negro Education*, 16 (Spring, 1947), 246-251.

Cohen, Arthur M. "The Process of Desegregation: A Case Study." *Journal of Negro Education*, 35 (Fall, 1966), 445-451.

Coleman, C. D. "The Christian Methodist Episcopal Church: The Rationale and Policies Upon Which Support of Its Colleges Is Predicated." *Journal of Negro Education*, 29 (Summer, 1960), 315-318.

Coleman, E. M. "The Teaching of Negro History in Negro Colleges." *Negro History Bulletin*, 12 : 3 (December, 1948),

53-54, 66-67.

"Colleges and Universities for Negroes." School and Society, 6 (August 25, 1917), 222-223.

Colson, Edna M. "The Negro Teachers' College and Normal School." Journal of Negro Education, 2 (July, 1933), 284-298.

_____. "Student Guidance at Virginia State." Opportunity, 16 (March, 1938), 77-78.

Colvin, Sandra. "Students Seek Black Unity." Southern Courier, May 11, 1968.

"Commencement At Livingstone College." A. M. E. Zion Quarterly Review, 24 (1914), 34.

"Congress Assigns Another Function to Bureau of Education." School Life, 14 (March, 1929), 127.

Connor, M. W. "The Facilities and Practices of Negro Tax-Supported Teacher-Training Institutions." Journal of Negro Education, 6 (October, 1937), 623-627.

Conyers, James E. "Negro Doctorates in Sociology: A Social Portrait." Phylon, 29 (Fall, 1968), 209-223.

Cook, Walter W., and Hartshorn, Herbert H. "Success of Lincoln University (Mo.) Graduates in Graduate School." Journal of Negro Education, 10 (January, 1941), 59-62.

Cooke, Anne. "The Atlanta University Summer Theatre." Opportunity, 19 (November, 1941), 331-333.

Cooke, Paul. "Desegregated Higher Education in the District of Columbia." Journal of Negro Education, 27 (Summer, 1958), 342-351.

Coombs, Orde. "Jackson State College." Change, 5 (October, 1973), 34-39.

Cooper, C. L. "The Vocational Choices of Negro College Students in North Carolina." Journal of Negro Education, 6 (October, 1937), 60-69.

Cooper, William M. "Adult Education Programs of Negro Colleges and Universities." Journal of Negro Education, 14 (Summer, 1945), 307-311.

Cornely, Paul B. "Administration of Health Education and Health Supervision in Negro Colleges." American Journal of Public Health, 26 (1936), 888-896.

_____. "Health Education Programs in Negro Colleges." Journal of Negro Education, 6 (July, 1937), 531-537.

_____. "The Status of Student Health Programs in Negro Colleges in 1938-1939." Journal of Negro Education, 10 (April, 1941), 151-167.

"Court Upset Student Ousters at 3 Colleges." Chronicle of Higher Education, 2 : 1 (September 13, 1967), 4.

Cox, Oliver Cromwell. "The Leadership of Booker T. Washington." Social Forces, 30 (October, 1951), 91-96.

_____. "Provisions for Graduate Education Among Negroes." Journal of Negro Education, 9 (January, 1940), 22-31.

Craig, Argentine S., and Cooke, Gwendolyn J. "The Federal Government as a Change Agent in Higher Education and a Black College's Response to that Role." Journal of Negro Education, 44 (Fall, 1975), 468-475.

Cranford, Clarence W. "The Furnishing of a Healthy Mind." Journal of Negro Education, 27 (Spring, 1958), 103-106.

Cronin, Joseph M. "Negroes in Catholic Schools." Commonweal, 85 (October 7, 1966), 13-16.

Crooks, Kenneth B. M. "Entrance Examinations for Negro Colleges." Southern Workman, 61 (July, 1932), 299-302. Ibid., Journal of Negro Education, 3 (October, 1934), 593-597.

Crouch, H. B., and Leathers, C. M. "The Validity of Students Opinions in Evaluating a Program of College Biology." Science Education, 35 (March, 1951), 73-76.

Crowl, John A. "Carnegie Commission Issues Its Recommendations for Black Colleges." Chronicle of Higher Education, 5 : 20 (February 22, 1971), 1-2.

_____. "Quality of Colleges for Negroes is Hit." Chronicle of Higher Education, 3 : 1 (September 2, 1968), 1, 3.

_____. "Negro Colleges Seen Needing Special Funds." Chronicle of Higher Education, 3 : 18 (May 19, 1969), 12.

_____. "Negro Students Scoring Gains With Sit-Inns." Chronicle of Higher Education, 2 : 15 (April 8, 1968), 1, 5.

_____. "Negro Colleges Seek to Boast Business Gifts." Chronicle of Higher Education, 2 : 9 (January 15, 1968), 3.

Crowell, Suzanne. "Trials of Bluefield Students Begin." Southern Patriot, May, 1969.

_____. "Why Bluefield State Students Rebelled." Southern Patriot, April, 1968.

Cureau, Harold G. "The Art Gallery, Museum: Their Availability as Educational Resources in the Historically Negro College." Journal of Negro Education, 42 (Fall, 1973), 452-

461.

_____. "The Visual Arts in the Historic Black Colleges." Journal of Negro Education, 58 (October, 1973), 441-451.

Curtis, Florence Rising. "The Library of the Negro College." Southern Workman, 55 (October, 1926), 472-474.

_____. "The Contribution of Library School to Negro Education." Southern Workman, 56 (August, 1927), 373-378.

_____. "Librarianship As A Field for Negroes." Journal of Negro Education, 4 (January, 1935), 94-98.

Curtis, L. Simington. "The Negro Publicly-Supported College in Missouri." Journal of Negro Education, 31 (Summer, 1962), 251-259.

Curtis, N. "Significance of Hampton's Fifty Years." Outlook, 12 (June 4, 1919), 197-198.

D'Amico, Louis A., and Reed, Maenylie M. "A Comparison of Tuition-and-Fee Charges in Negro Institutions with Charges in Institutions of the Southeast and of the Nation: 1962-1963." Journal of Negro Education, 33 (Spring, 1964), 186-190.

Daniel, Robert P. "Impact of the War Upon the Church Related College and University." Journal of Negro Education, 11 : 3 (July, 1942), 359-364.

_____. "The Relationship of the Negro Public College and the Negro Private and Church-Related College." Journal of Negro Education, 29 (Summer, 1960), 388-393.

Daniel, V. E. "Our Negro Colleges - Fisk University, Taugaloo, Wiley College." Opportunity, 1 (April, 1923), 12-14.

Daniel, Walter G., and Daniel, Robert P. "The Curriculum of the Negro College." Journal of Educational Sociology, 19 (April, 1946), 496-502.

Daniel, Walter G. "FERA Help for Negro Education." Journal of Negro Education, 4 (April, 1935), 278-283.

_____. "Federal Activities and Negro Education, and General Progress." Journal of Negro Education, 6 (January, 1937), 101-103.

_____. "The National Youth Administration." Journal of Negro Education, 6 (April, 1937), 230-233.

_____. "Negro Higher and Professional Education in Virginia." Journal of Negro Education, 17 (Summer, 1948), 382-392.

_____. "Liberal Arts and Teacher Education in the Negro

Public College." Journal of Negro Education, 31 (Summer, 1962), 404-413.

_____. "Negroes as Teaching Assistants in Some Publicly Supported Universities." Journal of Negro Education, 31 (Summer, 1962), 202-204.

Daniels, Virginia R. McDonald. "Reading Abilities of Southern University Freshmen." Southern University Bulletin, 27 (March, 1941), 54-83.

Davenport, Roy K. "A Negro College Examines Its Curricula by Measuring Improvement in Reading." Journal of Negro Education, 10 (April, 1941), 178-184.

_____. "A Background Study of a Negro College Freshmen Population." Journal of Negro Education, 8 (April, 1939), 186-197.

Davis, Arthur P. "The Negro College Student." Crisis, 37 (August, 1930), 270-271.

_____. "The Negro Student and World Revolution." Journal of Negro Education, 12 (Winter, 1973), 7-13.

_____. "Depression and the Small College." Virginia Union Bulletin, 34 (November, 1933), 3-5.

_____. "The Negro Professor." Crisis, 43 (April, 1936), 103-114.

Davis, C. R. "Library Club on a College Campus." Wilson Library Bulletin, 21 (September, 1946), 48, 51.

Davis, Clarence W. "Health Education Programs in Negro Colleges and Universities." Journal of Negro Education, 18 (Spring, 1949), 409-417.

Davis, Edward P. "The Negro Liberal Arts College." Journal of Negro Education, 2 (July, 1933), 299-311.

Davis, Jackson, et al. "Negro Land-Grant Colleges." School and Society, 47 (March, 1938), 411-413.

Davis, Jackson. "New Head of Jeanes and Slater Funds." Southern Workman, 60 (October, 1931), 404-406.

_____. "The Outlook for the Professional and Higher Education of Negroes." Journal of Negro Education, 2 (July, 1933), 403-410.

_____. "Outlook for Negro Colleges." Southern Workman, 57 (March, 1928), 129-136.

_____. "Livingstone Given High Tributes at A. M. E. Zion Sesquicentennial." Church School Hearld, 30 (November, 1946), 6.

Davis, Jane E. "A Maker of Hampton." *Southern Workman*, 54 (May, 1925), 193-199.

_____. "Some Hampton Builders." *Southern Workman*, 52 (July, 1923), 327.

Davis, John Warren. "The Negro Land-Grant College." *Journal of Negro Education*, 2 (July, 1933), 312-328.

Davis, John W. "Land-Grant Colleges for Negroes." *West Virginia State College Bulletin*, Series 21, No. 5 1934.

_____. "Education." *Opportunity*, 6 (July, 1928), 201.

_____. "The Unrest in Negro Colleges." *The New Student*, January, 1929.

_____. "Report of the Committee of Findings of the Conference of Presidents of the Negro Land-Grant Colleges." *Quarterly Review of Higher Education Among Negroes*, 6 (April, 1938), 156-159.

_____. "The Participation of Negro Land-Grant Colleges in Permanent Federal Education Funds." *Journal of Negro Education*, 7 (July, 1938), 282-291.

_____. "The Future Role of the Negro Public College." *Journal of Negro Education*, 31 (Summer, 1962), 421-428.

_____. "Current Changes in Negro Higher Education Meet the Immediate War Emergency." *Journal of Negro Education*, 11 (July, 1942), 292-296.

_____. "Problems in the Collegiate Education of Negroes." *West Virginia State College Bulletin*, Series 24, No. 4, 1937.

Davis, Ralph N. "Data on Negro Life Available at Tuskegee Institute." *Negro College Quarterly*, 1 (September, 1943), 87-91.

Davis, Thomas Edward. "A Study of Fisk University Freshmen From 1928 to 1930." *Journal of Negro Education*, 2 (October, 1933), 477-483.

_____. "Some Racial Attitudes of Negro College and Grade School Students." *Journal of Negro Education*, 6 (April, 1937), 157-165.

Day, Everett A., and Ready, I. E. "The Future of Black Colleges, an Articulation Challenge." *Community College Review*, Spring, 1974, 53-59.

Decker, Paul M. "A Study of Job Opportunities in the State of Florida for Negro College Graduates." *Journal of Negro Education*, 29 (Winter, 1960), 93-95.

_____. "Study of White Teachers in Selected Negro Colleges." Journal of Negro Education, 24 (Fall, 1955), 501-505.

DeCosta, Frank A. "Negro Higher and Professional Education in South Carolina." Journal of Negro Education, 17 (Summer, 1948), 350-360.

_____. "The Tax-Supported College for Negroes." Journal of Educational Sociology, 32 (February, 1958), 260-266.

DeMott, Benjamin. "Encounter in Mississippi: Tougaloo Summer Enrichment Program." Saturday Review, 51 (January, 20, 1968), 51-53.

Dent, Thomas C. "Blues for the Negro College." Freedomways, Fall, 1968.

Derbigny, Irving. "The Adaptation of Instructional Materials in Chemistry to the Needs of the Students in Negro Colleges." Quarterly Review of Higher Education Among Negroes, 2 (July, 1934), 175-178.

_____. "Selective College Admission in the Lower South." Journal of Negro Education, 9 (April, 1940), 154-161.

_____. "Vocational Orientation Among Tuskegee Institute Freshmen." Journal of Negro Education, 10 (October, 1941), 653-660.

_____. "Tuskegee Looks at Its Veterans." Quarterly Review of Higher Education Among Negroes, 14 (January, 1946), 11-18.

"Desegregation and the Negro College." Journal of Negro Education, 27 (Summer, 1958), 209-435.

Dickerson, G. Edward, and Imes, William Lloyd. "The Cheyney Training School." Crisis, May, 1923.

Dillard, James Hardy. "Fourteen Years of the Jeanes Fund." South Atlantic Quarterly, 22 (July, 1923), 193-201.

_____. "A Christian Philosopher, Booker T. Washington." Southern Workman, 54 (May, 1925), 209-214.

_____. "The Negro Goes to College." World's Work, 55 (January, 1928), 337-340.

_____. "Negro in Rural Education and Country Life." Journal of Rural Education, 1 (November, 1921), 97-99.

_____. "Negro Rural School Fund, Anna T. Jeanes Foundation." Indiana, 67 (December 2, 1909), 1250-1252.

Dinwiddie, Bob. "Revolution, Not Boycott, Says Miles [College] Protest Leader." Southern Courier, October 14, 1967.

Doddy, Hurley H. "The Status of the Negro Public College: A Statistical Summary." Journal of Negro Education, 31 (Summer, 1962), 370-385.

_____. "The 'Sit-In' Demonstrations and the Dilemma of the Negro College President." Journal of Negro Education, 30 (Winter, 1961), 1-3.

_____. "The Progress of the Negro in Higher Education, 1950-1960." Journal of Negro Education, 32 (Fall, 1963), 485-492.

Doggett, Allen B., Jr. "From Slave Farm to County Training School." Southern Workman, 55 (November, 1926), 500-508.

Donnell, William C. "Vocational Guidance; A Plan for the Small College." Quarterly Review of Higher Education Among Negroes, 1 (October, 1933), 4-11.

Dorey, Frank David. "Negro College Graduates in Schools of Religion." Christian Education, 29 (September, 1946), 350-358. Ibid., Journal of Negro Education, 15 (Fall, 1946), 689-694.

Doyle, Bertram W. "Introductory Course in Sociology in Negro Colleges and Universities." Journal of Educational Sociology, 7 (September, 1933), 30-36.

_____. "Sociology in Negro Schools and Colleges, 1926-1932." Quarterly Review of Higher Education Among Negroes, 1 (July, 1933), 7-14.

Drake, St. Clair. "The Black University in the American Social Order." Daedalus, 100 : 3 (Summer, 1971), 833-897.

Drain, Leonard Pack. "Fines-Rates and Payments: A Survey of Thirty-Seven Colleges and Universities for Negro Youth." Library Journal, 66 (April, 1941), 293-294.

"Drop in Enrollment at Negro Land-Grant Colleges." School and Society, 55 (April 11, 1942), 412.

Du Bois, W. E. B. "The Cultural Mission of Atlanta University." Phylon, 3 (2nd Quarter, 1942), 105-115.

_____. "Does the Negro Need Separate Schools?" Journal of Negro Education, 4 (July, 1935), 328-335.

_____. "Education and Work." Journal of Negro Education, 1 (April, 1932), 60-74. Ibid., Howard University Bulletin, 9 (January, 1931), 5-22.

_____. "The Future of Wilberforce University." Journal of Negro Education, 9 (October, 1940), 553-570.

_____. "The Laboratory in Sociology at Atlanta University." The Annals of the American Academy of Political and Social Science, 21 (May, 1903), 100-163.

_____. "A Crisis at Fisk." Nation, 163 (September 7, 1946), 269-270.

_____. "Negroes in College." Nation, 122 (March, 1926), 228-230.

_____. "The Hampton Strike." Nation, 125 (November 2, 1927), 471-472.

_____. "The Field and Function of the Negro College." Fisk University Herald, 6 (June, 1931), 1.

_____. "Negro Education." Crisis, 15 (February, 1918), 173-178.

_____. "Wilberforce." Crisis, 20 (August, 1920), 176-178.

_____. "A College President." Crisis, 9 (November, 1914), 12-13.

_____. "Hampton College." Crisis, 24 (July, 1922), 104-105.

_____. "A Graduate School." Crisis, June, 1929.

_____. "The Negro College." Crisis, 40 (August, 1933), 175-177.

_____. "The Future and Function of the Private Negro College." Crisis, 53 (August, 1946), 234-236, 253-254.

_____. "The Freedmen's Bureau." Atlantic Monthly, 87 (March, 1901), 354-365.

_____. "Reconstruction and Its Benefits." American Historical Review, 15 (July, 1910), 781-799.

_____. "Thomas Jesse Jones." Crisis, 22 (October, 1921), 252-256.

_____. "The Significance of Henry Hunt." The Fort Valley State College Bulletin, 1 (October, 1940), 15-16.

_____. "What Intellectual Training is Doing for the Negro." Mississippi Review, 27 (August, 1904), 574-582.

_____. "The Training of Negroes for Social Power." The Outlook, 75 (October, 1903), 409-414.

_____. "The Tragedy at Atlanta--From the Point of View of the Negro." The World Today, 11 (November, 1906), 173-175.

_____. "Wilberforce College." Chicago Defender, June 7, 1947, p. 19.

_____. "New Day at Lincoln University." Chicago Defender, May 18, 1946, p. 15.

_____. "The Future of the Negro State University." Wilberforce University Quarterly, 2 (April, 1941), 53-60.

Dummett, Clifton O. "The Negro in Dental Education: A Review of Important Occurrences." Phylon, 20 (4th Quarter, Winter, 1959), 379-388.

Dunbar, King and Christophe, Jr. "Teacher Evaluation by Students in Negro Colleges." Negro Educational Review, 3 : 3 (July, 1952), 108-110.

Duncan, Catherine J. Watkins. "Teacher Education at Fort Valley State College." Journal of Negro Education, 15 (Winter, 1946), 102-108.

_____. "Pre-Service Teacher Education for Negroes in Georgia." Journal of Negro Education, 19 (Spring, 1950), 159-166.

Dunlap, Mollie E. "Recreational Reading of Negro College Students." Journal of Negro Education, 2 (October, 1933), 448-459.

_____. "Special Collections of Negro Literature in the United States." Journal of Negro Education, 4 (October, 1935), 482-489.

Dunne, William Kailer. "The Roman Catholic Church: The Rationale and Policies Underlying the Maintenance of Higher Institutions for Negroes." Journal of Negro Education, 29 (Summer, 1960), 307-314.

Dyer, Henry S. "Toward More Effective Recruitment and Selection of Negroes for College." Journal of Negro Education, 36 (Summer, 1967), 216-229.

Dykes, Eva B. "Higher Training of Negroes." The Crisis, (July, 1921), 105-112.

Eagleson, Oran W., and Bell, Eleanor S. "The Values of Negro Women College Students." Journal of Social Psychology, 22 (November, 1945), 149-154.

Eaton, James A. "The Effects of the College 'Atmosphere' on the Personality of Students." Journal of Negro Education, 20 (Spring, 1951), 228-232.

Eberhardt, Harry G. "Individual Differences in Reading Ability Among College Freshmen." Journal of Negro Education, 7 (January, 1938), 55-59.

Editorial. "The Reclassification of Livingstone College." The Livingstone, May 15, 1926, 4.

Editorial. "The Negro College Libraries." Southern Workman, 55 (June, 1926), 245.

Editorial. "Fisk's New President." [Thomas Elsa Jones] Southern Workman, 56 (January, 1927), 3-5.

Editorial. "Fisk's Million Dollar Endowment Fund." Opportunity, 2 (August, 1924), 227-228.

Editorial. "More Student Unrest." Opportunity, 3 (June, 1925), 164.

Editorial. "Hampton Inaugurates A President." [Malcolm S. Mac Lean] Opportunity, 18 (December, 1940), 354-355.

Editorial. "Julius Rosenwald Fund, 1917-1948." Phylon, 9 (3rd Quarter, 1948), 195.

Editorial. "Livingstone College and Hood Seminary." The Star of Zion, November 22, 1945, 4.

Edley, Christopher F. "Black Education the Need for Black Support." Crisis, 83 (January, 1976), 14-16.

Edmonds, Randolph. "The Negro Little Theater Movement." Negro History Bulletin, 12 (January, 1949), 82-86, 92.

Edmonds, Randolph. "Fraternities at the Crossroads." Crisis, 46 (October, 1939), 301-302, 315.

_____. "What Good Are College Dramatics." Crisis, 41 (August, 1934), 232-234.

"Educating the Negro After the Civil War." Negro History Bulletin, 3 : 2 (November, 1939), 22-24.

Eells, Walter Crosby. "The Higher Education of Negroes in the United States." Journal of Negro Education, 24 (Fall, 1955), 426-434.

Eells, Walter C. "Highest Earned Degrees of Faculty Members in Institutions of Higher Education in the United States; 1954-1955." College And University, 34 (Fall, 1958), 5-38.

_____. "Surveys of Higher Education for Negroes." Journal of Negro Education, 5 (April, 1956), 245-251.

_____. "Results of Surveys of Negro Colleges and Universities." Journal of Negro Education, 4 (October, 1935), 476-481.

_____., and Hollis, Earnest V. "The Origin and Development of the Public College in the United States." Journal of Negro Education, 31 (Summer, 1962), 221-229.

Eggleston, G. K. "The Work of the Relief Societies During the Civil War." Journal of Negro History, 14 (July, 1929), 272-299.

Eichelberger, James William. "The African Methodist Episcopal Zion Church: The Rationale and Policies Upon Which Maintenance of Its Colleges is Based." Journal of Negro Education, 29 (Summer, 1960), 323-329.

Eisenberg, Bernard. "Kelley Miller: The Negro Leader as a Marginal Man." Journal of Negro History, 45 (July, 1960), 182-197.

Elam, Lloyd C. "Problems of the Predominantly Negro Medical School." Journal of the American Medical Association, 2 : 209 (August, 18, 1969), 1070-1072.

Elder, Alphonso. "A Plan to Improve the Academic Work at the North Carolina College for Negroes." Quarterly Review of Higher Education Among Negroes, 1 (January, 1933), 33-34.

_____. "Analysis of Some Major Problems Connected With Freshmen." North Carolina Teachers' Record, 2 (March, 1931), 24-27.

Eleazer, R. B. "Atlanta School of Social Work." Social Forces, 11 (December, 1932), 262.

Eliot, Charles W. "Hampton Idea of Education." Southern Workman, 39 (January, 1910), 12.

Ellis, A. W. "The Status of Health and Physical Education for Women in Negro Colleges and Universities." Journal of Negro Education, 8 (January, 1939), 58-63. Ibid., Research Quarterly, 10 (May, 1939), 135-141.

Ellis, L. B. "Georgia State Industrial College for Negroes." Gunton's Magazine, 25 : 218-226.

Ellison, John M. "The Policies and Rationale Underlying the Support of Colleges Maintained by the Baptist Denomination." Journal of Negro Education, 29 (Summer, 1960), 330-338.

Ellsworth, Clayton S. "Oberlin College." Negro History Bulletin, 7 (February, 1944), 113-115.

Elton, Charles F. "Black and White Colleges: A Comparative Analysis." Journal of Negro Education, 43 (Winter, 1941), 111-116.

"End of Night of Terror at Tennessee State University." Crisis, 78 (January-February, 1971), 11-14.

"Enrollment in Negro Universities and Colleges." School and Society, 28 (September 29, 1928), 401-402. Ibid., 50 (July, 1939), 141.

"Enrollment of Students in Negro Colleges." Quarterly Review of Higher Education Among Negroes, 1 (January, 1933), 26-29.

Ernst, Harry and Calloway, Andrew. "Reverse Integration." New York Times, January 6, 1957.

"Establishment of a School of Law by Lincoln University." School and Society, 50 (September, 1939), 339.

Evans, James C. "The Contribution of Negro Higher Education to the War Effort." Journal of Negro Education, 11 (July, 1942), 304-313.

_____. "The Negro College and the War." Negro College Quarterly, 1 (June, 1943), 35-44.

Evans, James C., and Parker, Albert J. "ROTC Programs and Negro Youth." Journal of Negro Education, 25 (Spring, 1956), 130-138.

"Everyday Life at Hampton." Southern Workman, 54 (March, 1925), 123-126.

Farrell, H. Alfred. "What Lincoln University is Now Trying to Do With the Assistance of the Association for the Study of Negro Life and History." Negro History Bulletin, 17 (December, 1953), 50, 68.

Farrison, W. Edward. "Booker T. Washington: A Study in Educational Leadership." South Atlantic Quarterly, 41 (July, 1942), 312-319.

_____. "Negro Scholarship." Crisis, 40 (February, 1934), 33-34.

_____. "A Note on Negro Education." Opportunity, 2 (March, 1924), 75-77.

Fauset, Jessie. "In Talladega." Crisis, 35 (February, 1928), 47-48.

Favort, Leo M. "Schools for Negro Children: Past Practices and Present Hopes." Nation's Schools, 10 (October, 1932), 59-65.

_____. "Provisions for Preparation and Training of Negro Teachers." Bulletin of the National Association of Teachers in Colored Schools, 11 (January, 1931), 15-17.

"Federal City First Class Operation in a Second Class Context." Chronicle of Higher Education, 8 : 40 (August 19, 1974), 6.

"Federal Jury Probes Slaying at Southern U." Chronicle of Higher Education, 8 : 33 (May 20, 1974), 1.

Fen, Sing-Nan. "Notes on the Education of Negroes at Norfolk and Portsmouth, Virginia During the Civil War." Phylon, 28 (Summer, 1967), 197-201.

_____. "Notes on the Education of Negroes in North Carolina During the Civil War." Journal of Negro Education, 36 (Winter, 1967), 24-31.

_____. "Liberal Education for Negroes: As Viewed in the General Context of American Higher Education." Journal of Negro Education, 30 (Winter, 1961), 17-24.

Fenner, Wildred Sandison, and Soule, Jean Conder. "George Washington Carver--The Wizard of Tuskegee." Journal of the National Education Association, 35 (December, 1946), 580-581.

Fichter, Joseph H. "Career Preparation and Expectations of Negro College Seniors." Journal of Negro Education, 35 (Fall, 1966), 322-335.

Fields, Cheryl M. "Negro College Presidents Ask More U. S. Aid." Chronicle of Higher Education, 4 : 22 (March 9, 1970), 7.

_____. "Black Colleges Receive Only Small Amounts of Extra $30 Million Promised by Nixon." Chronicle of Higher Education, 5 : 9 (November 23, 1970), 2.

"Fifty Years of Tuskegee." School and Society, 33 (April 18, 1931), 537-538.

Finan, Christopher M. "Tornado Rips Central State University, Hanover College." Chronicle of Higher Education, 8 : 28 (April 15, 1974), 1, 2.

_____. "Tornado-Battered University Reopens in Trailers, Dorms." Chronicle of Higher Education, 8 : 29 (April 22, 1974), 2.

Fisher, Isaac. "Florida Builds Its Negro College." Southern Workman, 58 (November, 1929), 507-512.

_____. "Armstrong's Unique Philosophy." Southern Workman, 62 (May, 1933), 203-208.

_____. "Tuskegee's Fiftieth Anniversary: A Review of the Founder's Philosophy." Southern Workman, 60 (June, 1931), 242-254.

_____. "School Problems of the Southern Negro." Fisk University News, October, 1922.

Fisher, J. W. "The Veterans Program at Southern University." *Quarterly Review of Higher Education Among Negroes*, 14 (January, 1946), 1-2.

Fisher, Miles Mark. "Lincoln, Wilberforce, and Integration." *Crisis*, 60 (December, 1953), 602-604.

Fisher, R. Farley. "Lincoln University's Contribution to Livingstone College." *A. M. E. Zion Quarterly Review*, 42 (July-September, 1932), 12.

"Fisk University: 1865-1940." *Crisis*, 47 (August, 1940), 239.

Fitchett, E. H. "The Occupational Preferences and Opportunities of Negro College Students." *Journal of Negro Education*, 7 (October, 1938), 498-513.

8 _____. "The Influence of Claflin College on Negro Family Life." *Journal of Negro History*, 29 (October, 1944) 43-60.

_____. "The Role of Claflin College in Negro Life in South Carolina." *Journal of Negro Education*, 12 (Winter, 1943), 46-49.

_____. "The Claflin College Graduate and the Community." *Negro History Bulletin*, 7 (October, 1944), 1-12, 14-16.

Fleming, G. James. "Preacher-at-Large to Universities [H. Thurman]." *Crisis*, 46 (August, 1939), 233, 251, 253.

_____. "Desegregation in Higher Education in Maryland." *Journal of Negro Education*, 27 (Summer, 1958), 275-283.

_____. "The Negro Publicly-Supported Colleges in Delaware and Maryland." *Journal of Negro Education*, 31 (Summer, 1962), 260-274.

Fletcher, Thomas Fortune. "The Purpose and Function of A State University for Negroes." *Opportunity*, 20 (November, 1942), 337-338, 350-352.

"Florida Agricultural and Mechanical College, Tallahasse, Florida." *Crisis*, 47 (August, 1940), 240-267.

"Florida College President Awarded Ph.D." *Crisis*, 49 (August, 1942), 248-267.

Foley, Albert S. "The Negro and Catholic Higher Education." *Crisis*, 64 (August-September, 1957), 413-419.

Foner, Philip S. ed. "Is Booker T. Washington's Idea Correct?" *Journal of Negro History*, 55 (October, 1970), 343-347.

Ford, Nick Aaron. "The Negro Junior College." *Journal of Negro Education*, 5 (October, 1936), 591-594.

_____. "Student Writing and Faculty Attitudes." *Journal of Higher Education*, 28 (January, 1957), 38-41.

_____. "I Teach Negro Literature." *College English*, 2 (March, 1941), 530-541.

Foster, Luther H., and Prothro, Charles E. "Minimum Income Necessary to Maintain a Small College Effectively." *Journal of Negro Education*, 29 (Summer, 1960), 345-355.

_____. "Recent Trends in Financing Negro Colleges." *Negro Educational Review*, 10 (July, 1959), 130-140.

Franklin, John Hope. "George Washington Williams, Historian." *Journal of Negro History*, 31 (January, 1946), 60-90.

_____. "Courses Concerning the Negro in Negro Colleges." *Quarterly Review of Higher Education Among Negroes*, 8 (July, 1940), 138-144.

Fraser, Lionel B. "The Dilemma of Our Colleges and Universities." *Opportunity*, 15 (June, 1937), 167-171.

Fraser, Thomas P. "Science Surveys in Accredited Negro Colleges." *Journal of Negro Education*, 9 (January, 1940), 13-21.

_____. "A Study of the Opinion of Students on College General Education Science." *Science Education*, 39 (April, 1955), 213-219.

Francis, Cyrus W. "Our College Record--Atlanta University Exercises." *American Missionary*, 20 (August, 1876), 172-174.

_____. "Religious Work at Atlanta University." *American Missionary*, 40 (April, 1886), 106.

_____. "The Atlanta Mission." *American Missionary*, 12 (November, 1868), 243-244.

Francois, William. "A Living Laboratory of Human Relations [West Virginia State College]." *Saturday Review*, May 21, 1966.

Frazier, E. Franklin. "A Community School." *Southern Workman*, 54 (October, 1925), 459-464.

Fraizer, E. Franklin. "Role of Negro Schools in the Post-War World." *Journal of Negro Education*, 13 (October, 1944), 464-473.

_____. "Graduate Education in Negro Colleges and Universities." *Journal of Negro Education*, 2 (July, 1933), 329-341.

Friedman, Lawrence J. "Life 'In the Lion's Mouth':

Another Look at Booker T. Washington." Journal of Negro History, 59 (October, 1974), 337-351.

Friedman, Neil. "Learning in Black Colleges." Wilson Library Bulletin, 44 (September, 1969), 49-74,

_____. "The Miles College Freshmen Social Science Program: Educational Innovation in a Negro College." Journal of Negro Education, 38 (Fall, 1969), 361-369.

Frissell, H. B. "What Industrial Education is Doing for the Negro." Missionary Review, 27: 578-582.

_____. "The Training of Negro Teachers." Southern Workman, 29 (November, 1900), 612-615.

Frissell, H. B. "Negro Education." Outlook, 74 (August 15, 1903), 937-939.

Frissell, Sidney D. "Hampton A Training Station for Two Races." Survey, June 7, 1913.

Froe, Otis D. "A Comparative Study of a Population of 'Disadvantaged' College Freshmen." Journal of Negro Education, 37 (Fall, 1968), 372-382.

_____. "Educational Planning for Disadvantaged College Youth." Journal of Negro Education, 33 (Summer, 1964), 290-303.

_____. "Meeting the Needs of College Youth: The Morgan State College Program." Journal of Negro Education, 35 (Fall, 1966), 422-429.

Fullerton, Garry. "Two More Negro Colleges are Given Accreditation." Southern School News, 6 (January, 1960), 13.

"Fundless Campus; United Negro College Fund." Newsweek, 27 (June 24, 1946), 93.

Funke, Loretta. "The Negro in Education." Journal of Negro History, 5 (January, 1920), 20.

Funkhouser, W. D. "Conferences on Graduate Work in Negro Institutions in the South." Journal of Negro Education, 15 (Winter, 1946), 122-127.

"Future of Private Negro Colleges." Ebony, 16 (July, 1961), 88-90.

Gale, Mary Ellen. "Can Governor Keep Tuskegee Money?" Southern Courier, September 16, 1967.

Gallagher, Buell G. "The Impact of the War Upon Privately Controlled Colleges and Universities for Negroes." Journal of Negro Education, 11 (July, 1942), 346-358.

_____. "Talladega Library: Weapon Against Caste." Crisis, 46 (April, 1939), 110-111, 126.

_____. "The Function of the Negro College." Opportunity, 11 (November, 1933), 345-346.

_____. "College Training for the Negro---To What End?" Opportunity, 15 (September, 1937), 273-275.

Galloway, Thomas J. "Booker T. Washington and the Tuskegee Institute." The New England Magazine, 17 (October, 1897), 131-146.

Gamble, H. F. "Report of Committee on Medical Education and Negro Medical Schools." Journal of the National Medical Association, October-December, 1909.

Gandy, John M. "The Program of Education of Virginia State College: Vindication." Virginia State College Gazette, 45 (December, 1939), 3-9.

Gandy, Samuel L. "Desegregation of Higher Education in Louisiana." Journal of Negro Education, 27 (Summer, 1958), 269-274.

Gardner, Booker T. "Educational Contributions of Booker T. Washington." Journal of Negro Education, 44 (Fall, 1975), 502-518.

Garrison, K. C., and Burch, Viola S. "A Study of the Racial Attitudes of College Students." Journal of Social Psychology, 4 (May, 1933), 230-235.

Gates, Maurice. "Negro Students Challenge Social Forces." Crisis, 42 (August, 1935), 233.

Gatewood, Willard B. "Booker T. Washington and the Ulrick Affair." Phylon, 30 (Fall, 3rd Quarter, 1969), 286-302.

Gay, Dorothy A. "Crisis of Identity: The Negro Community in Raleigh, 1890-1900." North Carolina Historical Review, 50 (April, 1973), 121-140.

Gellhorn, E. "Law Schools and the Negro." Duke Law Journal, 6 (December, 1968), 1069.

Georgia Conference on Educational Opportunities. "Georgia's Education: Separate and Unequal." New South, 15 (December, 1960), 9-11.

Gerber, David A. "Segregation, Separatism, and Sectarianism: Ohio Blacks and Wilberforce University's Effort to Obtain Federal Funds, 1891." Journal of Negro Education, 45 (Winter, 1976), 1-20.

Gibbs, Warmoth T. "Engineering Education in Land-Grant

Colleges." Journal of Negro Education, 21 (Fall, 1952), 546-550.

Gideonse, Harry D. "The Function of Higher Education in the Present War Crisis." Journal of Negro Education, 11 (July, 1942), 247-256.

Gipson, Theodore H. "Relationship of Teaching Aptitude to Age, Sex, and Classification of Students at Southern University." Journal of Negro Education, 29 (Winter, 1960), 96-99.

Gleason, Eliza A. "The Atlanta University School of Library Service--Its Aims and Objectives." Library Quarterly, 12 (July, 1942), 504-510.

Gloster, Hugh M. "The Southern Regional School Plan." Crisis, 55 (August, 1948), 233-236, 252.

Golden, Harry. "The American Negro and Higher Education." Crisis, 70 (August-September, 1963), 405-409.

Golightly, Cornelius L. "Negro Higher Education and Democratic Negro Morale." Journal of Negro Education, 11 (July, 1942), 322-328.

Good, Carter V. "The Social Crisis and Reconstruction in Higher Education." Journal of Negro Education, 11 (July, 1942), 267-273.

Godwin, Winfred. "Southern State Government and Higher Education for Blacks." Daedalus, 100 (Summer, 1971), 783-790.

Goins, Alvin E., and Meenes, Max. "Ethnic and Class Preferences Among College Negroes." Journal of Negro Education, 29 (Spring, 1960), 128-133.

Gordon, Milton A. "An Analysis of Enrollment Data for Black Students in Institutions of Higher Education, 1940-1972." Journal of Negro Education, 45 (Spring, 1976), 117-121.

Gore, George W., Jr. "Scholarship Societies in Negro Colleges." School and Society, 46 (August 7, 1937), 180-181.

Gore, George W. "The Comprehensive Examination and the Negro College." Quarterly Review of Higher Education Among Negroes, 1 (July, 1933), 15-18.

_____. "Tennessee A. & I. State College and Its President." Wilberforce University Quarterly, 2 (April, 1941), 49-52.

_____. "A Functional Program for the State Teachers College." Negro College Quarterly, 2 (June, 1944), 54-61.

"Graduate Work in Negro Institutions." Higher Education, 2 (January 1, 1946), 8-9.

Graham, James L. "A Quantitative Comparison of Rational Responses of Negro and White College Students." Journal of Social Psychology, 1 (February, 1930), 267-285.

Graham, William L. "Relation of Paine College to Its Community." Quarterly Review of Higher Education Among Negroes, 4 (July, 1936), 129.

Grant, George C. "An Approach to Democratizing a Phase of College Education." Journal of Negro Education, 27 (Fall, 1958), 463-475.

Grant, Jim. "Save Black Colleges in North Carolina." Integrated Education, 10 (March, 1972), 36-40.

"Grants to Negro Colleges Follow Ford Fund Pledge." Chronicle of Higher Education, 2 : 12 (February 26, 1968), 8.

Gray, William H., Jr. "Trends in the Control of Private Negro Colleges." Journal of Negro Education, 11 (January, 1942), 18-28.

_____. "Recommendation of An Out-of-State Scholarship Fund for Negroes in Florida." Journal of Negro Education, 16 (Fall, 1947), 604-609.

Gregg, James E. "Fifty-Ninth Annual Report of the Principal." [Hampton Institute] Southern Workman, 56 (June, 1927), 261-281.

Green, Dan S., and Driver, Edwin F. "W. E. B. Du Bois: A Core in Sociology of Sociological Negation." Phylon, 37 (4th Quarter, Winter, 1976), 308-333.

Green, Dan S. "Resurrection of the Writings of [Du Bois] an American Scholar." Crisis, 79 (November, 1972), 311-313.

Green, John W. "Did Black Colleges Kill Dial Access?" Journal of Negro Education, 45 (Spring, 1976), 204-211.

Green, Robert L. "Why the Push to 'Upgrade' Negro Colleges?" Southern Education Report, July-August, 1967.

Green, Sherman L., Jr. "The Rationale Underlying the Support of the Colleges Maintained by the African Methodist Episcopal Church." Journal of Negro Education, 29 (Summer, 1960), 319-322.

Greene, Harry W. "The Education of Negro Leaders." School and Society, 42 (July 27, 1935), 134-136.

_____. "Two Decades of Research and Creative Writings at West Virginia State College." West Virginia State College Bulletin, Series 33 : No. 1 February, 1946. Ibid., Series 26 : No. 4 August-November, 1939.

_____. "Negro Colleges in the Southwest." Opportunity, 5 (November, 1927), 322-325.

_____. "The Present Status of Negro Doctorates." School and Society, 40 (September, 1934), 388-389.

_____. "The Negro College and Social Change." Opportunity, 14 (August, 1936), 235-238.

_____. "An Adventure in Experimental Cooperative Teaching: A General Account of Recent Work in Progressive Education Conducted Jointly by Members of the Department of Education of the Ohio State University and the West Virginia State College." West Virginia State College Bulletin, Series 25, No. 6. 1938.

_____. "The Ph.D. and the Negro." Opportunity, 6 (September, 1928), 267-269, 284.

_____. "Sixty Years of Doctorates Conferred Upon Negroes." Journal of Negro Education, 6 (January, 1937), 30-37.

_____. "Higher Standards for the Negro College." Opportunity, 9 (January, 1931), 8-11.

_____. "Negro Holders of the Ph.D. Degree." School and Society, 35 (April 16, 1932), 542-544.

_____. "The Number of Negro Doctorates." School and Society, 38 (September 16, 1933), 375.

_____. "Highlights in Higher Education, 1946." Negro College Quarterly, 5 (March, 1947), 8-15.

_____. "Negro Higher and Professional Education in West Virginia." Journal of Negro Education, 17 (Summer, 1948), 393-399.

_____. "Crucial Problems in the Higher Education of Negroes." School and Society, 46 (August 21, 1937), 245-246.

Greenleaf, Walter S. "Aiding College Students." School Life, 20 (January, 1935), 110.

Grimke, Francis J. "Colored Men as Professors in Colored Institutions." A. M. E. Church Review, 4 (1885), 142-149.

Gurin, Patricia. "Social Class Constraints on the Occupational Aspirations of Students Attending Some Predominantly Negro Colleges." Journal of Negro Education, 35 (Fall, 1966), 336-350.

_____, and Epps, Edgar. "Some Characteristics of Students From Poverty Backgrounds Attending Predominantly Negro Colleges in the Deep South." Social Forces, 45 (September, 1966), 27-40.

Guzman, Jessie P. "Twenty Years of Court Decisions Affecting Higher Education in the South: 1938-1958." Journal of Educational Sociology, 32 (February, 1958), 247-253.

Hale, E. E. "Education and Civilization of Freedmen." North American Review, 101 (1865), 528.

Hall, Gwendolyn Midlo. "Rural Black College." Negro Digest, March, 1969.

Hamilton, Charles V. "The Place of the Black College in the Human Rights Struggle." Negro Digest, September, 1967.

_____. "The Constitutional Status of the 'Colored' Youth Provision in State Charters for Private Negro Colleges." Journal of Negro Education, 28 (Fall, 1969), 467-471.

Hamilton, Cleo Erma. "Problems of Negro College Students." Journal of Negro Education, 23 (Winter, 1954), 88-91.

"Hampton: College by the Sea." Our World, 4 (May, 1949), 43-49.

"Hampton in Brunswick." Southern Workman, 54 (Fall, 1925), 49-58.

"Hampton Summer School." Southern Workman, 50 (August, 1921), 389.

Hampton, Le Rosa. "Personnel Service in Negro State Colleges--The Extent to Which it is Developed." Quarterly Journal, 10 (April, 1941), 5-13.

Harding, Lowry W. "White Consultants to a Negro College Workshop." School and Society, 57 (April 10, 1943), 413-415.

Harding, Vincent. "Black Brain Drain." Columbia Forum, 11 (Winter, 1968), 38-39.

_____. "Toward a Black University." Ebony Magazine, 25 (August, 1970), 156-159.

_____. "Some International Implications of the Black University." Negro Digest, 17 (March, 1968), 33-38.

Hare, Nathan. "Black Students and Negro Colleges: The Legacy of Paternalism." Saturday Review, 51 (July 20, 1968), 44-45.

_____. "Behind Black College Revolt." Ebony, (August, 1967).

Hargrett, Andrew J. "Teaching of Religion in State Colleges for Negroes." Journal of Negro Education, 22 (Winter, 1953), 88-90.

_____. "Feelings of Depression Among Students of Savannah State College, 1957-1958." Journal of Negro Education, 27 (Fall, 1958), 537-543.

_____. "Religious Attitudes as Expressed by Students of Savannah State College." Journal of Negro Education, 20 (Spring, 1951), 237-240.

Harlan, Louis R. "The Secret Life of Booker T. Washington." Journal of Southern History, 37 (August, 1971), 393-416.

_____, and Daniel, Pete. "A Dark and Stormy Night in the Life of Booker T. Washington." University of Maryland Graduate School Chronicle, 3 (February, 1970), 4-7. Reprinted in the Negro History Bulletin, 33 (November, 1970), 159-161.

Harper, Conrad K. "The Legal Status of the Black College." Daedalus, 100 : 3 (Summer, 1971), 772-782.

Harper, R. M. "Matrimonial Prospects of Southern College Women." Journal of Heredity, 21 (1930), 29-33.

Harrington, Eugene M. "Negro Law Schools: The Liberals Dilemma." Commonweal, 88 (April 12, 1968), 94-95.

Harris, Edward E. "Some Comparisons Among Negro-White College Students: Social Ambition and Estimated Social Mobility." Journal of Negro Education, 35 (Fall, 1966), 351-368.

Harris, Nelson H. "Desegregation in North Carolina Institutions of Higher Learning." Journal of Negro Education, 27 (Summer, 1958), 295-299.

_____. "Honor Societies in Negro Four-Year Colleges." Journal of Negro Education, 11 (January, 1942), 60-63.

_____. "Negro Higher and Professional Education in North Carolina." Journal of Negro Education, 17 (Summer, 1948), 335-340.

_____. "Publicly Supported Negro Higher Institutions in North Carolina." Journal of Negro Education, 31 (Summer, 1962), 284-292.

_____. "In-Service Teacher Training Facilities of North Carolina Negro Institutions." Journal of Negro Education, 9 (January, 1940), 44-50.

_____. "Student Teaching in the Negro Colleges of North Carolina." Journal of Negro Education, 17 (Winter, 1948), 91-97.

Harris, Patricia R. "The Negro College and Its Community." Daedalus, 100 : 3 (Summer, 1971), 720-731.

Harrison, E. C. "A Faculty Acts to Improve Instruction for Freshmen." Educational Record, 37 (July, 1956), 224-228.

Harrison, E. C. "The Negro College in a Changing Economy, the Need for a New Educational Pattern." Journal of Higher Education, 36 (May, 1965), 259-265.

_____. "Improving Instruction Through Pilot Studies." Association of American Colleges Bulletin, 42 (October, 1956), 424-430.

_____. "Student Unrest on the Black College Campus." Journal of Negro Education, 41 (Spring, 1972), 113-120.

Harrison, Madeline G. "A Study of the Community Services of the Libraries in State Supported Negro Colleges and Universities Approved by the Southern Association of Colleges and Secondary Schools." Savannah State College Bulletin, Faculty Research Edition, 9 (October, 1955), 36-60.

Hart, T. A. "Status and Trends of Physical Education Programs in Negro Junior Colleges." Junior College Journal, 22 (March, 1952), 393-395.

Hartnett, Rodney T. "Differences in Selected Attitudes and College Orientations Between Black Students Attending Traditionally Negro and Traditionally White Institutions." Sociology of Education, 43 (1970), 419-436.

Hartson, Louis D. "The Occupations of Oberlin's Colored Alumni." Oberlin Alumni Magazine, 28 (July, 1932), 10.

Havice, Doris Webster. "Learning the Black Student: A White Teacher in a Black College." Soundings, 52 (Summer, 1969), 154-161.

Hawkins, Thomas E. "A Volunteer Tutorial System." Journal of Higher Education, 16 (April, 1945), 209-211.

_____. "Some Factors Which Made for Occupational Maladjustment Among 38 Negro Freshmen." Journal of Negro Education, 11 (April, 1942), 154-157.

Hawkins, Thomas E. "A Guidance Program to Aid Students to Fully Appreciate College Life." Journal of Negro Education, 20 (Winter, 1951), 122-125.

Haynes, C. H. "Adapting Instructional Materials to the Needs of Students in Negro Colleges--Political Science." Quarterly Review of Higher Education Among Negroes, 2 (July, 1934), 186-189.

Hazen, Henry H. "Twenty-Three Years of Teaching in a Negro Medical School." Social Forces, 12 (May, 1934), 570-575.

Hazerdorn, Herman. "Black Ambassador to White America." Negro Digest, September, 1946, 77.

Head, M. E. "Hand Weaving in a College Course." Southern Workman, 58 (May, 1929), 209-211.

Heckman, Richard Allen and Hall, Betty Jean. "Berea College and the Day Law." Register of the Kentucky Historical Society, 66 : 1 (1968), 35-52.

Heggie, Sarah. "[Why Negro Teacher Group Opposes New State College in Montgomery, Alabama.]" Southern Courier, September 23, 1967.

Henderson, Stephen E. "The Black University: Toward Its Realization." Negro Digest, March, 1968.

Henderson, Thomas H. "The Future of the Non-Land-Grant Negro Public College." Journal of Negro Education, 27 (Summer, 1958), 392-397.

_____. "The Role of the Negro College in Retrospect and Prospect." Journal of Negro Education, 27 (Spring, 1958), 136-140.

Henderson, Vivian W. "Unique Problems of Black Colleges." Liberal Education, 56 (October, 1970), 375.

_____. "Blacks and Change in Higher Education." Daedalus, 103 (Fall, 1974), 72-79.

_____. "Role of Predominantly Negro Institutions." Journal of Negro Education, 36 (Summer, 1967), 266-273.

_____. "Negro Colleges Face the Future." Daedalus, 100 (Summer, 1971), 630-646.

Henry, J. L. "The Problems Facing Negroes in Dental Education." Journal of the American College of Dentistry, 36 (October, 1969), 233-243.

Henry, Oliver. "A Negro Student on Campus Turmoil." Dissent, 16 (July-August, 1969), 297-300.

Heninburg, Alphonse. "The Relation of Tuskegee to Education in the Lower South." Journal of Educational Sociology, 7 (November, 1933), 157-162.

"Herman Sweatt's Victory." Life, 29 (October 16, 1950), 64.

Herron, Leonora E. "Dramatic Clubs at Hampton Institute." Southern Workman, 53 (October, 1924), 461-463.

Heslip, Constance Ridley. "The Study of the Negro in College and University Curricula." Negro History Bulletin, 7 (December, 1943), 59-60, 67-70.

"Higher Education for the Negro." The Outlook, 64 (January 13, 1900), 97.

"Higher Education for Negroes." School Life, 24 (November, 1938), 42.

"The Higher Education of Negro Americans: Prospects and Programs." Journal of Negro Education, 36 (Summer, 1967), 187-347.

"Higher Education of the Negro: Bestowal of the First Spingarn Medal Upon Professor Just." Nation, 100 (February 18, 1915), 187-188.

"High Enrollments in Negro Colleges Reported." School and Society, 65 (May 10, 1947), 341.

"Higher Training of Negroes." Crisis, 22 (July, 1921), 105-113.

Hill, Charles L. "The Case for a Christian Liberal Arts College Like Wilberforce University." The A. M. E. Review, 72 (April-June, 1956), 11-16.

Hill, John R. "Presidential Perceptions: Administrative Problems and Needs of Public Black Colleges." Journal of Negro Education, 44 (Winter, 1975), 53-62.

Hill, J. Newton. "The Negro College Faces Desegregation." College and University, 31 (Spring, 1956), 291-297.

Hill, Leslie Pinckney. "The State Teachers College at Cheyney and Its Relation to Segregation in the North." Journal of Negro Education, 1 (October, 1932), 408-413.

Hill, Mozell C., and Ackiss, Thelma D. "Some Idealogical Confusion Among Negro College Students." Journal of Negro Education, 12 (February, 1943), 600-606.

Himes, Joseph S. "Teacher of Sociology in the Negro College." Social Forces, 29 (March, 1951), 302-305.

_____. "Mate Selection Among Negro College Students." Sociology and Social Research, 33 (January-February, 1949), 204-211.

Hinchiff, William F. "Urban Problems and Higher Education, Federal City College." Wilson Library Bulletin, (February, 1969).

Holmes, Dwight O. W. "Seventy Years of the Negro College-1860-1930." Phylon, 10 (4th Quarter, 1949), 307-313.

_____. "Problems Facing Church-Related Colleges for Negroes Due to the Rapid Development of State Colleges." Wilberforce University Quarterly, 1 (July, 1940), 3-13.

_____. "Twenty-Five Years of Thomas Jesse Jones and the Phelps-Stokes Fund." Journal of Negro Education, 7 (October, 1938), 475-480.

Holmes, Dwight O. W. "Our Colleges--Howard University." Opportunity, 1 (March, 1923), 10-13.

_____. "The Role of the College in the Development of Character." Quarterly Review of Higher Education Among Negroes, 7 (October, 1939), 271-277.

_____. "The Beginnings of the Negro College." Journal of Negro Education, 3 (April, 1934), 167-192.

_____. "The Future Possibilities of Graduate Work in Negro Colleges and Universities." Journal of Negro Education, 7 (January, 1938), 5-11.

_____. "The Negro College Faces the Depression." Journal of Negro Education, 2 (January, 1933), 16-25.

_____. "The Present Status of College Education Among Negroes." Bulletin of the Association of Teachers in Colored Schools, 11 (January, 1931), 5.

Holmes, Defield T. "Provision for Adequate Academic Training for Secondary Biology Teachers at Central State College." Central State College Research Journal, 1 (July, 1962), 20-22.

Holmes, Jean Baxter. "A Study of Racial Attitudes Found in Four Colleges, Including a Scale to Measure These Attitudes." Journal of Negro Education, 12 (Winter, 1943), 69-75.

Holsendolph, Ernest. "Black Colleges Are Worth Saving." Fortune Magazine, 84 (October, 1971), 104-107, 118-122.

Hoover, Herbert C. "Address at the Tuskegee Institute." School and Society, 33 (April 25, 1931), 571-572.

Hope, Edward S. "How Howard is Training Engineers." Opportunity, 18 (April, 1940), 104-106.

Hope, John. "The Atlanta University Affiliation." Bulletin of the Association of American Colleges, May, 1933.

Hope, John, II. "The Negro College, Student Protest and the Future." Journal of Negro Education, 30 (Winter, 1961), 368-376.

Horowitz, Laura Godofsky. "A New College With a City View." Southern Education Report, May, 1969.

Horne, Frank. "The Industrial Schools of the South." Opportunity, 13 (May, 1935), 136-139. Ibid., 13 (June, 1935), 178-181.

Hornsby, Alton. "The 'Colored Branch University' Issue in Texas--Prelude to Sweatt vs. Painter." Journal of Negro History, 61 (January, 1976), 51-60.

Hotchkiss, Wesley Akin. "The Congregational and Christian Churches (AMA): The Rationale Underlying Support of Negro Private Colleges." Journal of Negro Education, 29 (Summer, 1960), 289-298.

Houston, G. David. "Weaknesses of the Negro College." Crisis, 20 (July, 1920), 122-225.

"Howard University." The Brown American, 4 (May, 1940), 10-11, 18.

"Howard University." Crisis, 47 (August, 1940), 243.

"Howard Lays Stress on Education." The Harvard Crimson, Special Supplement, June 14, 1956, 4-10.

"Howard Law Dean Explain Resignation---." Muhammad Speaks, March 14, 1969.

Howe, Arthur. "Report of the President of Hampton Institute." Southern Workman, 66 (June, 1937), 177-188.

_____. "President Howe and the Harrison-Fletcher-Black Bill." Southern Workman, 66 (April, 1937), 99.

_____. "New Fields of Opportunity and How the Land-Grant Colleges Can Meet Them." Southern Workman, 67 (February, 1938), 37-44.

Hubert, Benjamin F. "Tuskegee's Work in Agriculture." Southern Workman, 53 (October, 1942), 449.

Huge, Harry. "Inquest at Jackson State." New South, 25 (Summer, 1970), 65-70.

Hughes, Langston. "Cowards From the [Negro] Colleges." Crisis, 41 (August, 1934), 226-228.

_____. "Simple Discusses Colleges and Color." Phylon, 10 (4th Quarter, 1949), 399-400.

Hulbert, James A. "Some Observations on the Negro College Library." Virginia State College Gazette, 45 (December, 1939), 68-73.

_____. "The Negro College Library." Journal of Negro Education, 12 (Fall, 1943), 623-629.

Humphery, George Duke. "Improved Status of Land-Grant Colleges." School and Society, 86 (March 15, 1958), 135-136.

Hunter, Charlayne. "Black Colleges and the Black Mood." Southern Education Report, May, 1969.

Hunter, John M. "Adapting Instructional Materials in Physics to the Needs of Students in Negro Colleges." Quarterly Review of Higher Education Among Negroes, 2 (July, 1934), 168-174.

Hunter, John. "Virginia State College and the Returning Veteran." Quarterly Review of Higher Education Among Negroes, 14 (January, 1946), 9-10.

Hunter, Robert W. "Essential Elements Contributing to Instructional Effectiveness." Educational Administration and Supervision, 41 (May, 1955), 277-284.

Hurst, Charles G., Jr., and Jones, Wallace L. "Psychosocial Concomitants of Sub-Standard Speech." Journal of Negro Education, 35 (Fall, 1966), 409-421.

Hurt, Huber W. "The Land-Grant Colleges." Southern Workman, 53 (April, 1924), 147.

Hutchinson, W. E. "Place of Industrial Training in Higher Negro Education." Southern Workman, 35 (April, 1906), 204.

Huyck, Earl E. "Faculty in Predominantly White and Predominantly Negro Higher Institutions." Journal of Negro Education, 35 (Fall, 1966), 381-392.

Iles, R. E. "Standardizing the Negro College." Peabody Journal of Education, 6 (September, 1928), 96-101.

"Integration in Reverse." Look, April 21, 1964.

Irving, Florence B. "Segregation Legislation by Southern States." New South, 12 (February, 1957), 96-101.

Ivey, John E., Jr. "Facts About Regional Education." Crisis, 57 (November, 1950), 628-632, 674.

Ivey, John E. "Regional Education: An Experiment in Democracy." Phylon, 10 (4th Quarter, 1949), 381-388.

Jabs, Albert E. "Teaching Philosophy in a Black College." Crisis, 79 (December, 1972), 338-339.

Jabs, Albert E. "On Being a White Professor in a Black College." Negro Educational Review, 24 (July-October, 1973), 138-143.

Jackson, Jacqueline J. "Exploration of Attitudes Toward Faculty Desegregation at Negro Colleges." Phylon, 28 (Winter, 1967), 338-352.

Jackson, L. P. "The Educational Efforts of the Freedmen's Bureau and Freedmen's Aid Societies in South Carolina, 1862-1872." Journal of Negro History, 8 (January, 1923), 1-40.

Jackson, Lewis A. "An Experimental Study of Reading at Central State College." Central State College Research Journal, 1 (July, 1962), 36-39.

Jackson, Reid. "A Democratic Philosophy for Negro Teacher Education Institutions." Quarterly Review of Higher Education Among Negroes, 6 (April, 1938), 108-122.

Jackson, Reid E. "Background Factors for Negroes Listed as Leaders in Education." School and Society, 66 (August 30, 1947), 164-169.

_____. "Financial Aid Given by Southern States to Negroes for Out-of-State Study." Journal of Negro Education, 13 (Winter, 1944), 30-39.

_____. "Rise of Teacher Training for Negroes." Journal of Negro Education, 7 (October, 1938), 540-547.

Jackson, W. C. "College Instruction in Race Relations." Religious Education, 26 (February, 1931), 123.

Jackson, Wallace Van. "The Countee Cullen Memorial Collection at Atlanta University." Crisis, 54 (May, 1947), 140-142.

Jacobson, Robert L. "New Negro College Group to Seek More Influence." Chronicle of Higher Education, 4 : 4 (October 20, 1969), 6.

_____. "Negro College Winning Support for More Funds." Chronicle of Higher Education, 4 : 7 (November 10, 1969), 2.

Jaffe, A. J., et al. "The Sharply Stratified World of the Negro Colleges." College Board Review, Winter, 1967-1968.

James, Felix. "The Tuskegee Institute Movable School, 1906-1923." Agricultural History, 45 (July, 1971), 201-209.

James, Milton Morris. "A Note on Richard Humphreys." Negro History Bulletin, 23 (October, 1959), 4.

_____. "The Institute for Colored Youth." Negro History Bulletin, 21 (January, 1958), 83-85.

Jamison, Andrew. "Community College for the Capital." Harvard Crimson, October 19, 1968.

Jans, Ralph T. "Racial Integration at Berea College, 1950-1952." Journal of Negro Education, 22 (Winter, 1958), 26-37.

Janssen, Peter A. "Higher Education and the Black American." Chronicle of Higher Education, 6 : 3 (May 30, 1972), 1-2.

Jensen, V. L. "Higher Education for Negroes in Atlanta." Atlanta Historical Bulletin, 8 : 33 (October, 1948), 107-111.

Jencks, Christopher. "Social Stratification and Higher Education." Harvard Educational Review, 38 (Spring, 1968), 277-316.

_____, and Riesman, David. "The American Negro College." Harvard Educational Review, 37 (Winter, 1967), 3-60.

Jenkins, Henry R. "Apostle of Industrial Education." [B. T. Washington] Opportunity, 18 (May, 1940), 141-144.

Jenkins, Iredell. "Segregation and the Professor." Yale Review, 46 (Winter, 1957), 311-320.

Jenkins, Martin D. "The Cost of Attending Negro Colleges and Universities." Journal of Negro Education, 9 (January, 1940), 130-137.

_____. "Survey of Higher Education of Negroes, Progress Report." School Life, 26 (December, 1940), 85-86.

_____. "The Availability of Higher Education for Negroes in the Southern States." Journal of Negro Education, 16 (Summer, 1947), 459-473.

_____. "Problems Incident to Racial Integration and Some Suggested Approaches to These Problems." Journal of Negro Education, 21 (Summer, 1952), 411-421.

_____. "Graduate Work in Negro Institutions of Higher Education." Journal of Negro Education, 18 (June, 1947), 300-306.

_____. "The National Survey of Negro Higher and Post-War Reconstruction: The Resources of Negro Higher Education." Journal of Negro Education, 11 (July, 1942), 382-390.

_____. "The Future of the Desegregated Negro College: A Critical Summary." Journal of Negro Education, 27 (Summer, 1958), 419-429.

_____. "The Negro College." Howard University Magazine, 6 (January, 1964), 13-16.

_____. "Enrollment in Institutions of Higher Education." Journal of Negro Education, 6 (April, 1937), 240-248; 7 (April, 1938), 118-123; 8 (April, 1939), 247-253; 9 (April, 1940), 266-273; 10 (October, 1941), 718-725; 11 (April, 1942), 217-223; 12 (Fall, 1943), 678-693; 13 (September, 1944), 227-233; 15 (Spring, 1946), 231-239; 16 (Spring, 1947), 224-232;

20 (Spring, 1951), 207-222; 21 (Spring, 1952), 205-219; 22 (Spring, 1953), 188-200.

Jenkins, M. D., and Randall, C. N. "Differential Characteristics of Superior and Unselected Negro College Students." Journal of Social Psychology, 27 (May, 1948), 187-202.

"Johnson C. Smith University." Crisis, 47 (August, 1940), 256-267.

Johnson, Charles S. "The Faculty." Journal of Educational Sociology, 19 (April, 1946), 471-483.

_____. "The Social Philosophy of Booker T. Washington." Opportunity, 6 (April, 1928), 102-105, 115.

_____. "Racial Attitudes of College Students." Racial Contacts and Social Research, 28 (December, 27-30, 1933).

_____. "The Negro College Graduate: How and Where He is Employed." Journal of Negro Education, 4 (January, 1935), 5-22.

Johnson, Edward A. "A Student at Atlanta University." Phylon, 3 (2nd Quarter, 1942), 135-148.

Johnson, Guy B. "Education, Segregation, and Race Relations." Quarterly Review of Higher Education Among Negroes, 3 (April, 1935), 89-94.

_____. "Progress in the Desegregation of Higher Education." Journal of Educational Sociology, 32 (February, 1958), 254-259.

_____. "Desegregation and the Future of the Negro College: A Critical Summary." Journal of Negro Education, 27 (Summer, 1958), 430-435.

Johnson, James Weldon. "Relations of the Negro College to the American Race Question." Southern Workman, 62 (July, 1933), 291-298.

Johnson, Kenneth R. "The Peabody Fund: Its Role and Influence in Alabama." The Alabama Review, 27 (April, 1974), 101-126.

Johnson, Leonard, Jr. "History of the Education of Negro Physicians." The Journal of Medical Education, 42 (1967), 439-446.

Johnson, Marcia Lynn. "Student Protest at Fisk University." Negro History Bulletin, 33 (October, 1970), 137-140.

Johnson, Mordecai Wyatt. "Negro Education and the Present Crisis." Educational Record, 23 (July, 1942), 464-477.

Johnson, O. Clayton. "The Importance of Black Colleges." Educational Record, 52 (Spring, 1971), 165-170.

Johnson, Roosevelt. "Black Administrators and Higher Education." Black Scholar, 1 (November, 1969), 66-76.

Johnson, Tobe. "The Black College as a System." Daedalus, 100 (Summer, 1971), 798-812.

Johnson, William H. "Institute for Colored Youth." Pennsylvania School Journal, 5 (January, 1857), 287.

Johnston, J. Hugo. "Graduates of Northern High Schools as Students at a Southern Negro College." Journal of Negro Education, 2 (October, 1933), 484-486.

Jones, Allen W. "The Role of Tuskegee Institute in the Education of Black Farmers." Journal of Negro History, 60 (April, 1975), 252-267.

Jones, Charles, and Harris, Lynn J. "Differences in Perceived Sources of Academic Difficulties: Black Students in Predominantly Black and Predominantly White Colleges." Journal of Negro Education, 44 (Fall, 1975), 519-529.

Jones, David D. "The War and the Higher Education of Negro Women." Journal of Negro Education, 11 (July, 1942), 329-337.

Jones, Douglas L. "The Sweatt Case and the Development of Legal Education for Negroes in Texas." Texas Law Review, 47 (March, 1968), 677-693.

Jones, Edward A. "The Modernization of Foreign Language Teaching." Negro College Quarterly, 4 (June, 1946), 80-86.

Jones, E. D. W. "History of Zion Wesley Institute." The Star of Zion, September 22, 1932, 1.

Jones, Eugene Kinckle. "St. Paul School, Lawrenceville, Virginia." Southern Workman, 57 (August, 1928), 302-303.

Jones, George W. "The Negro Public Colleges in Alabama." Journal of Negro Education, 31 (Summer, 1962), 354-361.

Jones, Iva G. "The Morgan State College Experiment in the Humanities." College Language Association Journal, 5 (December, 1961), 148-152.

Jones, Lewis W. "Southern Higher Education Since the Gaines Decision: A Twenty Year Review." Journal of Educational Sociology, 22 (Fall, 1969).

Jones, M. Ashby. "Hampton's Gift to the South." Southern Workman, 48 (June, 1919), 289-294.

Jones, Mack H. "The Responsibility of the Black College to the Black Community Then and Now." Daedalus, 100 : 3 (Summer, 1971), 732-744.

Jones, Thomas Elsa. "Fisk University--Excerpts From the President's Inaugural Address Delivered at Fisk University December 7, 1926." Southern Workman, 56 (January, 1926), 9-13.

Jones, Thomas Jesse. "Comparison of the Past and Present Aims of Hampton Institute." Southern Workman, (March, 1903).

_____. "Trends in Negro Education." Southern Workman, (March, 1903), 243.

Jones, Thomas M. "The Lincoln Tradition in Africa." Lincoln University Bulletin, 65 (Winter, 1962), 26-27; 30-31.

Jordan, Lawrence V. "Desegregation of Higher Education in West Virginia." Journal of Negro Education, 27 (Summer, 1958), 332-341.

Jordan, Vernon E., Jr. "Black and Higher Education--Some Reflections." Daedalus, 104 (Winter, 1975), 160-165.

Josey, E. J. "The Future of the Black College Library." Library Journal, 94 (September 15, 1969), 3019-3022.

_____. "Negro College Libraries and ACRL Standards." Library Journal, 88 (September 1, 1963), 2989-2996.

_____. "Your College Library and Your College Education." Quarterly Review of Higher Education Among Negroes, 31 (January, 1963), 9.

Kampschmidt, William H. "Why the Evangelical Lutheran Church Established and Maintains Colleges for Negroes." Journal of Negro Education, 29 (Summer, 1960), 299-306.

Kashif, Lonnie. "D. C. City College Begins Community Involvement Test." Muhammad Speaks, October 25, 1968.

_____. "Howard Showdown Spells New Student Dynamics." Muhammad Speaks, May 23, 1969.

_____. "Howard University Medical School Target of Boycott." Muhammad Speaks, February 21, 1969.

_____. "Howard University Law School Emptied in Wake of Determined Student Protest." Muhammad Speaks, March 7, 1969.

_____. "New Trends Coming in Black Studies." Muhammad Speaks, June 27, 1969.

_____. "Students Continue Thurst Despite Threat by NAACP." Muhammad Speaks, February 7, 1969.

_____. "Unnoticed Student Protest Plows on at Howard University." *Muhammad Speaks*, May 9, 1969.

Kassel, C. "Educating the Slave; a Forgotten Chapter of Civil War History." *Open Court*, 41 (April, 1927), 239-256.

Katz, Daniel, and Braly, Kenneth. "Racial Stereotypes of One Hundred College Students." *Journal of Abnormal and Social Psychology*, 28 (October-December, 1933), 280-290.

Kelleher, Daniel T. "The Case of Lloyd Lionel Gaines: The Demise of the Separate But Equal Doctrine." *Journal of Negro History*, 56 (October, 1971), 262-271.

Kelly, Alfred H. "The Congressional Controversy Over School Segregation, 1867-1875." *American Historical Review*, 64 (April, 1959), 537-563.

Kendrick, Ruby Moyse. "Art at Howard University." *Crisis*, 39 (November, 1932), 348-349.

Kidd, Arthur L. "Problems Affecting the Higher Education of Negroes in Florida." *Quarterly Review of Higher Education Among Negroes*, 5 (October, 1937), 160-170.

Kidd, A. L. "The Florida Agricultural and Mechanical College." *Bulletin of the National Association of Teachers in Colored Schools*, 11 (April-May, 1931), 13-14, 28.

King, Kermit C. "Negro Students View Civil Rights." *Negro Educational Review*, 1 : 3&4 (July-October, 1950), 172-178.

King, William E. "Charles McIver Fights for the Tarheel Negro's Right to an Education." *North Carolina Historical Review*, 41 (Summer, 1964), 360-369.

King, Willye M. "Higher Negro Education in the State of Mississippi." *Quarterly Review of Higher Education Among Negroes*, 5 (October, 1937), 174-185.

Kirchner, Earl L. "Fixed Fees in Land-Grant Colleges for Negroes." *Journal of Higher Education*, 4 (January 15, 1948), 113-114.

Kittrell, Flemmie P. "Home Economics at Bennett College for Women." *Southern Workman*, 60 (1931), 381-384.

Klein, Arthur J. "The Federal Government and Negro Education: A Critical Summary." *Journal of Negro Education*, 7 (July, 1938), 463-467.

Knox, Ellis O. "The Negro as a Subject of University Research." *Journal of Negro Education*, 2 (1933), 165-174; 3 (1934), 233-244; 4 (1935), 213-229; 5 (1926), 252-262, 612-625; 6 (1937), 166-171; 7 (1938), 172-179; 8 (1939), 198-204;

11 (1942), 170-183; 16 (1947), 180-189; 21 (1952), 484-491.

_____. "Federal Support of Special Institutions--Columbia Institution for the Deaf and Howard University." Journal of Negro Education, 7 (July, 1938), 413-422.

_____. "State Supported Colleges for Negroes." Negro History Bulletin, 14 (January, 1951), 75-79, 88-89.

Kopkind, Andrew. "Black Blacklash [Negro Colleges]." New Statesman, 73 (May 26, 1967), 708.

Kuritz, Hayman. "Integration on Negro College Campuses." Phylon, 28 (2nd Quarter, Summer, 1967), 121-130.

Kuyper, George A. "The Voorhees School." Southern Workman, 61 (April, 1932), 146-154.

Lamon, Lester C. "The Black Community in Nashville and Fisk University Student Strike of 1924-1925." Journal of Southern History, 40 (May, 1974), 225-244.

"Lane College, 1882-1940." Crisis, 47 (August, 1940), 244, 267.

Lane, David A., Jr. "Student and Collegiate Contracts: Some Legal Relationships of a Private College to Its Students." Journal of Higher Education, 4 (February, 1933), 77-84.

_____. "The Development of the Present Relationship of the Federal Government to Negro Education." Journal of Negro Education, 7 (July, 1938), 273-281.

_____. "The Junior College Movement Among Negroes." Journal of Negro Education, 2 (July, 1933), 272-283.

Lane, Hugh., et al. "What Black Students Want From You." College Management, March, 1969.

Langhorne, Joseph L. "Contrasts in Enrollments in Industrial and Liberal Arts Programs in Land-Grant Colleges, 1938-1939." Quarterly Journal, 8 (July, 1939), 23-25.

Lanier, R. G. "Reorganization and Redirection of Negro Education in Terms of Articulation and Integration." Journal of Negro Education, 5 (July, 1936), 369-374.

Lash, John S. "The Literature of the Negro in Negro Colleges: Its Status and Curricular Accommodation [1925-1948]." Quarterly Review of Higher Education Among Negroes, 16 (April, 1948), 66-76.

"Late Arrivals; Negro College Professors." Time, 541 (July 11, 1949), 79.

"Law School Branch of Lincoln University." Newsweek, 14 (October, 1939), 32.

Lawson, James R.; Mays, Benjamin; Proctor, Samuel D., and Psyton, Benjamin F. "Educators Respond [to the Black University Concept]." Negro Digest, March, 1969.

Leavell, Ullin W. "Trends of Philanthropy in Negro Education: A Survey." Journal of Negro Education, 2 (January, 1938), 38-52.

Lee, Harold Fletcher. "The Educational and Social Implications of the Redirection of the Negro College." Negro College Quarterly, 2 (June, 1944), 92-103.

Lee, Harold Fletcher. "A Proposal Integrating Program for Liberal Arts College." Educational Record, 17 (January, 1941), 56-68.

_____. "Some Aspects of a Guidance Program for the Post-War Negro College." Negro College Quarterly, 2 (December, 1944), 144-147.

_____. "What Negro Colleges are Doing." Negro College Quarterly, 4 (June, 1946), 89-96. Ibid., 4 (September, 1946), 144-151.

Lee, Maurice A. "Results of a College All-Freshmen Reading Improvement Program." Journal of Developmental Reading, 2 (Autumn, 1958), 20-32.

Leeson, Jim. "Colleges and Choice." Southern Education Report, October, 1968.

_____. "Most Students See a Strong Future." Southern Education Report, June, 1969.

_____. "The Short Road Home." Southern Education Report, May, 1969.

Leffall, Dolores C., and Sims, Janet L. "Mary McLeod Bethune--The Educator; Also Including a Selected Annotated Bibliography." Journal of Negro Education, 45 (Summer, 1976), 342-359.

Lehfeldt, Martin C. "A Very Mixed Bag: White Teachers at Black Colleges." Soundings, 52 (Summer, 1969), 128-153.

Lewis, Elsie M. "The History of Management of Land Grants for Education in Mississippi Prior to the Civil War." Quarterly Review of Higher Education Among Negroes, 17 (January, 1949), 20-25.

Lewis, Emma. "Hampton the Beautiful." Southern Workman, 54 (May, 1925), 207-208.

Lewis, Hyland. "Higher Education for Negroes: A 'Tough' Situation." Phylon, 10 (4th Quarter, 1949), 356-361.

Lewis, Stephen J. "The Negro in the Field of Dentistry." Opportunity, 2 (July, 1924), 207-212.

Lincoln, C. Eric. "The Negro College and Cultural Change." Daedalus, 100 : 3 (Summer, 1971), 603-629.

Lincoln, Daniel P. "West Virginia State College Serving a National Need." The West Virginia Review, April, 1944.

"Lincoln and the Peace Corps." Lincoln University Bulletin, 65 (Winter, 1962), 24-25.

"Lincoln University of Missouri." Crisis, 47 (August, 1940), 245.

"Lincoln University [Penn]." Crisis, 47 (August, 1940), 250.

"List of Approved Colleges for Negro Youth." North Central Association Quarterly, 27 (July, 1952), 56-59.

Liston, Hardy. "Report of the Commission on Higher Education. A--Institutions of Higher Learning." Quarterly Review of Higher Education Among Negroes, 7 (April, 1939), 119-125.

Little, Harlee H. "Presenting Livingstone College--A Historical Retrospect." The Star of Zion, March 7, 1940.

"Livingstone College: The Gateway to a Christian Education." Crisis, 47 (August, 1940), 246.

"Livingstone Moves on Many Fronts." Negro Progress, 17 (Summer, 1962), 9.

Lloyd, R. Grann. "Administration of Graduate Schools for Negroes." Journal of Higher Education, 29 (November, 1958), 449-450, 470.

_____. "Are Remedial Writing Programs Needed in Negro Colleges and Universities?" Journal of Negro Education, 17 (Spring, 1948), 204-206.

_____. "Some Problems of Graduate Schools Operated Primarily for Negroes." Journal of Negro Education, 25 (Winter, 1956), 83-86.

_____. "Loyalty Oaths and Communistic Influences in Negro Colleges and Universities." School and Society, 75 (January 5, 1952), 8-9.

_____. "Practices of American Negro Colleges and Universities Regarding Graduate Training of Faculty Members Within the Employing Institutions." Journal of Negro Education, 21 (Spring, 1952), 224-225.

_____. "Retirement and Annuity Plans in Negro Colleges and Universities." Journal of Negro Education, 22 (Spring, 1953), 201-204.

_____. "Plight of Colleges and Universities Operated Primarily for Negroes." Negro Educational Review, 22 (July, 1971), 131-132.

_____, and Walker, George H., Jr. "Sabbatical Leave in Negro Colleges and Universities." School and Society, 68 (September 18, 1948), 190-191.

_____, and Walker, George H., Jr. "Teacher Supply and Demand in the Negro Colleges." Journal of Negro Education, 23 (Fall, 1954), 421-427.

Lockett, John L. "Virginia State College Presents Its Educational Program to the Nation Via N. B. C." Virginia State College Gazette, 45 (December, 1939), 83-86.

Logan, Frenise A. "The Movement in North Carolina to Establish a State Supported College for Negroes." North Carolina Historical Review, 35 (April, 1958), 167-180.

Logan, R. W. "The Evolution of Private Colleges for Negroes." Journal of Negro Education, 27 (Summer, 1958), 213-220.

Long, Herman H. "Perspectives on the Negro College Teacher's World: Crisis and Redefinition in Racial Perspective." College Language Association Journal, 1 (November, 1957), 16-22.

_____. "The Negro Public College in Tennessee." Journal of Negro Education, 31 (Summer, 1962), 341-348.

_____. "The Future of Private Black Colleges." The Enquirer [Philadelphia], February 5, 1972.

Loran, Charles T. "New Opportunities for the Negro College." Southern Workman, 6 (June, 1934), 168-176.

Lord, Nathalie. "Booker Washington's School Days at Hampton." Southern Workman, 31 (May, 1902), 255-259.

"Louisiana Resolution Ask Merger of Colleges." [Louisiana State Conference of the NAACP] Crisis, 80 (February, 1973), 66.

"Louisville University." Negro History Bulletin, 20 (January, 1957), 79-88.

Louisville Municipal College. "The Appeal of the

Louisville Municipal College Faculty to the Board of Trustees." Journal of Negro Education, 20 (Spring, 1951), 241-248.

Love, Theresa R. "Needs and Approaches for Developing Linguistic Abilities." Journal of Negro Education, 35 (Fall, 1966), 400-408.

Lovett, Robert. "Du Bois." Phylon, 2 (3rd Quarter, 1941), 214-217.

Low, W. A. "The Freedmen's Bureau Education in Maryland." Maryland Historical Magazine, 47 (March, 1952), 32-39.

Lowe, Gilbert A. "Howard University Students and the Community Service Project." Journal of Negro Education, 36 (Fall, 1967), 368-376.

_____, and McDowell, Sophia F. "Participation-Nonparticipation Differences in the Howard University Student Protest." Journal of Negro Education, 40 (Winter, 1971), 81-90.

Lowe, Keith. "Towards a Black University." Liberator, September, 1968.

Lowell, Lawrence. "Report of the President of Howard University to the Board of Overseers." School and Society, 26 (December 24, 1932), 29.

Lowery, Raymond. "11 Governors Back Negro College Plan." Chronicle of Higher Education, 2 : 2 (September 27, 1948), 8.

Lucas, Robert. "Jazz Goes to College." Negro Digest, 9 (August, 1951), 45-59.

Ludlow, Helen W. "Hampton Normal and Agricultural Institute." Harper's Monthly, October, 1873.

_____. "Indian Education at Hampton and Carlisle." Harper's Monthly, April, 1881.

_____. "Fourth Tuskegee Negro Conference." The Outlook, 51 (March 9, 1895), 400-401.

Lyda, Wesley J. "Some Factors in the Improvement of College Instruction." Educational Record, 33 (January, 1952), 19-104.

Lyells, Ruby E. Stutts. "The Library in Negro Land-Grant Colleges." Journal of Negro Education, 14 (Spring, 1945), 153-165.

Lyford, C. A. "Summer Course at Hampton." Home Economics, 9 (November, 1917), 496-497.

Lynch, C. Maude H. "The Negro College and Nursing." Opportunity, 13 (Summer, 1945), 124-125.

McAfee, Mildred H. "The War and the Higher Education of Women." Journal of Negro Education, 11 (July, 1942), 262-266.

McAllister, Dorothy M. "Library Resources for Graduate Study in Southern Universities for Negroes." Journal of Negro Education, 23 (Winter, 1954), 51-59.

McAllister, Jane E. "Educating the Exceptional Teacher at Miner Teachers College." Educational Administration and Supervision, 23 (March, 1937), 225-234.

_____. "A Venture in Rural Teacher Education Among Negroes in Louisiana." Journal of Negro Education, 7 (April, 1938), 132-143.

McBride, Ullysses. "The Status of Black Studies in Traditionally Black Institutions in America." Negro Educational Review, 25 (October, 1974), 208-212.

McClain, Edwin W. "Personality Characteristics of Negro College Students in the South--A Recent Appraisal." Journal of Negro Education, 36 (Summer, 1967), 320-325.

McClendon, William H. "Which College--White or Negro?" Crisis, 19 (September, 1934), 41.

McConnell, Roland C. "A Small College and the Archival Record." Journal of Negro Education, 32 (Winter, 1963), 84-86.

McCormick, J. Scott. "The Julius Rosenwald Fund." Journal of Negro Education, 3 (October, 1934), 605-626.

McCuistion, Fred. "The South's Negro Teaching Force." Journal of Negro Education, 1 (April, 1932), 16-24.

_____. "The Present Status of Higher Education of Negroes." Journal of Negro Education, 2 (July, 1933), 379-396.

McCulloch, Margaret C. "The Function of the Negro Cultural College." Journal of Negro Education, 6 (October, 1937), 617-622.

_____. "Crisis in College Study of the Negro." Journal of Negro Education, 11 (October, 1942), 471-475.

McDaniel, Vernon. "Negro Publicly-Supported Higher Institutions in Texas." Journal of Negro Education, 31 (Summer, 1962), 349-353.

McGeoch, Dorothy M. "Teacher Training Role in Various

Types of Institutions." Quarterly Review of Higher Education Among Negroes, 24 (July, 1956), 89-92.

McGinnis, F. A. "Negro Students in Ohio Colleges, School Year 1948-1949." Journal of Negro Education, 19 (Spring, 1950), 209-210.

McHugh, Robert. "Three Students Slain in S. C. Riot." Chronicle of Higher Education, 2 : 12 (February 26, 1968), 8.

McKinney, Richard Ishmael. "Religion in Negro Colleges." Journal of Negro Education, 13 (Fall, 1944), 509-519.

McKinney, Theophilus Elisha. "Report of the Commission on Higher Education of the Association of Colleges and Secondary Schools for Negroes." Quarterly Review of Higher Education Among Negroes, 7 (April, 1939), 116-118.

_____. "Some Aspects of the Report and Recommendations of the Commission to Study Public Schools and Colleges for Colored People in North Carolina." Quarterly Review of Higher Education Among Negroes, 7 (April, 1939), 83-86.

_____. "Significant Developments in the Higher Education of Negroes Since 1863." Quarterly Review of Higher Education Among Negroes, 16 (January, 1948), 28-33.

_____. "A Summary of Findings and Policies Bearing on Problems of Administration in Institutions of Higher Learning." Quarterly Review of Higher Education Among Negroes, 1 (January, 1933), 1.

_____. "Tenure of Presidents of Negro Colleges." Quarterly Review of Higher Education Among Negroes, 1 (July, 1933), 34-36.

McMillan, Lewis K. "Negro Higher Education as I Have Known It." Journal of Negro Education, 8 (January, 1939), 9-18.

_____. "The American Negro in American Higher Education." Crisis, 54 (August, 1947), 234-238, 253.

McMorries, James C. "A Study of New Students Admitted by a Negro College in 1936." Journal of Negro Education, 7 (October, 1938), 535-539.

McNeely, J. H. "Higher Education of Negroes is Making Marked Progress." School Life, 14 (October, 1928), 37.

McNett, Ian E. "Jackson State Shootings Stir New Wave of Unrest." Chronicle of Higher Education, 4 : 33 (May 25, 1970), 1-2.

McPheeters, A. A. "Interest of Methodist Church in Education of Negroes." Phylon, 10 (4th Quarter, 1959), 343-350.

_____. "Toward Improving College Instruction." Association of American College Bulletin, 38 (December, 1952), 564-573.

McPherson, James M. "White Liberals and Black Power in Negro Education, 1865-1915." American Historical Review, 75 (June, 1970), 1357-1386.

McWorter, Gerald. "The Nature and Needs of the Black University." Negro Digest, March, 1968.

_____. "Struggle, Ideology, and the Black University." Negro Digest, March, 1969.

Mackintosh, Barry. "George Washington Carver: The Making of a Myth." Journal of Southern History, 42 (November, 1976), 509-528.

Maclean, Malcolm S. "The Impact of World War II Upon Institutions for Higher Education of the Negro." Journal of Negro Education, 11 (July, 1942), 338-345.

Malson, Robert A. "The Black Power Rebellion at Howard University." Negro Digest, December, 1967.

Manley, Albert E. "The Role of the Negro College in Retrospect and Prospect." Journal of Negro Education, 27 (Spring, 1958), 132-135.

_____, and Himes, Joseph S. "The Success of Students in Negro Liberal Arts College." Journal of Negro Education, 19 (Fall, 1950), 566-473.

Markoe, William M. "Negro Higher Education." America, 26 (April 1, 1922), 558-560.

_____. "Negro Higher Education." Catholic Mind, 20 (April, 1922), 153-159.

Marks, Eli S. "The Negro College." Journal of Educational Sociology, 12 (January, 1939), 288-297.

Marr, Warren, II. "Death on the Campus: The Orangeburg Story." Crisis, 75 (March, 1968), 88.

Marsh, Georgia. "Junior Colleges and Negroes." Southern Education Report, 4 : 2 (1968), 10-17.

Marshall, Albert P. "Libraries in Institutions for the Higher Education of Negroes in North Carolina." North Carolina Libraries, 1948, 65-74.

_____. "New Demands on Negro College Librarians." Quarterly Review of Higher Education Among Negroes, 8 (October, 1940), 203-205.

_____. "The New Page Library at Lincoln University." Missouri Library Association Quarterly, 12 (March, 1951), 131-134.

_____. "The Children's Room [Library], Winston-Salem Teachers College." North Carolina Teachers Record, January, 1947.

Mason, C. T., and Wilkins, T. B. "Entrance Examinations and Success in College." Journal of Negro Education, 10 (April, 1941), 54-58.

Marteena, Constance H. "A College for Girls." Opportunity, 16 (October, 1938), 306-307.

Martin, W. H., and Clift, V. A. "The Place of Social Values in Education for Returning Veterans." Quarterly Review of Higher Education Among Negroes, 14 (January, 1946), 3-8.

Martin, William H. "The Land-Grant Function of the Negro Public College." Journal of Negro Education, 31 (Summer, 1962), 396-403.

_____. "Negro Higher and Professional Education in Arkansas." Journal of Negro Education, 17 (Summer, 1948), 255-264.

_____. "Recent Developments in the Education of Negro Teachers in Oklahoma." Journal of Negro Education, 18 (Winter, 1949), 77-80.

_____. "Providing Non-School Experiences in Teacher Education." Quarterly Review of Higher Education Among Negroes, 10 (April, 1942), 106-108.

_____, and Mason, James E. "Golden Anniversary." The Star of Zion, (July 28, and August 11, 1932), 1.

_____. "The Genesis of Livingstone College." The Star of Zion, (November 22, 1934), 1.

Massey, Estelle G. "The Training and Placement of Negro Nurses." Journal of Negro Education, 4 (January, 1935), 42-48.

Matheus, John F. "A Negro State College Looks at Foreign Languages." Journal of Negro Education, 7 (April, 1938), 155-159.

Mathews, John and Holsendolph, Earnest. "When Black Students Take Over a Campus." New Republic, April 13, 1968.

Mathews, Marcis M. "The Difference Between Black and White." Saturday Evening Post, 232 (January 16, 1960), 13-15, 56-57.

Mayer, Milton. "What's Wrong With Negro Colleges?" _Negro Digest_, 5 (December, 1946), 4-6.

Mayhew, Lewis B. "Problems of General Education for the Smaller Institutions." _Quarterly Review of Higher Education Among Negroes_, 24 (April, 1956), 77-81.

_____. "Neighboring Black and White Colleges." _Education Digest_, 37 (November, 1971), 29-31. _Ibid._, _Educational Record_, 52 (Spring, 1971), 159-164.

Mays, Benjamin Elijah. "After College What: For the Negro." _Crisis_, 37 (December, 1930), 408-410.

_____. "The Role and Future of the Negro College." _Crisis_, 72 (August-September, 1965), 419-422, 457.

Mays, Benjamin E. "Negro Land Grant Colleges Launch a Study of Social Problems; Three-Day Conference at Hampton Institute." _School and Society_, 56 (July 25, 1942), 77.

_____. "The Most Neglected Area in Negro [Higher] Education." _Crisis_, 45 (August, 1938), 268-269.

_____. "The Future of Negro Colleges." _Saturday Review_, (November 18, 1961), 53-54.

_____. "Segregation in Higher Education." _Phylon_, 10 (4th Quarter, 1949), 401-406.

_____. "The American Negro College." _Harvard Educational Review_, 37 : 3 (Summer, 1967), 451-468.

_____. "Financing of Private Negro Colleges." _Journal of Educational Sociology_, 19 (April, 1946), 466-470.

_____. "A Look at the Black Colleges." _Foundations_, 17 (July-September, 1974), 235-246.

_____. "The Role of the Negro Liberal Arts College in Post-War Reconstruction." _Journal of Negro Education_, 11 (July, 1942), 400-411.

_____. "Centennial Commencement Address (Higher Education and the American Negro)." _Journal of Religious Thought_, 24 : 2 (1967-1968), 4-12.

_____. "The Education of Negro Ministers." _Journal of Negro Education_, 2 (July, 1933), 342-351.

_____. "The Religious Life and Needs of Negro College Students." _Journal of Negro Education_, 9 (July, 1940), 332-343.

_____. "The Significance of the Negro Private and Church-Related College." _Journal of Negro Education_, 29 (Summer, 1960), 245-251.

Mays, Nebraska. "Rationale for Development of Urban Programs in Black Colleges." Negro Educational Review, 25 (October, 1974), 184-189.

Means, James H. "Contributions of Negroes to National Mathematics Magazines." Journal of Negro Education, 28 (Winter, 1959), 81-83.

Meeth, L. Richard. "The Report on Predominantly Negro Colleges One Year Later." Journal of Negro Education, 35 (Summer, 1966), 204-209.

_____. "The Transition of the Predominantly Negro College." Journal of Negro Education, 35 (Fall, 1966), 494-505.

"Meharry Medical College." Opportunity, 2 (April, 1924), 122-123.

Meier, August. "Toward Reinterpretation of Booker T. Washington." Journal of Southern History, 23 (May, 1957), 220-227.

_____. "The Racial and Educational Philosophy of Kelly Miller, 1895-1915." Journal of Negro Education, 29 (Spring, 1960), 121-127.

_____. "Race Relations at Negro Colleges." Crisis, 65 (November, 1958), 535-543.

_____. "Booker T. Washington and the Negro Press." Journal of Negro Education, 38 (January, 1953), 67-90.

_____. "Booker T. Washington and the Rise of the NAACP." Crisis, 61 (February, 1954), 69-76, 117-123.

_____. "Booker T. Washington and the Town of Mound Bayou." Phylon, 6 (4th Quarter, 1954), 396-401.

_____. "The Successful Sit-In in a Border City." Journal of Intergroup Relations, 2 (Summer, 1961), 230-232.

_____. "The Beginning of Industrial Education in Negro Schools." The Midwest Journal, 7 (Spring, 1955), 21-44.

Menchan, W. McKinley. "The Negro College Takes to the Nursery School." School and Society, 36 (September 10, 1932), 338-340.

_____. "Parent Education in a Negro College." School and Society, 37 (June 3, 1933), 713-714.

_____. "From 'Conservative to Radical': The Ideological Development of W. E. B. Du Bois, 1885-1905." Crisis, 66 (November, 1959), 527-536.

"A Merger of Two Methodist Negro Colleges." [Wiley College, Marshall, Texas and Samuel Huston College, Austin,

Texas] School and Society, 68 (July 31, 1948), 71.

Miles, Michael. "Colonialism on the Black Campus." New Republic, August 5, 1967.

Miller, Carroll L. "Issues and Problems in the Higher Education of Negro Americans." Journal of Negro Education, 35 (Fall, 1966), 485-493.

_____. "The Negro Publicly-Supported Junior College." Journal of Negro Education, 31 (Summer, 1962), 386-395.

Miller, Julius Sumner. "A Teaching Device." American Journal of Physics, 19 (February, 1951), 130.

_____. "Concerning Lecture-Demonstrations." American Journal of Physics, 17 (December, 1949), 582.

Miller, Kelly C. "Take Them Where You Find Them." Journal of Negro Education, 26 (Fall, 1957), 530-531.

_____. "Modern Foreign Languages in Negro Colleges." Journal of Negro Education, 23 (Winter, 1954), 40-50.

_____. "Function of the Negro College." Dial, 32 (April 16, 1902), 207-270.

_____. "The Historic Background of the Negro Physician." Journal of Negro History, 1 (April, 1916), 99-109.

_____. "Negro Education and the Depression." Journal of Negro Education, 2 (January, 1933), 1-4.

_____. "Practical Value of the Higher Education of the Negro." Education, 36 (December, 1915), 234-240. Ibid., Opportunity, 1 (March, 1923), 4-5.

_____. "Reorganization of Higher Education for Negroes in the Light of Changing Conditions." Journal of Negro Education, 5 (July, 1936), 484-494.

_____. "Education for Manhood." Monographic Magazine, April, 1913.

_____. "The Higher Education of the Negro is at the Crossroads." Educational Review, 72 (December, 1926), 272-278.

_____. "The Past, Present, and Future of the Negro College." Journal of Negro Education, 2 (July, 1933), 411-422.

Mills, James Alexander. "Changes in the Faculties of Negro Colleges, 1948-1958." Quarterly Review of Higher Education Among Negroes, 30 (July, 1962), 153-157.

"Miner Teachers College Centennial." Negro History Bulletin, 14 (January, 1951), 74, 87.

Mines, Stephanie and Frazier, Phil. "Sammy Younge, Jr. Brigin' [All Down Home]." *The Movement*, April, 1969.

Mitchell, Edward C. "Higher Education of the Negro." *Baptist Home Mission Monthly*, 18 (September, 1896), 301-310.

Mitchell, F. T. "Superior Teacher of Vocational Agriculture." *Southern Workman*, 59 (July, 1930), 313-317.

_____. "Vocational Agricultural Education in Arkansas." *Southern Workman*, 59 (August, 1930), 345-348.

Mitchell, James J. "Negro Higher Education: Years of Crisis." *Quarterly Review of Higher Education Among Negroes*, 30 (January, 1962), 18-21.

Mitchell, Samuel Chiles. "Booker Washington's Gospel." *Southern Workman*, 52 (May, 1923), 216.

Mommsen, Kent G. "Black Ph.D.'s in the Academic Market-Place." *Journal of Higher Education*, 45 (April, 1974), 253-267.

Mommsen, Kent G. "Professionalism and the Racial Context of Career Patterns Among Black American Doctorates: A Note on the Brain Drain Hypothesis." *Journal of Negro Education*, 42 (Spring, 1973), 191-204.

Monro, John U. "The Black College Dilemma." *Educational Record*, 53 (Spring, 1972), 132-137.

Moon, F. D. "Higher Education and Desegregation in Oklahoma." *Journal of Negro Education*, 27 (Summer, 1958), 300-310.

_____. "The Negro Public College in Kentucky and Oklahoma." *Journal of Negro Education*, 31 (Summer, 1962), 322-329.

Moore, Alice P. "Miner Teachers College in a Program of Personal Growth and Development as Related to Teacher Recruitment." *The Journal of the Columbian Educational Association*, 8 (May, 1944), 23-24.

"Morehouse College: Higher Education for Negro Men." *Crisis*, 47 (August, 1940), 251.

Morehouse, H. L. "American Baptist Home Mission Society: Sketches of Its Manifold Work." *Baptist Home Mission Monthly*, 19 (September, 1897), 312-326.

_____. "The Talented Tenth." *Baptist Home Mission Monthly*, 18 (August, 1896), 277.

"Morgan State College." *Ebony*, 12 (February, 1957), 71-74.

"Morgan State College." Crisis, 47 (August, 1940), 252.

"Morgan State College." Negro History Bulletin, 20 (January, 1957), 75.

Morgan, T. J. "The American Baptist Home Mission Society and the Negroes." University Journal, 1 (February, 1901), 6-8.

_____. "Education of the Afro-American." Baptist Home Mission Monthly, 19 (October, 1897), 346-347.

_____. "Industrial and Intellectual Education for the Negro." Baptist Home Mission Monthly, 24 (June, 1902), 170-171.

Moron, Alonzo G. "Maintaining the Solvency of the Private College Through Efficient Management." Journal of Negro Education, 27 (Spring, 1958), 141-144.

Morris, Carl. "Why 394 White Students Choose a Negro College." Color Magazine, October, 1955.

Morris, Eddie W. "Admissions in Predominantly Negro College: A View From the Inside." College and University, 44 (Winter, 1969), 130-144.

_____. "The Contemporary Negro College and the Brain Drain." Journal of Negro Education, 41 (Fall, 1972), 309-319.

Morris, S. S. "Religious Instruction in Negro Colleges." Wilberforce University Quarterly, 3 (July and October, 1942), 78-84.

Mortimer, Kingsley E. "The Melanoblasts of Fate: Aspects and Attitudes at the 'Black Harvard'." Journal of the National Medical Association, 60 (September, 1968), 357-365.

Moton, Jennie F. "Tuskegee Program for the Training of Women." Journal of Educational Sociology, 7 (November, 1933), 184-189.

Moton, Robert Russa. "Apostle of Good Will." Southern Workman, 46 (March, 1917).

Moton, Robert R. "Tuskegee Institute After Forty-Two Years." Opportunity, 1 (April, 1923), 17-18.

_____. "Character Building at Tuskegee and Hampton." Southern Workman, 52 (Fall, 1923), 62.

_____. "Frissell, the Builder." Southern Workman, (June, 1923), 259.

_____. "Hampton's Gift to the Negro." Southern Workman, 48 (June, 1919), 295-302.

_____. "Negro Higher and Professional Education in 1943." Journal of Negro Education, 2 (July, 1933), 397-402.

_____. "Student Life at Hampton Institute." World's Work, 14 (May, 1907), 8915-8918.

_____. "The Scope and Aim of Tuskegee." Journal of Educational Sociology, 7 (November, 1933), 151-156.

_____. "Tuskegee's Founder." Southern Workman, 51 (April, 1922), 692.

Muehl, Siegmar and Muehl, Lois. "A College Level Compensatory Program for Educationally Disadvantaged Black Students: Interim Findings and Reflections." Journal of Negro Education, 41 (Winter, 1972), 65-81.

Mullowney, John J. "Training for Medicine and Dentistry." Opportunity, 14 (December, 1936), 370-374.

"Municipal College for Negroes." School and Society, 32 (November 22, 1930), 692.

Munn, Merton D. "Role of the Dean in a Church-Related College." Quarterly Review of Higher Education Among Negroes, 25 (April, 1957), 79-85.

Munro, John U. "Escape From the Dark Cave." Nation, 209 (October 27, 1969), 434-439.

Murphy, Edward. "S. S. J., an Old Challenge Newly Met [Xavier University]." The Sign, 12 : 4 (November, 1932), 231-232.

Murry, Florence. "An Educational Experiment at Tuskegee." Opportunity, 19 (September, 1941), 277-278.

Murry, G. R. "Negro Education in North Carolina." School and Society, 14 (July 10, 1921), 53.

Murry, Walter I. "The Reading Workshop at Jackson College." Journal of Negro Education, 18 (Winter, 1949), 18-83.

_____, and Anthony, James K. "An Inventory of Student Opinion." Junior College Journal, 26 (December, 1955), 224-227.

Myers, A. F. "Colleges for Negroes." Survey, 86 (May, 1950), 233-239.

Nabrit, James M., Jr. "Howard University Looks to the Future." Journal of Negro Education, 29 (Fall, 1960), 412-420.

_____. "Legal Inventions and the Desegregation Process." Annals of the American Academy of Political and Social Science. 304 (1960-1967), 35-43.

_____. "The State of the University [Howard]." Howard University Magazine, 6 (January, 1964), 17-20.

Nabrit, S. Milton. "The Carnegie Grant-in-Aid Program." Phylon, 10 (4th Quarter, 1949), 389-391.

Nabrit, S. M. "Desegregation and the Future of Graduate and Professional Education in Negro Institutions." Journal of Negro Education, 27 (Summer, 1958), 414-418.

Nabrit, S. M. "Reflections on the Future of Black Colleges." Daedalus, 100 : 3 (Summer, 1971), 660-677.

"National Survey of the Higher Education of Negroes." School and Society, 50 (September, 1939), 429-430.

"Nazareth College." Negro History Bulletin, 20 (January, 1958), 78.

"Negro Colleges Added to Carnegie Foundation Program to Vitalize Teaching." School and Society, 65 (April 26, 1947), 303.

"Negro Colleges." School and Society, 22 (August 8, 1925), 164.

"Negro Colleges Surveyed." Southern Workman, 57 (December, 1928), 519.

"Negro Colleges--Their Outlook." U. S. News and World Report, June 3, 1968, 74-78.

"Negro Collegiate Organizations." Opportunity, 1 (February, 1923), 26.

"Negro Education at Tuskegee Institute." Journal of Educational Sociology, 7 (November, 1933), 151-205.

"Negro Education in North Carolina." School and Society, 14 (July 30; October 22, 1921), 53; 335-336.

"Negro Education." Crisis, 30 (August, 1925), 166.

"Negro Enrollments This Year on the Nation's Campuses." Chronicle of Higher Education, 3 : 16 (April 21, 1969), 3-4.

"Negro Higher Institutions in the South." Regional Action, 17 (June, 1966).

"Negroes in College: What the Figures Show." U. S. News and World Report, 55 (November 25, 1963), 81.

"Negro Professor." Newsweek, 30 (September 1, 1947), 74.

"Negro Universities and Colleges." School and Society, 17 (March 31, 1923), 350-351.

Nelson, Paul David. "Experiment in Interracial Education at Berea College, 1858-1908." Journal of Negro History, 59 (January, 1974), 13-27.

Nelson, William Stuart. "Can Negro Colleges Meet the Challenge of the Modern World?" Negro Digest, 12 (June, 1963), 8.

Nesbitt, George B. "W. E. B. Du Bois: An Apostle of Blackness." Crisis, 79 (June-July, 1972), 194-197.

"New Buildings at Atlanta University." School and Society, 34 (November 21, 1931), 693.

"New President [G. Lamar Harrison] Chosen for Langston University." Crisis, 47 (August, 1940), 248-249.

Newbold, N. C. "Negro Colleges and Life." Quarterly Review of Higher Education Among Negroes, 1 (October, 1933), 1-3.

_____. "The Public Education of Negroes and the Current Depression." Journal of Negro Education, 2 (January, 1933), 5-15.

_____. "Using Hampton in North Carolina." Southern Workman, 57 (September, 1928), 346-349.

_____. "The Work and Needs of Livingstone College." Official Journal of the 30th Quadrennial Session of General Conference of the A. M. E. Zion Church, 1936, 248-287.

Neyland, Leedell W. "The Educational Leadership of J. R. E. Lee." Negro History Bulletin, 25 : 4 (1962), 75-78.

_____. "State Supported Higher Education Among Negroes in the State of Florida." Florida Historical Quarterly, 43 : 2 (1964), 105-122.

_____. "Africa: New Frontier for Teaching in Negro Institutions of Higher Learning." Educational Record, 42 (January, 1961), 57-61.

"Ninth President [Herman H. Long]." The Talladegan, 81 (October, 1963), 1-2.

Nolan, David. "The 'Movement' Finally Arrives [Voorhees]." Nation, 208 (May 26, 1969), 654-656.

Norris, E. M. "Prairie View State College and Community Relations." Journal of Negro Education, 14 (Fall, 1945), 644-648.

North, Arthur A. "The Plessey Doctrine: Rise and Demise." Thought, 35 (Fall, 1960), 138.

Nyabongo, Virginia Simmons. "Achievement in Modern Foreign Languages in Negro Colleges of America." Journal of Negro Education, 15 (Winter, 1946), 153-160. Ibid., French Review, 20 (December, 1946), 153-158.

Oak, V. V. "Some Outstanding Defects in Institutions of Higher Learning for Negroes." School and Society, 46 (September 18, 1937), 357-362.

Oak, Vishnu V. "Commercial Education of the Negro." Journal of Negro Education, 1 (October, 1932), 400-404.

_____. "Business Education in Negro Colleges." Crisis, 45 (June, 1938), 175-176, 190.

_____. "Higher Education of the Negro." Education, 53 (November, 1932), 176-181.

_____. "Suggestions for the Improvement of Business Curricula." Negro College Quarterly, 4 (September, 1946), 125-133.

_____. "Recent Trends in Higher Education for Negroes." Wilberforce University Quarterly, 2 (October, 1941), 106-116.

_____. "Some Problems in Business Education in Negro Colleges." Wilberforce University Quarterly, 1 (December, 1939), 18-22.

_____, and Rochelle, Charles E. "A Functional Program for the Negro Graduate School." Negro College Quarterly, 2 (June, 1944), 62-76.

Oliver, C. A. "The Negro--How Can We Help Him?" The Catholic World, 42 (October, 1885), 85.

Oliver, Marie M. "What Hampton Had Done for My Community." Southern Workman, 54 (August, 1925), 373-376.

Oliver, W. "Stony Path to Learning: Colleges of the Atlanta University System." Saturday Evening Post, 217 (April 14, 1945), 22-23.

Oppenheimer, Martin. "Institutions of Higher Learning and the 1960 Sit-Ins: Some Clues for Social Action." Journal of Negro Education, 32 (Summer, 1963), 286-288.

_____. "The Southern Student Movement: Year I." Journal of Negro Education, 33 (Fall, 1964), 396-403.

Orbell, John M. "Protest Participation Among Southern Negro College Students." American Political Science Review, June, 1967.

Orr, Charles W. "The Evolution of Admission Practices in Negro Land-Grant Colleges, 1890-1950." The Negro Educational Review, 10 (April, 1959), 53-60.

"Our Negro Colleges." _Opportunity_, 1 (April, 1923), 12-18.

"Our Tasks and Our Responsibilities at Wilberforce." _Wilberforce University Quarterly_, 1 (December, 1939), 23-28.

Orum, Anthony M. "The Class and Status Bases of Negro Student Protest." _Social Science Quarterly_, December, 1968.

"Outlook for Graduates From Segregated School." _Negro History Bulletin_, 18 (February, 1955), 117.

Owen, Samuel A. "Our Negro Colleges--Roger Williams College." _Opportunity_, 1 (April, 1923), 14.

"Paine College." _Crisis_, 47 (August, 1940), 269.

Palmer, Archie M. "Long Term College Presidents." _Association of American Colleges_, 19 (March, 1933), 102-103.

Palmer, J. H. "Notes From Tuskegee." _Southern Workman_, 11 (January, 1882), 9.

Palmer, L. F. "Public Relations, New Development in Negro Colleges." _Journal of Negro Education_, 17 (Fall, 1948), 556-561.

Palmer, R. Roderick. "Colonial Statues and Present-Day Obstacles Restricting Negro Education." _Journal of Negro Education_, 26 (Fall, 1957), 525-529.

Parker, Franklin. "Negro Education in the U. S. A.: A Partial Bibliography of Doctoral Dissertations." _Negro History Bulletin_, 24 (May, 1961), 192, 190, 191.

_____. "Negro Education in the U. S. A. Additional Doctoral Dissertations." _Negro History Bulletin_, 25 (October, 1961), 24, 23.

Parker, John W. "The Place of the Teacher in American Higher Education." _Vital Speeches_, 19 (July, 1953), 605-606.

_____. "Problems Incident to the Higher Education of Negroes in Arkansas." _Journal of Negro Education_, 9 (April, 1940), 167-176.

_____. "Current Debate Practices in Thirty Negro Colleges." _Journal of Negro Education_, 9 (January, 1940), 32-38.

_____. "The Place of the Gifted Student on the Negro College Campus." _Quarterly Review of Higher Education Among Negroes_, 8 (January, 1940), 14-16.

_____. "A Bibliography of the Published Writings of Benjamin Griffith Brawley." _North Carolina Historical Review_, 34 (April, 1957), 165-178.

Parrish, Charles H., Jr. "Negro Higher and Professional Education in Kentucky." Journal of Negro Education, 17 (Summer, 1948), 289-295.

_____. "Desegregated Higher Education in Kentucky." Journal of Negro Education, 27 (Summer, 1958), 260-268.

Parrish, Carl. "Music in the Negro Colleges." Saturday Review of Literature, 29 (January 26, 1946), 10-11.

Parsons, Cynthia and Welch, W. Bruce. "Mississippi's Beehive College." American Education, 4 : 1 (1967), 19-22, 28.

Partridge, Deborah C. "Adult Education Projects Sponsored by Negro College Fraternities and Sororities." Journal of Negro Education, 14 (Summer, 1945), 374-380.

Patrick, J. R. and Sims, V. M. "Personality Differences Between Negro and White College Students, North and South." Journal of Abnormal and Social Psychology, 29 (1934), 181-201.

Patterson, Frederick D. "Duplication and Resources of Negro Church-Related Colleges." Journal of Negro Education, 29 (Summer, 1960), 368-376.

_____. "The Future of the Private Negro College." Journal of Human Relations, 4 (Summer, 1956), 51-60.

_____. "Commercial Dietetics at Tuskegee Institute." Practical Home Economics, 24 (October, 1946), 483.

_____. "Esteem and Enrichment of Vocational-Industrial and Technical Programs in Negro Land-Grant Colleges With Recommendations." Quarterly Review of Higher Education Among Negroes, 5 (January, 1937), 1-6.

_____. "The Private Negro College in a Racially Integrated System of Higher Education." Journal of Negro Education, 21 (Summer, 1952), 363-369.

_____. "Colleges for Negro Youth and the Future." Journal of Negro Education, 27 (Spring, 1958), 107-114.

_____. "Cooperation Among Predominantly Negro Colleges and Universities." Journal of Negro Education, 35 (Fall, 1966), 477-484.

_____. "Foundation Policies in Regard to Negro Institutions of Higher Learning." Journal of Educational Sociology, 32 (February, 1958), 290-296.

_____. "Negro Higher Education's Contribution to the War Effort From the Point of View of Agriculture." Journal of Negro Education, 11 (July, 1942), 314-321.

_____, and Others. "Report of the Findings Committee, Conference of Presidents of Negro Land-Grant Colleges." School and Society, 53 (April, 1941), 513-514.

Patterson, T. B. "Taking the School to the Farmer." Southern Workman, 57 (October, 1928), 392-394.

Pawley, Thomas D. "Stagecraft in Negro Colleges." Negro College Quarterly, 4 (December, 1946), 193-199.

Payne, D. A. "Morris Brown." The A. M. E. Review, 72 (July-September, 1956), 15-19.

Payne, Joseph A., Jr. "The Role of the Association of Colleges and Secondary Schools for Negroes From 1934-1954." Journal of Negro Education, 27 (Fall, 1958), 532-536.

_____. "The Role of the Negro College in Light of Integrative Trends." Journal of Negro Education, 22 (Winter, 1953), 80-83.

Payne, William. "Forgotten...But Not Gone: The Negro Land-Grant Colleges." Civil Rights Digest, 3 (Spring, 1970), 16.

Payton, Blanche Blaylark. "In Appreciation of Livingstone: Past and Present." The Star of Zion, January 30, 1941, 1.

Peacock, Joseph L. "Our Colleges--Shaw University." Opportunity, 1 (March, 1923), 15, 21.

Pendleton, Helen B. "Education for Social Work Among Negroes in the South." Southern Workman, 56 (February, 1927), 71-77.

Penrose, W. O. "Report From Pine Bluff: Point of View in Higher Education for Negroes." Harvard Educational Review, 18 (May, 1948), 146-150.

Peoples, John A. and Nabrit, Samuel M. "A Special Review--A Pair of Studies of the Negro College." Journal of Higher Education, 42 (November, 1971), 694-702.

Perry, Jennings. "Dillard University Today." The Christian Educator, January-February, May, 1952, 14-16.

Petrof, John V. "Business Administration Curricula in Predominantly Negro Colleges." Journal of Negro Education, 35 (Summer, 1966), 276-279.

Peters, E. C. "Paine College Serves Its Community." World Outlook, 28 : 9 (September, 1938).

Peters, James S., II. "A Study of the Wechsler-Bellevue Verbal Scores of Negro and White Males." Journal of Negro Education, 29 (Summer, 1960), 7-16.

Peterson, F. L. "Why the Seventh-Day Adventist Church Established and Maintains a Negro College and Schools for Negroes Below College Grade?" Journal of Negro Education, 29 (Summer, 1960), 284-288.

Pettigrew, Thomas F. "Social Psychological View of the Predominantly Negro College." Journal of Negro Education, 36 (Summer, 1967), 274-285.

_____. "The Role of Whites in Black Colleges of the Future." Daedalus, 100 (Summer, 1971), 813-832.

Phillips, Waldo B. "Educational Contributions of Booker T. Washington." Negro Educational Review, 14 (July-October, 1903), 143.

Picott, J. Rupert. "The Negro Public College in Virginia." Journal of Negro Education, 31 (Summer, 1962), 275-283.

_____. "Desegregation of Higher Education in Virginia." Journal of Negro Education, 27 (Summer, 1958), 324-331.

Pierce, Chester M., and West, Louis J. "Six Years of Sit-Ins: Psychodynamic Causes and Effects." International Journal of Social Psychology, Winter, 1966.

Pierce, Ponchitta. "Integration: Negro College's Newest Challenge." Ebony, March, 1966.

Pipes, William H. "College Students Flunk Teachers." Association of American Colleges Bulletin, 37 (May, 1951), 263-265.

Pittman, Joseph A. "A Study of the Academic Achievement of 415 College Students in Relation to Remedial Courses Taken." Journal of Negro Education, 29 (Fall, 1960), 426-437.

_____. "A Study of the Prediction of Academic Achievement in Publicly-Supported Colleges for Negroes." Journal of Negro Education, 23 (Spring, 1954), 123-132.

Pitts, Lucius H. "A Black College President Asks for Advice." Soundings, 54 (Spring, 1971), 29-33.

Plaut, Richard L. "Increasing the Quantity and Quality of Negro Enrollment in College." Harvard Educational Review, 30 (Summer, 1960), 270-280.

_____. "Plans for Assisting Negro Students to Enter and to Remain in College." Journal of Negro Education, 35 (Fall, 1966), 393-399.

_____. "Prospects for the Entrance and Scholastic Advancement of Negroes in Higher Educational Institutions." Journal of Negro Education, 36 (Summer, 1967), 230-237.

Poinsett, Alex. "The Brain Drain at Negro Colleges." Ebony, 25 (October, 1970), 74-84.

Pollard, John A. "Consolidating the Colleges." School and Society, 34 (September 19, 1931), 404-408.

Porter, Dorothy B. "The Organized Educational Activities of Negro Literary Societies, 1828-1846." Journal of Negro Education, 5 (October, 1936), 565.

Porter, Dorothy B. "Preservation of University Documents: With Special Reference to Negro Colleges and Universities." Journal of Negro Education, 11 (October, 1942), 527-528.

_____. "The First Negro Medical Society." Journal of Negro Education, 9 (April, 1940), 213-215.

Porter, Gilbert L. "Negro Publicly Supported Higher Institutions in Florida." Journal of Negro Education, 31 (Summer, 1962), 293-298.

Porter, Jennie D. "Evolution of the Harriet Beecher Stowe School." Southern Workman, 53 (May, 1924), 237-239.

Posey, Thomas E. "Workers' Education: A Challenge to Negro Colleges." Journal of Negro Education, 16 (Winter, 1947), 112-115.

_____. "The Socio-Economic Background of Freshmen at West Virginia State College." Journal of Negro Education, 2 (October, 1933), 466-476.

Posey, Thomas E. "Negro Land Grant Colleges." Opportunity, 10 (January, 1932), 14-17, 27.

Powell, A. Scott. "Group Identity and Book Interests of College Students." Journal of Negro Education, 21 (Fall, 1952), 535-540.

Preston, Delorus. "Teaching Race Appreciation at Edward Waters College." Quarterly Review of Higher Education Among Negroes, 7 (April, 1939), 138-142.

Price, J. St. Clair. "The Intelligence of Negro College Freshmen." School and Society, 30 (November 30, 1929), 749-754.

Pugh, Wesley C. "The Inflated Controversy: Du Bois vs. Washington." Crisis, 81 (April, 1974), 132-133.

Purcell, Blanche W. "Home Economics at Hampton Institute." Southern Workman, 53 (January, 1925), 9-15.

Quarles, Benjamin. "A Service to Students." Improving College and University Teaching, 5 (Spring, 1957), 37.

_____. "One Shortcoming in Negro Colleges." Journal of Negro Education, 12 (Fall, 1943), 700-702.

_____. "Salary, Tenure and Retirement in Negro Colleges." Quarterly Review of Higher Education Among Negroes, 13 (July, 1945), 175-182.

Raffalovich, George. "Piety Rules a Negro College." Outlook and Independent, 160 (January 13, 1932), 45-56.

Rafky, David M. "The Attitude of Black Scholars Toward Black Colleges." Journal of Negro Education, 41 (Fall, 1972), 320-330.

Ramaker, Robert. "Negro Colleges Train Too Many Teachers, Too Few Technicians; Job Openings for Grads go Begging." Wall Street Journal, 154 (July 15, 1959), 1.

Rand, E. W., and Cooper, M. N. "Sophomore College Students and the Conversion of Common Fractions, Decimals and Percents." Journal of Negro Education, 30 (Winter, 1961), 80-82.

Rand, E. W. "The Cost of Board, Room and Student Fees in a Selected Group of Negro Publicly Supported Colleges." Journal of Negro Education, 26 (Spring, 1957), 207-212.

_____. "Negro Private and Church College at Mid-Century." Journal of Negro Education, 22 (Winter, 1953), 77-79.

_____. "Selection of Board Members in Negro Church-Related Colleges." Journal of Negro Education, 25 (Winter, 1956), 79-82.

Randall, Rogers E. "Experimental Study on the Teaching of Scientific Thinking in Physical Science Course at the College Level." School Science and Mathematics, 55 (October, 1955), 535-539.

Ransom, Leon A. "Education and the Law: Aftermath of the Gaines Decision." Journal of Negro Education, 8 (April, 1939), 244-246.

_____. "Education and the Law: Gaines vs. the University of Missouri." Journal of Negro Education, 8 (January, 1939), 111-117.

Raper, Arthur. "College Graduates and Race Relations." Opportunity, 15 (December, 1937), 370-373.

Read, Florence M. "The Place of the Women's College in the Pattern of Negro Education." Opportunity, 15 (September, 1937), 267-270.

Reason, Joseph H. "Veterans in College: A Bibliography." Negro College Quarterly, 5 (March, 1947), 27-30.

"Recommendations of the Presidents of Land-Grant Colleges for Negroes." School and Society, 43 (March 28, 1936), 443-446.

"Reconstruction and Education in South Carolina." South Atlantic Quarterly, 18 (October, 1919), 350-364. Ibid., 19 (January, 1920), 55-56.

"Reconstruction and Education in Virginia." South Atlantic Quarterly, 15 (January-April, 1916), 25-40, 157-174.

Redd, George N., and Dummett, Clifton O. "A Dental Faculty Analyzes Its Teaching Program." Journal of Dental Education, 12 (December, 1947), 79-86.

Redd, George N. "Experimenting With the Workshop and Seminar in the Education of Teachers." Quarterly Review of Higher Education Among Negroes, 9 (January, 1941), 10-15.

_____. "Better Utilization of the Resources of the Negro Church-Related Colleges Through Curriculum Revision." Journal of Negro Education, 29 (Summer, 1960), 377-387.

_____. "Resources for Graduate Work for Negroes in the States of Alabama, Kentucky and Tennessee." Journal of Negro Education, 15 (Winter, 1946), 161-171.

_____. "Present Status of Negro Higher and Professional Education: A Critical Summary." Journal of Negro Education, 17 (Summer, 1948), 400-409.

Reddick, L. D. "The State vs. the Student." Dissent, 7 (Summer, 1960), 219-228.

Reddick, Lawrence D. "The Younger Negro Looks at His College." Opportunity, 12 (July, 1934), 210-211, 222.

_____. "Select [ed] Bibliography." Journal of Educational Sociology, 19 (April, 1946), 512-516.

_____. "Library Facilities for Research in Negro Colleges." Quarterly Review of Higher Education Among Negroes, 8 (July, 1940), 127-129.

_____. "Black Beauty and the University." Crisis, 46 (October, 1939), 303-304.

_____. "How Much Higher and Professional Education Does the Negro Need?" Journal of Negro Education, 17 (Summer, 1948), 236-239.

_____. "Real Research Barriers in the South." The Social Frontier, 4 (October, 1937), 85-86.

_____. "Critical Review: The Politics of Desegregation." Journal of Negro Education, 31 (Summer, 1962), 414-420.

Redding, Louis L. "Desegregation of Higher Education in Delaware." Journal of Negro Education, 27 (Summer, 1958), 253-259.

Reed, George N. "Analysis of Teacher-Education Trends in Negro Colleges." Educational Administration and Supervision, 35 (December, 1949), 461-474.

Reedy, Sidney J. "Higher Education and Desegregation in Missouri." Journal of Negro Education, 27 (Summer, 1958), 284-294.

_____. "Negro Higher and Professional Education in Missouri." Journal of Negro Education, 17 (Summer, 1948), 321-334.

_____. "Graduate Work in Selected White and Negro Institutions." Journal of Negro Education, 14 (Spring, 1945), 256-258.

_____. "Is Negro Teacher Education Functional?" Educational Administration and Supervision, 31 (April, 1945), 223-228.

Reid, Herbert O., and Nabrit, James M., Jr. "Remedies Under Statutes Granting Federal Aid to Land-Grant Colleges." Journal of Negro Education, 17 (Summer, 1948), 410-425.

Reid, Ira De A. "The Negro Private College." Crisis, 57 (August-September, 1950), 481-484, 538.

Reid, Ira De A. "Three Negro Teachers." Phylon, 2 (Second Quarter, 1941), 137-143.

Reid, Robert D. "Curricular Changes in Colleges and Universities for Negroes." Journal of Higher Education, 37 (March, 1967), 153-160.

"Report on Standards for Negro Schools and Colleges." High School Quarterly, 18 (January, 1930), 80-81.

"Resolution of the Faculty and Staff of the South Carolina State College." Journal of Negro Education, 25 (Spring, 1956), 197-199.

"Resolutions of Negro Land-Grant Colleges." School and Society, 78 (December 12, 1953), 188. Ibid., 64 (August 31, 1946), 153.

Reynolds, L. R. "The Curriculum of the Liberal Arts College for Negroes and the Demands of a Bi-Racial Society." Quarterly Review of Higher Education Among Negroes, 2 (April, 1934), 102-108.

Richards, Eugene S. "Negro Higher and Professional Education in Oklahoma." Journal of Negro Education, 17 (Summer, 1948), 341-349.

Richardson, Joe M. "Christian Abolitionism: The American Missionary Association and the Florida Negro." Journal of Negro Education, 40 (Winter, 1971), 34-44.

Richter, Jay. "The Origin and Development of the Land-Grant College in the United States." Journal of Negro Education, 31 (Summer, 1962), 230-239.

Riddle, Estelle Massey. "Progress of Negro Nursing." American Journal of Nursing, 38 (February, 1938), 162-169.

_____. "The Training and Placement of Negro Nurses." Journal of Negro Education, 4 (January, 1935), 42-48.

Rigler, G. W. "Our Negro Colleges--Hartshorn Memorial College." Opportunity, 1 (April, 1923), 15-16.

Rivers, W. Napoleon, Jr. "A Study of the Modern Foreign Languages in Thirty Negro Colleges." Journal of Negro Education, 2 (October, 1933), 487-493.

Roberts, S. O. "Negro Higher and Professional Education in Tennessee." Journal of Negro Education, 17 (Summer, 1948), 361-372.

Robinson, Annie Mae, and Allen, Francis W. "Community Service of a Negro College Library." Journal of Negro Education, 12 (Spring, 1943), 181-188.

Robinson, James R. "Development Reading Program at Talladega College." Journal of Negro Education, 16 (Winter, 1947), 104-107.

Robinson, William A. "North Carolina Rating of Negro Colleges Since 1923." Opportunity, 7 (January, 1929), 21-22.

Robinson, William H. "Desegregation in Higher Education in the South." School and Society, 88 (May, 1960), 234-239.

_____. "The Negro Colleges Face the Future." Journal of Negro Education, 21 (Spring, 1952), 167-172.

Rose, Harold M. "The Market for Negro Educators in Colleges and Universities." Journal of Negro Education, 30 (Fall, 1961), 432-435.

Rosenthal, Joel. "Southern Black Student Activism: Assimilation vs. Nationalism." Journal of Negro Education, 44 (Spring, 1975), 113-129.

Roth, Robert M. "The Adjustment of the Negro College Students at Hampton Institute." Journal of Negro Education, 30 (Winter, 1961), 72-74.

_____. "A Self-Selection Process by Northern Negroes Existing in a Southern Negro College." Journal of Negro Education, 28 (Spring, 1959), 185-186.

Rothrock, Thomas. "Joseph Carter Corbin and Negro Education in the University of Arkansas." The Arkansas Historical Quarterly, 30 (Summer, 1971), 277-314.

Roucek, Joseph S. "Milestones in the History of Education of the Negro in the United States." International Review of Education, 2 (1964), 162-178.

Rudwick, Elliott M. "Du Bois' Last Year as Crisis Editor." Journal of Negro Education, 27 (Fall, 1958), 526-533.

_____. "W. E. B. Du Bois and the Atlanta University Studies on the Negro." Journal of Negro Education, 26 (Fall, 1957), 466-476.

_____. "Note on a Forgotten Black Sociologist: W. E. B. Du Bois and the Sociological Profession." American Sociologist, 4 (November, 1969), 303-306.

_____. "Booker T. Washington's Relations With the National Association for the Advancement of Colored People." Journal of Negro Education, 29 (Summer, 1960), 134-144.

Russell, Charles E. "Autobiography of Dr. Du Bois." Crisis, 47 (December, 1940), 382.

Russell, James Solomon. "Letters of James Solomon Russell to Monroe N. Work." Journal of Negro History, 8 (July, 1923), 341-342.

Russell, Roger D. "Negro Publicly-Supported Colleges in Mississippi and South Carolina." Journal of Negro Education, 31 (Summer, 1962), 310-321.

_____. "Guidance Development in Negro Colleges." Occupations, 28 (October, 1949), 25-27.

Ryan, Stephen P. "The College Teacher." Catholic Educational Review, 55 (September, 1957), 389-396.

"Samuel Massey Gets North Carolina Presidency." Kappa Alpha Psi Journal, 49 (October, 1963), 88-89.

Samuel, Nadene and Laird, Dorothy S. "The Self Concepts of Two Groups of Black Female College Students." Journal of Negro Education, 43 (Spring, 1974), 228-233.

Saulsbury, Charles William. "Salary as One Phase of College Standardization." Quarterly Review of Higher Education Among Negroes, 13 (July, 1945), 191-194.

Saundle, J. S. "Non-Resident Students and Non-Resident Fees." Journal of Negro Education, 27 (Winter, 1958), 84-89.

Savage, W. Sherman. "The Influence of the Gaines Case on Higher Education in the South." Quarterly Review of Higher Education Among Negroes, 11 (July, 1943), 1-5.

_____. "Forty Years of a Negro College." Education, 57 (October, 1936), 110-115.

Sawyer, Broadus E. "Graduate Training of Twenty-One Selected College Faculties." Journal of Negro Education, 32 (Spring, 1963), 193-197.

_____. "The Baccalaureate Origins of the Faculties of the Twenty-One Selected Colleges." Journal of Negro Education, 31 (Winter, 1962), 83-87.

Scales, Eldridge E. "A Study of College Student Retention and Withdrawal." Journal of Negro Education, 29 (Fall, 1960), 438-444.

_____. "Grading Practices at Fort Valley State College." Journal of Negro Education, 25 (Spring, 1956), 185-190.

_____. "A Report of the Persistence of a Group of Entering College Freshmen." The Savannah State College Bulletin, 11 (October, 1957), 12-19.

_____. "Variability of Grading Practices Among Instructors of a Multiple-Section English Course." College and University, 33 (Spring, 1958), 334-336.

Scanlon, John. "Luther Foster of Tuskegee." Saturday Review of Literature, 47 (May 16, 1964), 76-88.

Schroeder, P. B. "A Social Studies Program in the Negro College." Journal of Negro History, 27 (January, 1942), 71-82.

Schuler, Edgar A. "Southern Students' Dilemma." Phylon, 6 (1st Quarter, 1945), 70-77.

Schuyler, George S. "Was Booker T. Wrong?" Negro Digest, 4 (February, 1947), 86-90.

Scott, Emmett J. "Howard, the National University of the Negro Race." School Life, 9 (June, 1924), 243-244.

_____. "Mrs. Booker T. Washington's Part in Her Husband's Work." Ladies Home Journal, 24 (May, 1907), 494-512.

_____. "Twenty Years After: An Appraisal of Booker T. Washington." Journal of Negro Education, 5 (October, 1936), 543-544.

Scott, J. Irving. "Academic Preparation of Negroes Above the Master's Degree." Negro Education Review, 2 (July-October, 1951), 135-140.

_____. "Research in Negro Colleges and Universities for the Decade 1950-1960." Negro Educational Review, 11 (January, 1960), 32-42.

Scott, J. Irving, and Scott, H. R. "Foreign Students in Negro Colleges and Universities in the United States of America, 1951-1952." Journal of Negro Education, 22 (Fall, 1953), 484-492.

Scott, J. I. E., and Jordan, H. "Honorary Degrees Conferred by Negro Colleges." School and Society, 75 (March, 1952), 153-154.

Scott, Roy V. "Land Grants for Higher Education in Mississippi: A Survey." Agricultural History, 43 (1969), 357-368.

Scully, Malcolm G. "After a Year of Crises, Federal City College Drops Experiments for Traditional Forms." Chronicle of Higher Education, 4 : 5 (October 27, 1969), 3.

_____. "City is Concern of Land-Grant College No. 69." Chronicle of Higher Education, 3 : 2 (September 23, 1968), 5.

_____. "Black Studies Plan Sparks Bitter Debate at Federal City College." Chronicle of Higher Education, 3 : 14 (March 24, 1969), 5.

Searles, Ruth and Williams, J. Allen, Jr. "Negro College Students' Participation in Sit-Ins." Social Forces, 40 (March, 1962), 215-220.

Sekora, John. "Murder Relentless and Impassive: The American Academic Community and the Negro College." Soundings, 51 (Fall, 1968), 237-271.

_____. "On Negro Colleges: A Reply to Jencks and Riesman." Antioch Review, 28 (Spring, 1968), 5-26.

Semas, Philip W. "Public Negro Colleges Launch Campaigns for Private Funds." Chronicle of Higher Education, 4 : 11 (December 8, 1969), 1, 4.

"Seventy-Fifth Anniversary [Fisk University]." School and Society, 54 (August 30, 1941), 136-137.

Sewell, George A. "Alcorn A. & M.: Pioneer in Black Pride." Crisis, 79 (April, 1972), 121-126.

Shannon, Irwin V. "The Teaching of Negro Life and History in Relation to Some Views of Educators on Race Adjustment." Journal of Negro Education, 2 (January, 1933), 53-64.

Shaw, Albert. "Learning by Doing." American Review of Reviews, April, 1900.

_____. "What Hampton Means by Education." American Review of Reviews, September, 1906.

Shockley, Ann Allen. "Negro Librarians in Predominantly Negro Colleges." College and Research Libraries, 28 (November, 1967), 423-426.

_____. "Does the Negro College Library Need a Special Negro Collection?" Library Journal, 86 (June 1, 1961), 2048-2050.

Shores, Louis. "Comparison of the Reading Interests of Negro and White College Students." Journal of Negro Education, 2 (October, 1933), 460-465.

_____. "Fisk University's New Library." Library Journal, 56 (February, 1931), 107-110.

"Should Negro Colleges Be Perpetuated or Should There Be Integration in Education?" Harlem Quarterly, 1 (Spring, 1950), 3-12.

Sievert, William A. "Black Junior College Leaders Ask for Affiliate Organization." Chronicle of Higher Education, 5 : 23 (November 15, 1971), 9.

Simkins, Francis B. "New Viewpoints of Southern Reconstruction." Journal of Southern History, 5 (February, 1939), 49-61.

Simmons, Sidney B. "Control and Supervision of Smith Hughes Work and Its Effect on the Development of the Negro Land-Grant College." Quarterly Review of Higher Education Among Negroes, 2 (October, 1934), 253-255.

Sims, David H. "Religious Education in Negro Colleges and Universities." Journal of Negro History, 5 (April, 1920), 166-207.

Sims, William E. "Black Colleges--Bicentennial Offers Little Hope." Journal of Negro Education, 45 (Summer, 1976), 219-224.

Singletary, James D. "Individualized Instruction in College?" Journal of Negro Education, 19 (Winter, 1950), 103-107.

Sisk, Glenn. "Morehouse College." Journal of Negro Education, 27 (Spring, 1958), 201-208.

_____. "The Negro Colleges in Atlanta." Journal of Negro Education, 33 (Spring, 1964), 131-135, 404-408.

"[Six] 6 Negro Colleges in Texas Try Team Approach to Problems." Chronicle of Higher Education, 2 : 1 (September 13, 1967), 9.

Slattery, J. R. "College for Roman Catholic Negro Catechists." Catholic World, 70 : 1.

Slowe, Lucy D. "Higher Education of Negro Women." Journal of Negro Education, 2 (July, 1933), 352-358.

_____. "The Colored Girl Enters College." Opportunity, 15 (September, 1937), 276-279.

Smith, Alice W. "Adapting a College Course to Racial and Community Needs." Journal of Home Economics, 25 (December, 1933), 875-876.

Smith, H. S. "Kentucky State College and Its President." Wilberforce Quarterly, 2 (July, 1941), 77-80.

Smith, Paul M., Jr. "The Realism of Counseling for Scholarship Aid With Freshmen in the Negro College." Journal of Negro Education, 33 (Winter, 1964), 93-96.

_____. "Head Librarians in Negro Colleges and Universities." Journal of Negro Education, 20 (Spring, 1951), 169-173.

Smith, Stanley H. "Academic Freedom in Higher Education in the Deep South." Journal of Educational Sociology, 32 (February, 1959), 297-308.

Smith, S. L. "Development of a Health Education Program for Negro Teachers." Journal of Negro Education, 6 (July, 1937), 538-547.

Smythe, Hugh H., and Smythe, Mabel M. "Inbreeding in Negro College Faculties." School and Society, 59 (June 17, 1944), 430-432.

_____. "The Negro College and the Negro Veteran." Negro College Quarterly, 2 (September, 1944), 116-128.

Smythe, Mabel M. "Teaching of Economics in the Negro College." Negro College Quarterly, 2 (March, 1944), 15-18.

Sorkin, Alan L. "A Comparison of Quality Characteristics in Negro and White Public Colleges and Universities in the South." Journal of Negro Education, 38 (Spring, 1969), 112-119.

Southall, Eugene P. "The Attitude of the Methodist Church, South Toward the Negro From 1844 to 1870." Journal of Negro History, 16 (October, 1931), 359-370.

Southern Association of Colleges and Secondary Schools. Committee on Approval of Negro Schools, "Report of the Committee on Approval of Negro Schools: Approved List of Colleges and Secondary Schools for Negro Youth." Southern Association Quarterly, 11 (February, 1947), 109-114.

"Southern University is Largest Negro University." Ebony, 13 (April, 1958), 62-66.

Spaulding, C. C. "Editorial in Behalf of the National Training School." Durham Morning Herald, September 24, 1919.

Spellman, C. L. "Health Education in Negro Colleges." Journal of the American Association for Health, Physical Education and Recreation, 21 (May, 1950), 286-287.

_____. "Some Top Level Academic and Personnel Problems in Negro Colleges." Association of American Colleges Bulletin, 36 (May, 1950), 273-279.

Stanfiel, James D. "A Profile of the 1972 Freshmen Class at Howard University." Journal of Negro Education, 45 (Winter, 1976), 61-69.

_____. "Education and Income of Parents of Students at Predominantly Black Colleges." Journal of Negro Education, 41 (Spring, 1972), 170-176.

Start, Edwin A. "General Armstrong and the Hampton Institute." New England Magazine, June, 1892.

"State of Missouri at the Relation of Lloyd Gaines, Petitioner, vs. S. W. Canada, Registrar of the University of Missouri and Curators of the University of Missouri, U. S. Supreme Court No. 57, October Term, 1938." Journal of Negro Education, 8 (January, 1939), 112-117.

Steif, William. "Federal City College: Will It Become the Prototype for Black Institutions?" College and University Business, February, 1969.

Stembridge, Barbara Penn. "A Student's Appraisal of the Adequacy of Higher Education for Black Americans." Journal of Negro Education, 37 (Summer, 1968), 316-322.

Stephan, A. Stephen. "Desegregation of Higher Education in Arkansas." Journal of Negro Education, 27 (Summer, 1958), 243-252.

_____. "The Negro Public College in Arkansas." Journal of Negro Education, 31 (Summer, 1962), 362-369.

Stephens, Earnest. "The Black University in America Today: A Student's Viewpoint." Freedomways, 7 (Spring, 1967), 131-138.

Stevenson, Janet. "Ignorant Armies." Atlantic, 224 (October, 1969), 57-63.

Stevenson, J. D. "Tuskegee's Religious Work." Southern Workman, 39 (July, 1910), 401.

Steward, Ollie. "Too Much of Nothing!" Southern Workman, 61 (August, 1932), 333-337.

Stewart, Paul Allen. "How Georgia State Remained a College." Negro Digest, 7 (June, 1949), 7-8.

Stewart, Robert B. "Offerings in Language and Literature for Majors and Minors--A Study and Criticism of the Practice of the State Colleges." Quarterly Review of Higher Education Among Negroes, 7 (July, 1939), 231-233.

"Stieglitz Collection at Fisk University." Crisis, 57 (March, 1950), 157-159.

Stienberg, David. "Black Power Roots on Black Campuses." Commonweal, April 19, 1967.

Stokes, Maurice S. "A Brief Survey of Higher Education for Negroes." Social Studies, 55 : 6 (1964), 214-220.

_____. "Educational Techniques and Devices: The Need and Purpose." Educational Administration and Supervision, 41 (October, 1955), 361-363.

"Storer College: In John Brown Land." Crisis, 47 (August, 1940), 253.

Streator, George W. "Football in Negro Colleges." Crisis, 39 (April, 1932), 129-130, 139.

_____. "Negro Football Standards." Crisis, 38 (March, 1931), 85-86.

"Strengthening Negro Colleges." School and Society, 92 (March 7, 1964), 94.

"Study of Negro Students Cites Severe Handicaps." Chronicle of Higher Education, 2 : 2 (September 27, 1967), 8.

Sumner, Francis C. "Philosophy of Negro Education." Educational Review, 71 (January, 1926), 42-45.

_____. "Morale of the Negro College." Educational Review, 73 (March, 1927), 168-172.

_____. "Mental Health Statistics of Negro College Freshmen." School and Society, 33 (April 25, 1931), 574-576.

_____. "Environmental Factors Which Prohibit Creative Scholarship Among Negroes." School and Society, 22 (September 5, 1925), 294-296.

"Survey of Negro Colleges." School and Society, 25 (February 19, 1927), 221-222. Ibid., (April 2, 1927), 397.

Sutton, W. S. "The Contribution of Booker T. Washington to the Education of the Negro." School and Society, 4 (September, 1916), 460-463.

Swanston, David. "Education for Relevance: First Year at Federal City." Nation, 208 (May 12, 1969), 594-596.

Talley, M. A. "The Problem of Religion in Negro Colleges in Our Country." The Sunday School Informer, 5 (April, 1938), 6-11.

Tambe, Naren. "Booker T. Washington and Mahatma Gandhi as Educationists." Peabody Journal of Education, 45 (September, 1967), 94-97.

Tapley, Lucy Hale. "Our Negro Colleges--Spelman Seminary." Opportunity, 1 (April, 1923), 16-17.

Taylor, Alrutheus Ambush. "The Negro in the Reconstruction of Virginia." Journal of Negro History, 11 (April, 1926), 243-415.

_____. "The Negro in South Carolina During the Reconstruction." Journal of Negro History, 9 (October, 1924), 383.

Taylor, Andress. "Beyond Rehabilitation: The Federal City College Lorton Project--A Model Prison Higher Education Program." Journal of Negro Education, 43 (Spring, 1974), 172-178.

_____, and Sekora, John. "A Woodrow Wilson Teaching Internship Program." Improving College and University Teaching, 16 (Autumn, 1968), 260-264.

Taylor, Dalmas A. "The Relationship Between Authoritarianism and Ethnocentrism in Negro College Students." Journal of Negro Education, 31 (Fall, 1962), 455-459.

Taylor, Graves. "Hampton Institute, an Everlasting Inspiration." Pulse, 5, 22-23, 30.

Taylor, Ivan E. "Negro Teachers in White Colleges." School and Society, 65 (May 24, 1947), 369-372.

Taylor, Lois. "Social Action at Bennett College." Opportunity, 20 (January, 1942), 8-10.

Taylor, Lois. "Nurse Education at Hampton Institute." Opportunity, 22 (April-June, 1944), 83, 100.

Taylor, Robert R. "Tuskegee's Mechanical Department." Southern Workman, 50 (October, 1921), 457.

Teele, Arthur Earle. "Education of the Negro in North Carolina 1862-1872." Quarterly Review of Higher Education Among Negroes, 27 (October, 1959), 204-206.

Terrell, Robert L. "Black Awareness Versus Negro Traditions: Atlanta University Center." New South, 24 (Winter, 1969), 29-40.

_____. "Lane College: The Fires of Discontent." New South, 24 (Spring, 1969), 2-16.

"Texas vs. Herman Sweatt." Newsweek, 28 (December 30, 1946), 74.

"Texas Southern University." Negro History Bulletin, 20 (February, 1957), 118.

"The Appeal of the Louisville Municipal College Faculty to the Board of Trustees." Journal of Negro Education, 20 (Spring, 1951), 241-248.

"The English Program at Morgan College." The Morgan State College Bulletin, 21 (October, 1955), 1-26.

"The Higher Education of Negro Americans: Prospects and Programs." Journal of Negro Education, 36 (Summer, 1967).

"The N. A. A. C. P. Speaks to the Troubled Campus." Crisis, 77 (August-September, 1970), 268-269.

"The Negro Public College." Journal of Negro Education, 31 (Summer, 1962), 215-428.

"The School That Was Too Good to Die: Lincoln University in Jefferson City, Mo." Ebony, 13 (March, 1958), 17-24.

"The Scranton Report, The Black Student Movement." Chronicle of Higher Education, 4 : 2 (October 5, 1970), 11-14.

Thomas, James S. "The Rationale Underlying Support of Negro Private Colleges by the Methodist Church." Journal of Negro Education, 29 (Summer, 1960), 252-259.

Thomas, Jesse O. "A New School in an Old Town." Opportunity, 6 (March, 1928), 82-83.

Thompson, Charles H. "The Negro Private and Church Related College." Journal of Negro Education, 29 (Summer, 1960), 211-216.

_____. "Are There Too Many Negro Colleges?" Journal of Negro Education, 3 (April, 1934), 159-166.

_____. "Negro Higher and Professional Education in the United States." Journal of Negro Education, 17 (Summer, 1948), 221-223.

_____. "Administrators of Negro Colleges and the Color Line in Higher Education in the South." Journal of Negro Education, 17 (Fall, 1948), 437-445.

_____. "Negro Higher Education in the War and Post-War Reconstruction." Journal of Negro Education, 11 (January, 1942), 1-3.

_____. "The U. S. Office of Education Survey of Negro

Higher Education." Journal of Negro Education, 8 (October, 1939), 617-619.

_____. "The Educational and Administrative Reorganization of Hampton Institute." Journal of Negro Education, 9 (April, 1940), 139-143.

_____. "Some Critical Aspects of the Problems of Higher and Professional Education for Negroes." Journal of Negro Education, 15 (Fall, 1945), 509-526.

_____. "Booker T. Washington is Elected to the Hall of Fame." Journal of Negro Education, 15 (Winter, 1946), 1-3.

_____. "The Improvement of the Negro College Faculty." Journal of Negro Education, 16 (Winter, 1947), 1-9.

_____. "Negro Higher Education in Maryland." Journal of Negro Education, 16 (Fall, 1947), 481-490.

_____. "The Critical Situation in Negro Higher and Professional Education." Journal of Negro Education, 15 (Fall, 1946), 579-584.

_____. "The 125th Anniversary of the American Baptist Home Mission Society." Journal of Negro Education, 27 (Spring, 1958), 101-102.

_____. "Present Status of the Negro Private and Church Related College." Journal of Negro Education, 29 (Summer, 1960), 227-244.

_____. "Howard University Changes Leadership." Journal of Negro Education, 29 (Fall, 1960), 409-411.

_____. "Why Negroes are Opposed to Segregated Regional Schools." Journal of Negro Education, 18 (Winter, 1948), 1-8.

_____. "The Control and Administration of the Negro College." Journal of Educational Sociology, 19 (April, 1946), 484-495.

_____. "The Negro College: In Retrospect and in Prospect." Journal of Negro Education, 27 (Spring, 1958), 127-131.

_____. "The Problem of Negro Higher Education." Journal of Negro Education, 2 (July, 1933), 257-271.

_____. "The Prospect of Negro Higher Education." Journal of Educational Sociology, 32 (February, 1959), 309-316.

_____. "Rank, Tenure and Retirement of Teachers in Negro Colleges." Journal of Negro Education, 10 (April, 1941), 139-150.

_____. "The War and Negro Higher Education in 1942." Journal of Negro Higher Education, 12 (Winter, 1943), 1-6.

_____. "The University of Maryland vs. Donald Gaines Murry." Journal of Negro Education, 5 (April, 1936), 166-174.

_____. "The Socio-Economic Status of Negro College Students." Journal of Negro Education, 2 (January, 1933), 26-37.

_____. "The Southern Association and Negro College Membership." Journal of Negro Education, 27 (Winter, 1958), 1-3.

_____. "The Southern Association and the Predominantly Negro High School and College." Journal of Negro Education, 31 (Spring, 1962), 105-107.

_____. "Why a Class 'B' Negro College?" Journal of Negro Education, 2 (October, 1933), 427-431.

_____. "The Negro Private Church Related College." Journal of Negro Education, 39 (Summer, 1960), 211-216.

Thompson, Daniel C. "Our Wasted Potential." The Dillard Bulletin, 24 (April, 1960), 4.

_____. "Problems of Faculty Morale." Journal of Negro Education, 29 (Winter, 1960), 37-46.

_____. "Career Patterns of Teachers in Negro Colleges." Social Forces, 36 (March, 1958), 270-276.

Thompson, L. Lemar. "A College Student Looks at the Problem of Teaching Negro History to Negro College Students." Negro History Bulletin, 6 (December, 1942), 62-64.

Thornbrough, Emma L. "Booker T. Washington as Seen by His White Contemporaries." Journal of Negro History, 53 (April, 1968), 161-182.

Thorpe, Earl E. "The Washington-Du Bois Controversy." Quarterly Review of Higher Education Among Negroes, 23 (October, 1955), 157-167.

_____. "Frederick Douglass, W. E. B. Du Bois and Booker T. Washington." Negro History Bulletin, 20 (1956-1957), 39-42.

Tilford, Michael P., and Allen Donald E. "Science and Non-Science Majors in Three Predominantly Black Colleges." Journal of Negro Education, 43 (Winter, 1974), 117-126.

Toffler, A. "West Virginia State College Has Reversed Desegregation." Labor's Daily, August 5, 1955.

Tolten, Herman L. "A Survey of the Academic Status of Black College and University Librarians." Journal of Negro Education, 40 (Fall, 1971), 342-346.

"Tougaloo College." Crisis, 47 (August, 1940), 257.

Townes, Ross E. "Professional Education in Physical Education in Selected Negro Colleges." Journal of Negro Education, 20 (Spring, 1951), 174-180.

Towns, George A. "The Sources of the Traditions of Atlanta University." Phylon, 3 (2nd Quarter, 1942), 117-134.

Trenholm, H. Councill. "The Role of the Negro Teachers College in Post-War Reconstruction." Journal of Negro Education, 11 (July, 1942), 412-422.

Trent, William J., Jr., and Patterson, F. D. "Financial Support of the Private Negro College." Journal of Negro Education, 27 (Summer, 1958), 398-405.

Trent, William J., Jr. "The Problems of Financing Private Negro Colleges." Journal of Negro Education, 18 (Spring, 1949), 114-122.

Trent, W. J., Jr. "An Adventure in Cooperation." Journal of Educational Sociology, 19 (April, 1946), 517-520.

_____. "Relative Adequacy of Sources of Income of the Negro Church-Related Colleges." Journal of Negro Education, 29 (Summer, 1960), 365-367.

_____. "Cooperative Fund Raising in Higher Education." Journal of Negro Education, 24 (Winter, 1955), 6-15.

_____. "The Future Role of the Negro College and Its Financing." Daedalus, 100 (Summer, 1971), 647-659.

_____. "The Fiftieth Anniversary of Livingstone College." A. M. E. Zion Quarterly Review, 42 (July-September, 1932), 3.

_____. "Solvency of the Private Colleges." Journal of Negro Education, 27 (Spring, 1958), 145-150.

_____. "Private Negro Colleges Since the Gaines Decision." Journal of Educational Sociology, 32 (February, 1958), 267-274.

_____. "The United Negro College Fund's Scholarship Program." Journal of Negro Education, 31 (Spring, 1962), 205-209.

Trigg, Frank. "Bennett College." Southern Workman, 55 (February, 1926), 84-85.

Troup, Cornelius V. "Building Construction on Negro College Campuses." Journal of Negro Education, 23 (Winter, 1954), 92-96.

_____. "Some Significant Programs Initiated at Negro

Colleges and Universities During the School-Year, 1948-1949." Journal of Negro Education, 18 (Fall, 1949), 576-582.

Turner, Albert L. "Higher Education in Alabama." Quarterly Review of Higher Education Among Negroes, 5 (October, 1937), 153-159.

Turner, B. A. "Some Problems Affecting Industrial Education in Negro Colleges." Journal of Negro Education, 12 (Winter, 1943), 31-41.

Turner, Darwin T. "The Black University: A Practical Approach." Negro Digest, 17 (March, 1968), 14-20.

Turner, John A. "Dental Health Conditions in Negro Colleges." Journal of Negro Education, 11 (April, 1942), 258-259.

Turner, John G. "Radio at Bennett College." Opportunity, 21 (January, 1943), 8-10, 29.

Turner, Thomas W. "Science Teaching in Negro Colleges." Journal of Negro Education, 15 (Winter, 1946), 36-42.

_____. "Actual Conditions of Catholic Education Among the Colored Laymen." Catholic Educational Association Bulletin, November, 1919, 431-440.

"Tuskegee Institute." Negro History Bulletin, 21 (January, 1958), 80.

"Tuskegee's Traveling Nurses." Sepia, 12 (February, 1963), 33-38.

"Tuskegee Trains for Living and Making a Living." Crisis, 47 (August, 1940), 258-259.

"Tuskegee Inspires Community Business." Crisis, 48 (April, 1941), 129, 140.

"Twenty-Fifth Anniversary of the Presidency of H. Councill Trenholm." Negro History Bulletin, 14 (January, 1951), 80, 91.

"[Twenty-Five] 25 Years to Go; Texas State University for Negroes." Time, 50 (September 22, 1947), 60.

"University Education for Negroes." The Independent, 68 (March 24, 1910), 613-618.

"Upgrading Negro Colleges in the South." School and Society, 97 (October, 1969), 350-351.

Vairo, Philip D. "The Dilemma in Negro Higher Education." Journal of Higher Education, 38 (November, 1967), 448-450.

Valien, Preston. "Improving Programs in Graduate Education for Negroes." Journal of Negro Education, 36 (Summer, 1967), 238-248.

_____. "Desegregation in Higher Education: A Critical Summary." Journal of Negro Education, 27 (Summer, 1958), 373-380.

"Value of Higher Education to the Negroes." The Independent, 52 (May 15, 1900), 238-248.

Van Wright, Aaron, Jr. "Negro Land-Grant Institutions." Improving College and University Teaching, 15 (Autumn, 1967), 254-259.

Vaughn, William P. "Separate and Unequal: The Civil Rights Act of 1875 and Defeat of the School Integration Clause." Southwestern Social Science Quarterly, 48 (September, 1967), 146-154.

Villard, Oswald G. "Higher Education of Negroes." The Nation, 74 (January-June, 1902), 381-382.

Viorst, Milton. "Howard University: Campus and Cause." Harper's Magazine, 223 (November, 1961), 51-52.

"Virginia College Upgrading Held Integration Bar." Chronicle of Higher Education, 5 : 33 (May 24, 1971), 1, 2.

"Virginia State College and the Returning Veterans." Quarterly Review of Higher Education Among Negroes, 14 (January 1946), 9-10.

Voorhees, Lillian W. "Speech in the Negro College." The Talladegan, 57 (May, 1940), 4-6.

_____. "A Program of Speech Education for Talladega College." Journal of Negro Education, 15 (Winter, 1946), 109-116.

Vontress, Clemont E. "Should Your Child Attend a Negro College?" Negro Digest, March, 1968.

Votaw, Dow and Sethi S. Prakash. "Some Paradoxed in the Support of Predominantly Black Colleges." Journal of Higher Education, 41 (December, 1970), 673-694.

Walden, Daniel. "Contemporary Opposition to the Political and Educational Ideas of Booker T. Washington." Journal of Negro History, 45 (April, 1960), 103-115.

Walker, Alexander J. "Vocation Choices of Negro College Students." Journal of Negro Education, 15 (Winter, 1946), 146-152.

Walker, George H., Jr. "Analysis of Junior College

Growth." Junior College Journal, 30 (January, 1960), 264-267.

_____. "An Analysis of Junior College Growth." Junior College Journal, 27 (January, 1957), 256-259.

_____. "Legal Education in Negro Institutions of Higher Education." School and Society, 73 (May 26, 1951), 326-327.

_____. "Analysis of Negro Junior College Growth." Junior College Journal, 22 (November, 1951), 150-152.

_____. "The English Proficiency Test in Fifteen Negro Colleges." Journal of Negro Education, 22 (Winter, 1953), 84-87.

_____. "Master's Theses Under Way in Negro Colleges and Universities, 1959-1960." Negro Educational Review, 11 (April, 1960), 82-95. Ibid., 1960-1961, 12 (July, 1961), 85-95; 1961-1962, 13 (July-October), 127-141.

_____. "Master's Theses Under Way in Selected Colleges and Universities, 1972-1973." Negro Educational Review, 24 (July-October, 1973), 144-156. Ibid., 1973-1974, 25 (April-July, 1974), 146-166; 1974-1975, 26 (April-July, 1975), 72-84.

_____. "Extent and Types of Master's Research in Negro Colleges and Universities, 1950-1960." Negro Educational Review, 10 (July, 1959), 189-193.

_____. "Remedial Reading Programs in Negro Colleges and Universities." Journal of Negro Education, 15 (Winter, 1946),

_____. "Negro Educators Consider Problems of Reading on the College Level--With Statements of Future Institutional Plans." Journal of Negro Education, 16 (Spring, 1947), 233-235.

_____. "Some Internal Barriers Facing the Negro Researcher." Journal of Educational Research, 49 (March, 1956), 546-550.

_____, and Hazel, David W. "Integration in the Junior College." Journal of Negro Education, 29 (Spring, 1960), 204-206.

Wallace, J. W. "The Reference Paper and In-Class Writing." College English, 19 (January, 1958), 160-161.

Wallace, William J. L. "Some Outstanding Teachers of Chemistry in Negro Colleges and Universities." Journal of Chemical Education, 22 (October, 1945), 503-504.

_____. "Chemistry in Negro Colleges." West Virginia State College Bulletin, Series No. 2, April, 1940.

Walls, W. J. "J. C. Price a Social Thinker and Prophet." A. M. E. Zion Quarterly Review, 47 : 2 (April, 1938), 39-47.

Walsh, J. D. "Educational Work of the M. E. Church in the South." Methodist Quarterly Review, 46 (1886), 329.

Ware, Edward T. "Higher Education of Negroes in the United States." Annals of the American Academy of Political Science, 49 (September, 1915), 209-218.

Ware, Gilbert, and Determan, Dean W. "The Federal Dollar, The Negro College, and the Negro Student." Journal of Negro Education, 35 (Fall, 1966), 459-468.

Warnot, Winifred I. "The Role of White Faculty on the Black College Campus." Journal of Negro Education, 45 (Summer, 1976), 334-338.

Washington, Booker T. "Tuskegee: A Retrospect and Prospect." North American Review, 182 (April, 1906), 513-523.

_____. "Atlanta Speech." Southern Workman, 52 (May, 1922), 209.

Washington, Booker T. "The Successful Training of the Negro." World's Work, 6 (July, 1903), 3731-3751.

_____. "Some Results of the Armstrong Idea." Southern Workman, 38 (March, 1909).

_____. "Observations on Negro Colleges." World's Work, 21 (April, 1911), 1230-1238.

Washington, Booker T. "A Negro College Town." (The Uplifting Influence of Fifty Year's Growth of Wilberforce, O.) World's Work, 14 (September, 1907), 9361-9367.

_____. "University Education for Negroes." The Independent, 68 (March 24, 1910), 613-618.

_____. "Industrial Education, Public Schools and the Negroes." Annals of the American Academy of Political and Social Science, 49 (September, 1913), 219-233.

Washington, Margaret J. "Dorothy Hall." Southern Workman, 54 (May, 1925), 200-206.

Wasserman, Miriam. "The Loud, Proud, Black Kids." Progressive, 32 (April, 1968), 35-38.

Watson, H. R. "Arkansas' New College." Crisis, 39 (September, 1932), 297-298, 320.

Watson, J. B. "A Tired College President." Crisis, 39 (November, 1932), 344, 364.

_____. "Louisiana Negroes are Advancing." Southern Workman, 57 (May, 1928), 224-230.

_____. "The Negro Graduate School." Journal of Negro Education, 7 (October, 1938), 533-534.

Wayland, H. L. "Higher Education of Negroes." American Journal of Social Science, 34 : 68.

Weatherford, Allen Ericson. "The Status of Graduate Offering in Health Education, Physical Education, and Recreation in Negro Colleges and Universities." Journal of Negro Education, 21 (Spring, 1952), 220-223.

_____. "Professional Health, Physical Education, and Recreation in Negro Colleges, 1948-1949." Journal of Negro Education, 22 (Fall, 1953), 527-533.

Weaver, George L. "The New Challenge to Negro Colleges." Negro Digest, 11 (July, 1962), 33-37.

Weaver, Robert. "The Negro Private and Church Related College: A Critical Summary." Journal of Negro Education, 29 (Summer, 1960), 394-400.

_____. "The Private Negro Colleges and Universities--An Appraisal." Journal of Negro Education, 29 (Spring, 1960), 113-120.

"W. E. B. Du Bois Dies in Ghana." Christian Century, 80 (September 11, 1963), 1092.

Weisberger, Bernard A. "The Dark and Bloody Ground of Reconstruction Historiography." Journal of Southern History, 25 (November, 1959), 427-447.

Welsh, Constance Davis. "Leisure-Time Activities of Langston University Faculty Members." Research Quarterly, 24 (October, 1953), 368-369.

Wesley, Charles H. "The Outlook for the Graduate and Professional Education of Negroes." Journal of Negro Education, 11 (July, 1942), 423-434.

_____. "Graduate Education for Negroes in Southern Universities." Harvard Educational Review, 10 (January, 1940), 82-94.

West, Earle H. "Peabody Education Fund and Negro Education, 1867-1880." History of Education Quarterly, 6 (Summer, 1966), 3-21.

White, Amos J. "Bishop Richard Robert Wright, Acting President of Wilberforce University." Wilberforce University Quarterly, 3 (April, 1942), 40-43.

White, Emma L. "Report of Proposed Grading System at Meharry Medical College, 1939-1940." Journal of National Medical Association, 23 (January, 1941), 42-45.

White, Forrest P. "Tuition Grants: Strange Fruit of Southern School Integration." South Atlantic Quarterly, 60 (Spring, 1961), 226-229.

White, Lucien H. "Negro Music-A Review." Crisis, 45 (July, 1938), 217-219.

"White, Negro Undergraduates at Colleges Enrolling 500 or More as Compiled From Reports to U. S. Office for Civil Rights." Chronicle of Higher Education, 2 : 16 (April 22, 1968), 3.

Whitehead, Matthew J. "Are You Afraid of Student Ratings." Journal of Teacher Education, 4 (June, 1953), 135-136.

_____. "Significant Achievements of Negroes in Education, 1907-1947." Quarterly Review of Higher Education Among Negroes, 16 (January, 1948), 1-6.

_____. "Origin and Establishment of the Negro College Deanship." Journal of Negro Education, 14 (Winter, 1945), 167-173.

_____. "Impact of the War Upon Negro Teachers Colleges." School and Society, 59 (May 6, 1944), 334-335.

"Whites Said to Rule Negro Colleges' Boards." Chronicle of Higher Education, 4 : 30 (May 4, 1970), 2.

Whiting, Helen A. "The Teaching Practice Program of the Atlanta Negro Colleges." Journal of Negro Education, 15 (Summer, 1946), 246-251.

Whiting, Joseph L. "Tuskegee Trade Graduates." Southern Workman, 52 (December, 1923), 597.

Whiting, Joseph L. "Tuskegee Ideals in Industrial Education." Opportunity, 4 (February, 1926), 58-60.

"Who's Who Among Atlanta University Graduates and Former Students." Phylon, 3 (2nd Quarter, 1942), 163-169.

Wickersham, J. P. "Education as an Element in Reconstruction After the Rebellion." American Journal of Education, (1886), 283.

Wickey, Gould, and Eckhart, Ruth A. "The National Survey of Courses in Bible and Religion." Christian Education, 20 (October, 1936), 9-45.

Wiggins, Sam P. "Dilemmas in Desegregation in Higher

Education." Journal of Negro Education, 35 (Fall, 1966), 430-438.

"Wilberforce University as Seen by the North Central Association in 1940." Wilberforce University Quarterly, 1 (July, 1940), 32-39.

"Wilberforce University Makes Progress." Crisis, 47 (August, 1940), 260-267.

"Wiley College, 1873-1940." Crisis, 47 (August, 1940), 261.

Wilkerson, Doxey Alphonso. "The Vocational Education, Guidance, and Placement of Negroes in the United States." Journal of Negro Education, 8 (July, 1939), 462-488.

_____. "The Curriculum of the Negro [Liberal] Arts College and the Demands of a Bi-Racial Society." Quarterly Review of Higher Education Among Negroes, 2 (April, 1934), 108-115.

Wilkerson, D. A. "The Role of the Negro College on the Home Front." Negro College Quarterly, 1 (March, 1943), 15-20.

Wilkerson, Doxey Alphonso. "Drop in Enrollment at Negro Land-Grant Colleges." School and Society, 55 (April 11, 1942), 412.

_____. "Social Relation of Students at Virginia State College." Southern Workman, 63 (December, 1934), 357-366.

_____. "A Determination of the Peculiar Problems of the Negro in American Society." Journal of Negro Education, 5 (July, 1936), 324-350.

_____. "American Caste and the Social Studies Curriculum." Quarterly Review of Higher Education Among Negroes, 5 (April, 1937), 67-74.

Wilkins, Ernest H. "The Contribution of the Liberal Arts College to the War Program." Journal of Negro Education, 11 (July, 1942), 257-261.

Wilkins, Theresa B. "Late Afternoon and Evening Classes in Colleges for Negroes." Journal of Negro Education, 11 (October, 1942), 507-516.

Williams, Charles H. "Twenty Years' Work of the C. I. A. A." The Bulletin of the Colored Intercollegiate Athletic Association, 1932, 1-22. Ibid., Southern Workman, 61 (February, 1932), 65-76.

Williams, Elson K. "Degrees Earned by Social Science Teachers in Negro Schools." Journal of Negro Education, 20 (Winter, 1951), 119-121.

Williams, F. A. "A War-Time Negro Land-Grant College." Negro College Quarterly, 1 (March, 1943), 26-31.

Williams, Henry S. "The Development of the Negro Public School System in Missouri." Journal of Negro History, 5 (April, 1920), 137-165.

Williams, Richard A. "The Language Laboratory." Central State College Research Journal, 1 (July, 1962), 23-31.

Williams, Roger Kenton. "A Study of Personnel Programs in Eleven Accredited Negro Colleges." Journal of Negro Education, 10 (April, 1941), 168-177.

Williams, Sidney D. "How the Colleges May Use the Report of Dr. Ina C. Brown Dealing With the Socio-Economic Status of the Negroes." Quarterly Review of Higher Education Among Negroes, 10 (July, 1942), 169-172.

Williams, William Taylor Burwell. "The Yankee School Ma'am in Negro Education." Southern Workman, 44 (Fall, 1915), 73.

_____. "Higher Education for Negroes." Tuskegee Messenger, 8 (August, 1932), 6-7.

_____. "Is Tuskegee Just Another College?" Journal of Educational Sociology, 7 (November, 1933), 170-174.

Williamson, Anne O'H. "Effective Teaching at the College Level." Association of American Colleges Bulletin, 33 (December, 1947), 645-651.

_____. "What the Negro Colleges Are Doing." Negro College Quarterly, 2 (December, 1944), 158-164.

Williamson, Juanita. "A Look at Black English." Crisis, 78 (August, 1971), 169-173, 185.

_____. "What Can We Do About It?--The Contribution of Linguistics to the Teaching of English." College Language Association Journal, 1 (November, 1957), 23-27.

Willie, Charles V. "Researchers to Work! Education of Negroes in Predominantly White Colleges." Integrated Education, 7 (September, 1969), 32-38.

Willie, Charles V., and Mac Leish, Marlene Y. "Priorities of Black College Presidents." Educational Record, 57 (Spring, 1976), 92-100.

Wilson, G. D. "Plan of Endowment--Administration for Negro Colleges." School and Society, 53 (January 11, 1941), 57-58.

Wilson, H. A. "Black Colleges Have a Chance if They

Break With Tradition." College and University Business, 52 (June, 1972), 33-36.

Wilson, Ruth D. "Negro Colleges of Liberal Arts." American Scholar, 19 (October, 1950), 461-470.

_____. "Phi Beta Kappa at Howard University." Crisis, 60 (August-September, 1953), 393-395.

Wilson, W. W. "The Methodist Episcopal Church in Her Relations to the Negro in the South." Methodist Review, 75 (September-October, 1941), 713-723.

Winston, Michael R. "Through the Back Door: Academic Racism and the Negro Scholar in Historical Perspective." Daedalus, 100 : 3 (Summer, 1971), 678-719.

Wish, Harvey. "Negro Education and the Progressive Movement." Journal of Negro History, 49 (July, 1964), 184-200.

Withers, John D. "The Male Student at Barber-Scotia College." Negro Educational Review, 9 (January, 1958).

Woodruff, Bertram. "Curriculum Adjustments for the Improvement of English in Negro Colleges." Quarterly Review of Higher Education Among Negroes, 1 (July, 1933), 1-7.

_____. "A Critical Study of the Offerings in Language and Literature for Majors and Minors in Private Negro Colleges." Quarterly Review of Higher Education Among Negroes, 7 (July, 1939), 226-230.

_____. "Socio-Economic Status of Negro College Students." Journal of Negro Education, 2 (January, 1933), 16.

Woodruff, Hale. "Presidents of Atlanta University." Phylon, 3 (2nd Quarter, 1942), 123, 127, 131, 137, 141, 145.

Woods, L. L. "The Negro College and Wartime Training Program." School and Society, 57 (January 2, 1943), 19-20.

Woods, L. L. "The Negro in Chemistry." School and Society, 52 (July 6, 1940), 11-12.

Woodson, Carter G. "Anniversary Celebrated." Negro History Bulletin, 4 (1940-1941), 198-215.

_____. "The Anniversary Celebration (Address Delivered on the Opening Day of the West Virginia State College Semi-Centennial Celebration, March 17, 1941)." West Virginia State College Bulletin, 3 (August-November, 1941), 7-8, 21-24.

Woodson, Grace I. "Community Related Programs at West Virginia State College." Journal of Negro Education, 16 (Fall, 1947), 594-596.

Woodson, Harold W. "A Survey of Chemistry Curricula in Negro Colleges." Journal of Negro Education, 8 (October, 1939), 644-648.

_____. "The Present Status of Physics in Negro Colleges." American Journal of Physics, 9 (June, 1941), 180-183.

Woodward, Isaiah H. "Methods of Teaching Freshmen History at Morgan." Social Studies, 48 (December, 1957), 273-275.

Woolfolk, E. O., and Smith, L. S. "Chemical Education in Negro Colleges." Negro History Bulletin, 30 (February, 1967), 7-11.

Work, Monroe N. "Tuskegee Institute More Than an Educational Institution." Journal of Educational Sociology, 7 (November, 1933), 197-205.

"Work of the Jeanes Fund in 1922." School and Society, 16 (October 21, 1922), 467.

Worthington, Marguerite, and Carter, William T. "The Results of Placement Tests in French for Virginia State College Freshmen." Virginia State College Gazette, 47 (November, 1941), 87-92.

Wright, J. Skelly. "Hobson vs. Hansen." Congressional Record, June 21, 1967. H7655-H7697.

Wright, Marion Thompson. "Negro Higher and Professional Education in Delaware." Journal of Negro Education, 17 (Summer, 1948), 265-271.

Wright, Patricia S., and Huyck, Earl E. "Faculty in White and Negro Colleges." Health, Education and Welfare Indicators, February, 1965.

Wright, R. R., Jr. "Wilberforce in South Africa." Opportunity, 15 (October, 1937), 306-310.

Wright, Stephen J. et al. "The American Negro College." Four Responses and a Reply. Harvard Educational Review, 37 (Summer, 1967), 451-459.

Wright, Stephen J. "The Negro College in America." Harvard Educational Review, 30 (Summer, 1960), 280-297.

_____. "The Dilemma of Negro Colleges; Transition and Brain." Journal of Education, 153 (December, 1970), 49.

_____. "The Promise of Equality." Saturday Review, 51 (July 20, 1968), 45-46.

_____. "The Development of the Hampton-Tuskegee Pattern of Higher Education." Phylon, 10 (4th Quarter, 1949), 334-342.

_____. "Problems, Developments and Issues Incident to Equality of Opportunity in the Higher Education of Negroes: A Critical Summary of the 1966 Yearbook." Journal of Negro Education, 35 (Fall, 1966), 506-513.

_____. "Some Critical Problems Faced by the Negro Church-Related College." Journal of Negro Education, 29 (Summer, 1960), 399-444.

_____. "The Future of the Negro Private College: Philosophy and Program." Journal of Negro Education, 27 (Summer, 1958), 406-413.

Yago, John W. "West Virginia State College." Charleston Gazette, May 12, 1963.

_____. "West Virginia State Integration Story." Charleston Gazette, May 17, 1964.

_____. "White 'Take Over' Irks W. Va., Students." Chronicle of Higher Education, 2 : 4 (October 26, 1967), 8.

_____. "Negro Colleges Must be Kept, South is Told." Chronicle of Higher Education, 2 : 1 (September 13, 1967), 1, 9.

Yerby, Frank G. "Problems Confronting the Little Theater in Negro Colleges." Southern University Bulletin, 27 (March, 1941), 96-103.

_____. "A Brief Historical Sketch of the Little Theater in the Negro College." Quarterly Journal of Florida Agricultural and Mechanical College, 9 (April, 1940), 27-32.

Yette, Samuel F. "The Tuskegee Story." Negro Digest, 11 (July, 1962), 25-32.

Young, Alfred. "The Educational Philosophy of Booker T. Washington A Perspective for Black Liberation." Phylon, 37 (3rd Quarter, Fall, 1976), 224-235.

Young, Harding B. "The College Administrator's Dilemma: Problems Involved in Balancing Anticipated Income and Expenses." Negro Educational Review, 10 (April, 1959), 61-71.

Young, Sadye Pearl. "Looking at Home Economics for Negroes in Higher Education." Negro Educational Review, 12 (July, 1961), 96-107.

Zinn, Howard. "A New Direction for Negro Colleges." Harper's, May, 1966.

Zook, George F. "The Role of Higher Education in Post-War Reconstruction." Journal of Negro Education, 11 (July, 1942), 274-278.

MASTERS' THESES 4

1922–1974

Abbott, Jessie Ellen. "Teacher Preparation for Physical Education in Twelve Representative Accredited Negro Colleges With Special Reference to Women: A Comparative Survey." University of Wisconsin, 1942.

Ackiss, Thelma Davis. "The Negro and the Supreme Court to 1900." Howard University, 1936.

Adair, Margaret Smith. "An Index to the _Spelman Messenger_ for the Period March, 1885, through June, 1891." Atlanta University, 1963.

Adams, Marguerite Minor. "The Participation of Negroes in Federal Education Grants in the State of North Carolina." Howard University, 1938.

Aiken, Margaret Harding. "A Study of the Counseling Techniques Used in Personnel Services to Students at Clark College, Atlanta, Georgia, 1946 to 1951." Atlanta University, 1952.

Albey, Mary Louise. "A Study of What Fisk Students Read." Fisk University, 1939.

Alexander, Herald Wilburn. "English Studies in Colleges for Negroes in Georgia." The State University of Iowa, 1948.

Alexander, Mae T. "Recent Trends in the Home Economics College Curriculum." Howard University, 1945.

Allen, La Mar. "A Proposed Program of Intramurals for Arkansas State Agricultural, Mechanical and Normal College." University of Southern California, Los Angeles, 1951.

Allen, Leroy B. "A Study of the Attitudes Towards Certain Principles of Religion as Shown by 200 Students of Howard University." Atlanta University, 1947.

Allgood, William I. "A Study of the Relationship Between Scores Made by Selected University Students on a Racial Attitude Scale and on a Neurotic Tendencies Scale." Emory University, 1947.

Anderson, Frederick T. "A Survey of College Reading Improvement Programs With Findings Related to Specific Installations in the United Negro College Fund Program." Atlanta University, 1965.

Anderson, Leroy Frederick. "The Analysis of Differences in Performance Over a Two Year Period on ACE of Negro College Students, 'North and South'." Fisk University, 1948.

Armstrong, James Lionel. "An Analysis of the Influences That Were Responsible for the Development of Vocational Agricultural Programs for Negroes in Georgia." Howard University, 1938.

Arnold, Clarence Edward. "Guidance Received by Virginia State College Students While in High School." Virginia State College, 1950.

Bailey, J. W. "A Study Pertaining to the Organization and Administration of Intercollegiate Athletics in Colleges and Universities for Negroes." Springfield College, 1942.

Baily, Flavius J. "The Policies of the American Missionary Association in Relation to Negro Education." Howard University, 1933.

Baker, Orestes Jeremiah. "A Study of Senior College Library Facilities for Negroes in Texas." Columbia University, 1937.

Ballard, Robert Melvyn. "A Job History of the Atlanta University School of Library Science Graduates, 1948-1959." Atlanta University, 1961.

Banning, Magnolia Lowe. "The Contribution of the Julius Rosenwald Fund to Negro Education and Better Race Relations." University of Arizona, 1947.

Barksdale, Florence A. "Present Status of Graduates of Atlanta Negro Colleges, 1937-1938, Who Received National Youth Administration Assistance During These Two Years." Atlanta University, 1941.

Bashful, Emmett W. "W. E. B. Du Bois and Booker T. Washington - A Study of Techniques in Race Relations." University of Illinois, 1949.

Batey, M. Grant. "John Chavis: His Contributions to Education in North Carolina." North Carolina College [Durham, N.C.], 1954.

Bayton, James Arthur. "Personality Traits of Negro College Students." Howard University, 1936.

Beasley, Stella Tarner. "An Item Analysis of American Literature: Test Scores for Five Selected Years of the Academic Meet at Alabama State Teachers College." Alabama [Montgomery] State Teachers College, 1944.

Bell, Jereline Ryus. "A Limited Study of the Contributions of the American Missionary Association to Negro Education in Alabama." The State College for Negroes at Montgomery, Alabama, 1949.

Bennett, Finis Hercules. "Some Religious Beliefs and Practices Among College Students." Atlanta University, 1948.

Blair, Dorothy Reeves. "A Study of the Vocational Interests of Women Students at Clark College, 1942-1943, in Relation to the Position Available to Negro Women in the War Program." Atlanta University, 1943.

Blackman, Myrtle. "An Analytical Study of the 1946-1947 Testing Program in the Survey of Literature Course at Tennessee A. & I. State College." Tennessee Agricultural and Industrial State College, 1948.

Bolton, Ruth. "A Study of Home Economics in Fourteen Land Grant Colleges of Southern States." George Peabody College for Teachers, 1931.

Bond, James M. "Negro Education in Kentucky." University of Cincinnati, 1930.

Bond, Julia Washington. "A Bibliography of Works on Africa in the Negro Collection of the Trevor Arnett Library of Atlanta University, Published 1900-1925." Atlanta University, 1964.

Boone, Elwood Bernard. "Present Practices in the Supervision of Directed Teaching in Physical Education in Negro Institutions of Higher Learning." University of Michigan, 1937.

Boone, F. Theressa. "Higher Education for the Negro." University of Southern California, Los Angeles, 1925.

Bowen, Margaret Davis. "Educational Work of a National Professional Sorority for Negro College Women." University of Cincinnati, 1935.

Boyce, Joseph Anthony. "A Survey of Periodical Holding in the Atlanta University Center in the Field of Religion." Atlanta University, 1964.

Bozeman, Alva L. "The Scholastic Attainment of Home Economics Students at Virginia State College." Virgina State College, 1944.

Bradley, Mattie Lena. "An Analysis of the Sociology Graduates of Atlanta University, Atlanta, Georgia, for the Years 1933 to 1961." Atlanta University, 1963.

Branford, Pat Audrey. "Training and Opportunities for Negro Women in the Field of Physical Education." University of Iowa, 1939.

Brannon, Rena Arvette. "A Study of Religious Beliefs, Attitudes and Practices Among College Students." Howard University, 1941.

Brazil, Doris J. "Curriculum Development in Home Economic at Tuskegee Institute Since 1899." Tuskegee Institute, 1949.

Brant, Gwendolyn Eloise. "Recent Trends in Racial Attitudes of Negro College Students." University of Michigan, 1938.

Brent, Rose Shaw. "An Appraisal of the Integrated Arts Program of the State Teachers College Laboratory Schools at Montgomery, Alabama." The State Teachers College, 1947. [Montgomery, Alabama]

Britton Lawrence M. "A Survey of Liesure Time Activities of the Male Students of Prairie View Agricultural and Mechanical College with Suggestions for Improvement." Prairie A. & M. College, 1950.

Brock, Charles V. "A Study of Vocabulary Achievement in Three Selected Groups of College Freshmen." Ohio University, 1949.

Brooks, Henry Lindsay. "An Analysis of the Academic Achievement of the Lowest Quartile of the Freshmen Classes at Morehouse College for the Years 1945 and 1946 on the Basis of the Iowa Silent Reading Test." Atlanta University, 1950.

Brown, A. S. "Opportunities in Higher Education in North Carolina for Negro Students." North Carolina College [Durham, N.C.], 1954.

Brown, Charles C. "The History of Negro Education in Tennessee." Washington University, 1929.

Brown, Ethel Randolph. "A Study of the Faculties of the Negro Land-Grant Colleges." Virginia State College, 1941.

Brown, Genevieve Swann. "An Analytical and Statistical Study of Higher Education for Negroes During the Period 1877-1900." Howard University,

Brown, Georgia C. "Student Problems Encountered Daily by Deans of Women in Sixteen Colleges for Negroes." University of Michigan, 1948.

Brown, Mayme Gibson. "The Effect of Intelligence Upon the Relationship Between Certain High School Factors and the Acheivement of College Freshmen." Howard University, 1939.

Brown, Otyce Clementine. "Extra-Curricular Duties of Negro Home Economics High School Teachers With Reference to their Teacher-Training Courses." Howard University, 1942.

Brown, Thelma Barrett. "Ten Great Negro Educators." Atlanta University, 1936.

Brumfield, Louise Crouch. "A Study of the Financial Aid Received by Selected Negro Church-Related High Schools and Colleges in Georgia, 1945-50." Atlanta University, 1951.

Brummell, Mildred Lee. "The Best Friend: A Study of Friendship Patterns of College Students." Atlanta University, 1949.

Buchanan, Singer A. "The Development of the Educational Theater in Negro Colleges and Universities from 1925 to 1949." Tennessee A. & I. State College, 1949.

Bullock, Merles L. A. "A Personality Study of Student Leaders at Prairie View College." University of Michigan, 1939.

Burghardt, William F. "Safety in the Teacher Education College." New York University, 1950.

Burnside, Mary Haynes. "Relationship Among High School and College Performances of Students Who Major in Mathematics, Biology and Chemistry." Atlanta University, 1963.

Burr, J. H., Jr. "A Survey of Physical Education in Negro Colleges and Universities." International YMCA College, 1932.

Burrell, Fannie Mae. "A Study of the Publications of a Selected Group of College and University Libraries." Atlanta University, 1950.

Burton, Mary Lillian. "A Survey of Guidance Problems in Four-Year Negro Colleges and Universities." University of Southern California, Los Angeles, 1952.

Butcher, Beatrice Bowen. "The Evolution of Negro Women's Schools in the United States." Howard University, 1936.

Butcher, Charles P. "Charles W. Cable: Early Realist of Negro Life." Howard University, 1947.

Butler, Roxie Beatrice. "The Status of Home Economics Teacher-Education in Twenty-Four Negro Colleges." Ohio State University, 1946.

Caldwell, Joe Louis. "A Study of the Development of William Edward Burghardt Du Bois Pan-African Ideas." Atlanta University, 1969.

Calhoun, Anne E. "Teacher Training Programs for Negroes in Maryland." Howard University, 1948.

Callendar, Theresa Maria. "An Evaluation of the Supervised Student Practice Program of Teachers College, Fayetteville, North Carolina." Virginia State College, 1950.

Calloway, Ina E. "An Annotated Bibliography of Books in the Trevor Arnett Library Negro Collection Related to the Civil War." Atlanta University, 1963.

Campbell, Astrea S. "Attitude of 1082 College Students Toward the Administration of Justice." Howard University, 1939.

Campbelle, Margaret Rose. "A Bibliography of Senior Projects at Tennessee Agricultural and Industrial State College, 1938-1945, With Special Annotated References in the Division of Education." Tennessee A. & I. State College, 1949.

Campbelle, Roy B. Jr. "An Appraisal of the Business Education Division of Tennessee State College." Tennessee Agricultural and Industrial State College, 1945.

Carey, Ora L. Randall. "Improving the English Usage of the Students of Jarvis Christian College, 1947-1948." Prairie View A. & M. College, 1948.

Carson, Suzanne. "J. L. M. Curry and the Peabody Fund." The John Hopkins University, 1948.

Carter, William Henry. "Two Groups of College Students" Their Relationship to Socio-Economic Status, Scholarship and Personality Adjustment." Fisk University, 1956.

Carver, Savannah Joyce. "A Study of the Relative Effectiveness of Two Methods of Teaching General Biology to a College Class at Clark College, Atlanta, Georgia." Atlanta University, 1951.

Cash, Rubye Singleton. "A Follow-Up Study of the Graduates of Spelman College for the Years 1947-1958." Atlanta University, 1960.

Caswell, Arlie Ann Bernice. "A Comparative Study of Ford Scholars and Comparisons Entering A Southern College 1951-1954 Inclusive." Fisk University, 1961.

Chavis, J. D., Jr. "A History of the Preparation and Professional Training of Negro Secondary School Teachers in Tennessee." Fisk University, 1933.

Christter, Ethel Maude. "The Atlanta University Participation of Negroes In the Government of Georgia, 1867-1870." Atlanta University, 1932.

Church, Zelmera. "The Participation of Negro Land-Grant Colleges and Universities in Federal Emergency and Regular Educational Funds." Howard University, 1939.

Churchwell, Charles Darrett. "An Evaluation of the Library of Alabama State College for Negroes, 1952-1953." Atlanta University, 1953.

Clark, E. E. "A Study of Certain Attitudes of Negro College Students." University of Iowa, 1935.

Clark, Kenneth Bancroft. "The Attitude of Negro College Students Toward Their Parents." Howard University, 1936.

Clark, Laron Jefferson, Jr. "A Study of the Independent Reading Interest and Habits of the Students at Clark College." Atlanta University, 1965.

Clark, Velma Green. "Performance on Tests of General Ability and Achievement in Predominantly Negro Church-Related Liberal Arts Colleges." Fisk University, 1961.

Clater, Marie. "An Analysis and Appraisal of the Aims of Negro Teacher-Colleges in Texas in Relation to Their Curriculum Offerings." Prairie View State College, 1941.

Clement, Rufus. "The Educational Work of the African Methodist Episcopal Zion Church, 1820-1920." Northwestern University, 1922.

Clemons, Veotis Evelyn. "The Relationship of Reading Achievement to Academic Status of Select Group of College Freshmen." Atlanta University, 1962.

Coan, Josephus Roosevelt. "Daniel Alexander Payne: Christian Educator." Yale University, 1934.

Cole, William H., Jr. "The Effect, if Any, of Commercial High School Courses Upon the Success of North Carolina College Graduates in the Commercial Department." North Carolina College [Durham, N.C.], 1954.

Coleman, Clarence D. "A Study of Jobs Held by One-Hundred Graduates of Atlanta School of Social Work From 1942-1946." Atlanta University, 1947.

Coleman, Jamye Harris. "Speech Training in Negro Colleges." Fisk University, 1939.

Coleman, Zelia Simington. "Needs and Interests of Students in Home Management at Bishop College." Kansas State College, 1944.

Collins, E. Lillian. "A Study of Professional Program for Women in Health and Physical Education in Negro Teacher-Training Colleges and Universities." Boston University, 1950.

Collins, Leslie Morgan. "W. E. B. Du Bois' View on Education." Fisk University, 1937.

Colston, James Allen. "A Comparison of the Gross Scores of One Hundred College Freshmen, Fifty Girls and Fifty Boys, on the Thurstone Psychological Examination With Their Time and Error Scores on a Motor Learning Test." Atlanta University, 1933.

_____. "State Financial Support of Higher Education in Georgia From 1932 to 1949 With Specific Reference to Higher Education for the Negro." New York University, 1950.

Conley, Binford Harrison. "A Study of the Adequacy of the Resources of Trevor Arnett Library to Support the Instruction in English in the Atlanta University Center, Atlanta, Georgia." Atlanta University, 1960.

Conyers, James E. "Musical Tastes and Interests of College Students." Atlanta University, 1956.

Cook, Geraldine H. "A Diagnostic Analysis of the Performance of 80 College Freshmen in the Fundamentals of Arithmetic." Atlanta University, 1947.

Cooper, Nina Georgette. "The Relationship Between Adjustment and Attitudes of College Freshmen." Fisk University, 1960.

Cotton, June Rosella. "Historical Development of United Presbyterian Schools for Southern Negroes." University of Cincinnati, 1937.

Cowan, Frank, Jr. "A Study of the Impact of Participation in Civil Rights Demonstrations on Negro College Students of the Atlanta University Center." Atlanta University, 1966.

Craft, Guy Calvin. "An Evaluation of the Florida Normal and Industrial Memorial College Library." Atlanta University, 1961.

Crawford, Claudine. "A Suggested Course of Study in Clothing for College Students - Based Upon the Clothing Problem of a Selected Group of Howard University Women Students." Howard University, 1948.

Creditt, Adelaid Louise. "An Exploratory Study of Freshman Over-and-Under Achievement." Fisk University, 1951.

Crooks, Clinton D. "A Study of the Physical Defects Found Among Students at State College for Colored Students, Dover, Delaware: To Study Physical Defects; to Compare Defects." University of Michigan, 1941.

Crutchfield, M. Inez. "An Analytical Study of the Attitudes of the Undergraduate Students at Tennessee A. & I. State

College Toward Sex Education." Tennessee A. & I. State College, 1949.

Cummings, Mildred Moss. "A Comparison of the Relationships Among Reading Abilities and Mathematical Aptitude Manifested by College Freshmen." Atlanta University, 1963.

Dailey, Mozelle E. "A Study of the Success of Booker T. Washington High School Students Who Entered Spelman College During the Years 1936-1941." Atlanta University, 1947.

Darden, Rose Etta. "The Occupational Status of Prairie View Sociology Major and Minor Graduates 1929-1949." Prairie A. & M. College, 1950.

Davenport, P. Eugene. "Improvement of Faculty Personnel and Training in Negro Colleges." University of Minnesota, 1933.

Davis, Alma Lucille. "An Analysis of the Persuasive Techniques Employed by Booker T. Washington in Five Occasional Addresses." The State University of Iowa, 1948.

Davis, Betty Faye McDowell. "A Study of the Treatment of Libraries in a Selected Group of College Catalogs." Atlanta University, 1964.

Davis, George W. "A Study of the Graduates of the Division of Trade and Industries of Hampton Institute From 1920 Through 1939: Their Occupations, Community Interests, and Their Recommendations for the Division." Pennsylvania State College, 1945.

Davis, Gwendolyn Lucille. "An Investigation of Student Attitudes Toward the School of Education Which Might be Related to Withdrawals From Atlanta University." Atlanta University, 1962.

Davis, Sarah E. "Elementary Student Teaching Practices in Louisiana." University of Cincinnati, 1938.

Davis, Thomas Edward. "A Study of Fisk Freshmen, 1928-1930." Fisk University, 1932.

Davis, Willie Cowan. "Current Practices in the Teaching of Remedial Freshmen Composition." Atlanta University, 1954.

Day, Marie Dansby. "An Index to the Spelman Messenger, November, 1891, Through June, 1898." Atlanta University, 1963.

Dean, Julia K. "A Study of the Analysis of the Errors Made by the Prairie View Freshmen for the Year 1944-1945." Prairie State College, 1945.

Dease, Ruth Roseman. "A Study of the Level of Social

Maturity of the Children Attending Jackson College Nursery-Kindergarten." Atlanta University, 1952.

Debes, Robert Randolph. "A Sociological Study of Paul Quinn College." Baylor University, 1949.

Demons, Leona Marie. "Graduates of Spelman, Clark and Morris Brown Colleges Who Have Earned Doctoral Degrees." Atlanta University, 1965.

Dixon, Jessie Gaither. "A Dietary Study of 200 Undergraduate Men of Howard University." Howard University, 1951.

Doddy, Hurley Herman. "Socio-Economic Status and Performance on the A. C. E. of Freshmen Male Students, Veterans and Non-Veterans, North and South." Fisk University, 1948.

Douyon, Chavannes. "Vocational Interest Patterns of Medical College Students." Fisk University, 1955.

Dozier, Ruth Edith. "A Plan for Teaching Arts and Crafts Through Home Economics Courses in a Small Liberal Arts College for Negroes." State University of Iowa, 1940.

Drake, Mary Mean. "W. E. Burghardt Du Bois as a Man of Letters." Fisk University, 1934.

Drewry, Bessie Boyd. "A Study of the Ability of Two Groups of Freshmen Students at Morehouse College to Use the Trevor Arnett Library." Atlanta University, 1953.

Duncan, Annie Elizabeth. "A Study to Determine the Stage of Development at Which 53 Pupils of the 6th, 7th, and 8th Grades in 1938 and the 8th, 9th, and 10th Grades in 1940, of the Atlanta University Laboratory Schools, Atlanta, Georgia, Show Indications of Acceleration or Retardation in Scholastic Achievement." Atlanta University, 1941.

Durvan, K. I. G. "Status of Guidance in the Thirteen Negro Colleges of Texas With a Proposed Program of Guidance for St. Phillip's Junior College." University of Colorado (Boulder), 1940.

Earl, Charlotte Alma. "Racial Attitudes of One Hundred Negro College Students." Atlanta University, 1938.

Ebanks, Jessie Bentley. "A Study of Personal Values Manifested by Ninety Graduate Students in Varying Fields of Specialization." Atlanta University, 1961.

Eberhardt, Dorthy Nell. "A Study of Two Anthropometric Measures of the Children of the Spelman College Nursery School, Atlanta, Georgia." Atlanta University, 1942.

Echols, James Robert. "An Analysis of Higher Education for Negroes in the Commonwealth of Virginia." University of Virginia, 1948.

Edmonds, Helen Gray. "A Movement in Negro Education for Fifty Years Under the Influence of the Episcopal Church: St. Paul School." Ohio State University, 1938.

Edmonds, William Sylvestre. "A Comparative Study of the Vocational Offerings of the Southern Land-Grant Colleges." Virginia State College, 1942.

Edwards, Earnest W. "An Analysis of the Thesis Submitted and Accepted in the Graduate Program at Florida A. & M. University, August, 1947 Through August, 1953." Florida A. & M. College, 1953.

Ellington, Margaret. "A Survey of the Student Use of the William H. Sheppard Library, Stillman College, Tuscaloosa, Alabama." Atlanta University, 1964.

El-Sayeh, Hassein Bayoumi. "Booker T. Washington; A Study of His Educational Experiments in Tuskegee Normal and Industrial Institute." California State University, Fresno, 1964.

Emanuel, Samuel. "A Study to Determine the Amount of Agriculture That Should be Offered at Grambling College Where Negro Teachers Are Educated for Work in Elementary Schools of Rural Louisiana." University of Wisconsin, 1946.

Epps, E. W. "Comparative Study of Motor Ability of High School, College, and Varsity Negro Boys." Springfield College, 1936.

Fancher, Evelyn Pitts. "A Survey of the Oakwood College Library, Huntsville, Alabama." Atlanta University, 1961.

Few, Moses Clinton. "A Comparative Study of School Achievement and Personality Between Groups (Equated on Intelligence) of Graduates From Accredited and Non-Accredited High Schools Enrolled in the Freshmen Class of Morris Brown College, Atlanta, Georgia, 1953-1954." Atlanta University, 1954.

Fisher, Charles C. "A Study of the Educational Contributions of the Presbyterian Church, U. S. to Negro Education in Alabama From 1876-1952." Alabama State College, 1953.

Fisher, Dwight Hillis. "A Study of Athletic Conferences Among Negro Colleges of the United States." Ohio State University, 1936.

Fisher, Gordon Everett. "A Study of the Relations Among College Placement Test, Sophomore General Examinations, and Course Grades." Fisk University, 1961.

Fisher, John Eastham. "Atticus Greene Haygood and Negro Education in the South." Vanderbilt University, 1951.

Flagg, Lucy Williams. "Use of the Circulation Department of the Trevor Arnett Library by Morehouse College Undergraduate Students, September, 1954, Through May, 1955." Atlanta University, 1959.

Fleming, Oliver Wendell. "The Trend of Thought Regarding Negro Education as Revealed in the Journal of Negro Education From 1932 to 1940 Inclusive." University of Michigan, 1948.

Fletcher, Jennie A. "Health and Physical Education in Negro Colleges and Universities." University of Cincinnati, 1935.

Floyd, Raymond B. "Growth in Professional Training of Negro Teachers and the Improvement of Teacher Training Facilities in the State of Louisiana, 1929-1939." Xavier University, 1941.

Flood, James J. "A Study of the Vocational Guidance Program of Tuskegee Industrial Institute." University of Michigan, 1941.

Franklin, Bostic Josiah. "The Politico-Economic Theories of Three Negro Leaders: Douglass, Washington, Du Bois." Howard University, 1936.

Franklin, Ethel Viola. "A Study of the Literacy of Two Classes of Morehouse Students." Atlanta University, 1953.

Frazier, Annie L. "A Follow-Up Study of the Graduates of the High School Department of the Mississippi Industrial College, Holly Springs, Mississippi, 1937 to 1946 Inclusive." Atlanta University, 1950.

Frazier, Lorraine Mortel. "The Relationship of Selected Factors to the Social Attitudes of College Students." Howard University, 1942.

Frazier, Ruth Naomi. "Health Misconceptions of Certain High School and Junior College Students." Fisk University, 1941.

Freeman, George Albert. "The Socio-Economic Background of a Selected Group of Male Negro College Students." Kansas State College, 1949.

Gandy, John Manuel, Jr. "Study of Racial Attitudes of Negro College Students." Ohio State University, 1938.

Garrett, Ernestine Louise. "Influence of the Du Bois-Washington Controversy on Higher Education for Negroes. Shall Higher Education for Negroes be Cultural or Industrial?" Fisk University, 1937.

Gibson, Louise Edna. "A Study of the Vocational Guidance Materials of the Atlanta University, Spelman, Morris Brown and

Clark College Libraries." Atlanta University, 1952.

Gist, Grace Perry. "The Educational Work of the African Methodist Episcopal Church Prior to 1900." Howard University, 1949.

Glover, Carolyn May. "A Curriculum of Music for Kentucky State College Based on the Public School System of Kentucky." Ohio State University, 1938.

Gottschalk, Matthew Thomas. "A Comparative Study of the Values of Fisk Students and Catholic Seminarians." Fisk University, 1963.

Gould, Pauline W. "Personnel Practices in a Selected Group of Negro Colleges and Universities." Tennessee Agricultural and Industrial State College, 1945.

Grady, Margaret O. "Why College Students Fail to Meet the Required Scholastic Attainment." Virginia State College, 1941.

Grant, George Calvin. "A Study of the Extracurricular Reading Interests and Habits of Morehouse College Students." Atlanta University, 1962.

Grant, Jason Clifton, III. "A Content Analysis of Serial Publications in English Philology for a Four-Year Liberal Arts College Library." Atlanta University, 1952.

Graves, Ann R. C. "Higher Education for Negroes in Atlanta: An Example of Academic Affiliation and Cooperation." University of Chicago, 1941.

Graves, Harry Cornelius. "The Contribution of a Curriculum for the Preparation of Teachers of Health and Physical Education for Wilberforce University." Ohio State University, 1933.

Gray, Grant Sylvester. "Survey and Evaluation of the Health and Physical Education Program at Kentucky State College for Negroes." Ohio State University, 1947.

Green, William Tecumseh. "A Critical Analysis and Evaluation of the Preparation of Elementary Teachers in Health Education as it is Carried on in Two Negro Colleges of Georgia." Ohio State University, 1950.

Greene, Harry W. "Educational and Social Background of Prominent Negro Leaders." West Virginia State College, 1935.

Griffin, Helen Montgomery. "The Relation Between High School Record and Freshman Achievement." Fisk University, 1935.

Griffin, James Morgan. "Teacher Training in Health Education in Schools Belonging to the Colored Intercollegiate

Athletic Association." Springfield College, 1949.

Griggs, Mary E. W. "Cooperative Intercollegiate Program Scores and Other Selected Factors for the Prediction of College Success." Atlanta University, 1960.

Haines, James E. "A Critical Appraisal of the Service Program of Physical Education for Men in Colleges of the Southern Intercollegiate and Athletic Conference." Springfield College, 1950.

Hall, Clyde Woodrow. "Undergraduate Offerings in Industrial Education in Negro Land-Grant Colleges." Iowa State College, 1949.

Hall, Sylvester Raymond. "The Evolution of Intramural Sports for Men in American Colleges and Universities." Howard University, 1936.

Hamilton, Henry C. "An Experimental Study of Factors Conditioning the Effectiveness of College Orientation Courses." University of Cincinnati, 1937.

Hamilton, Marion Murphy. "A Comparison of the Academic Achievement of 10th and 11th grade Early Admission Students at Morehouse College, 1952-1959." Atlanta University, 1960.

Hams, Henry Lewis. "Higher Education for Negroes in the State of Missouri Analyzed From the Standpoint of a Social Movement." University of Kansas, 1949.

Handy, Kathryn Lawson. "The Evolution of the Negro Teachers College." Howard University, 1951.

Hanigan, (Sr.) Maria G. "The Problem of Higher Education for Negroes in Catholic Colleges, Universities and Seminaries." Marquette University, 1940. [1941]

Hankins, Irene Barham. "The Stability of Educational Goals Among College Students." Atlanta University, 1962.

Hardeman, Veoria M. "An Analysis and Evaluation of the Freshman Reading Program of Prairie View University for the Year 1945-1946." Prairie View A. & M. College, 1946.

Harden, Rubye Browne. "A Follow-Up Study of Two Groups of Home Economics Students Who Withdrew From Prairie View College Before Graduation: 1933 and 1943." Prairie View A. & M. College, 1948.

Hardison, Henry L. "A Study of the Academic Failures of Veterans at Tennessee A. & I. State College." Tennessee Agricultural and Industrial State College, 1947.

Hardy, Blanch Brewster. "The Relation of Scholastic Aptitude and English Test Performance to Academic Achievement of One Hundred Freshmen Women." Fisk University, 1949.

Hargrett, Andrew Joshua. "Religious Attitudes of Post-War College Students at Florida Agricultural and Mechanical College." Atlanta University, 1949.

Harper, Armesia Celeste. "The Organization and Management of Certain Negro College Food Services." Kansas State College, 1954.

Harpole, Ellsworth Henry. "A Survey of Instructional Practices in Physical Education for Men in 64 Higher Institutions of Learning." University of Minnesota, 1939.

Harris, James Otis, Jr. "A Comparative Study of the Performance of a Group of College Sophomores on Timed and Untimed Administrations of Two Different Tests of Mental Ability." Atlanta University, 1952.

Harris, M. Sylvia. "An Index to the Bulletin of Atlanta University for the Period June, 1883, Through December, 1891." Atlanta University, 1962.

Harris, Thomas. "A Comparison of Physical Education Courses Offered at the University of Tennessee With Physical Education Courses Offered at Negro Colleges in Tennessee Granting Degrees in Physical Education." Tennessee A. & I. College, 1950.

Harrison, G. L. "Teacher Training in the Negro Land-Grant Colleges." University of Cincinnati, 1929.

Harrison, Violet Gertrude. "A Study of Negro Colleges and Other Educational Institutions Founded by the Methodist Episcopal Church." University of Cincinnati, 1937.

Harvey, Jeannette Wynn. "Changing Opportunities in Social Work as Shown by a Study of the Placements of the Graduates From Atlanta University School of Social Work From June, 1934 Through June, 1943." Atlanta University, 1944.

Hassock, Toni Overton. "The Prediction of Academic Achievement of College Students From Two Aptitude Tests." Fisk University, 1962.

Hasty, John Bruner. "A Study of Admission Practices of Negro Colleges and Universities." University of Cincinnati, 1939.

Hawkins, James E. "A History and Survey of Physical Education and Athletics in the Colored Intercollegiate Athletic Association." State University of Iowa, 1947.

Hawkins, John, Jr. "The Educational Development of Bishop Payne Divinity School." Virginia State College, 1945.

Haywood, Sylvia Nadene. "A Study of College and University Library Clubs in the State of Georgia." Atlanta University, 1960.

Hearn, R. D. "The Development of Higher Education for Negroes With Special Reference to the Denominational Schools." Prairie View A. & M. College, 1948.

Hemphill, Dianne Adaire. "Aptitude Tests and High School Record in Predicting Academic Achievement in College." Fisk University, 1963.

Henderson, Mae E. Shaw. "An Experiment Conducted in Spelling Among the Prairie View Freshmen, 1947-1948." Prairie View A. & M. College, 1948.

Henry, Ephriam Madison. "An Interpretative and Evaluative Analysis of the Literature Dealing With the Philosophy, Techniques, and Approaches Employed by Booker T. Washington." Atlanta University, 1950.

Herbert, Cleopatra Adyrnne. "An Evaluation of the Results of Teaching Certain Phases of Home Economics at Howard University as Determined by the Food Selection of a Selected Group of Students." Howard University, 1944.

Higgins, Frances Louise. "A Survey of the Alabama Agricultural and Mechanical College Library, Normal, Alabama." Atlanta University, 1954.

Hill, Milton. "Certain Factors Associated With Withdrawal From the Atlanta University School of Education." Atlanta University, 1963.

Hillier, George Arlington. "History of Educational Legislation in Alabama, 1860-1910." University of Chicago, 1924.

Hilton, Eva Tanguay. "A Psychological and Statistical Study of One Hundred College Freshmen." Howard University, 1928.

Hines, Emory Wellington. "A Survey of Programs of Physical Education and Athletic Facilities in Negro Colleges." The State University of Iowa, 1948.

Hinson, Rosalind Olivia. "Certain Characteristics Manifested by the Enrollees in the National Defense Education Act Guidance and Counseling Institute, Atlanta University." Atlanta University, 1961.

Holland, La Verne. "A Study of the Results and Implications of the Chemistry Tests Given Freshmen at Tennessee A. & I. State College." Tennessee Agricultural and Industrial State College, 1947.

Holston, L. Oliver. "The Personality Characteristics of a Group of Eighty-Five First Summer Graduate Students of the State Teachers College." Alabama State Teachers College, 1946. [Montgomery]

Hood, Hanna Melbane. "A Study of the Performances of 261 College Freshmen in Arithmetic." Atlanta University, 1940.

Horne, Frank Smith. "The Present Status of Negro Education in Certain Southern States, Particularly Georgia." University of Southern California, Los Angeles, 1932.

Horner, Juanita. "Types and Frequencies of Problems of Adjustment of Negro Students During the First Year of College Life as Reported in Current Literature From 1937-1947." University of Michigan, 1948.

Hoursey, Alphonso W. "A Follow-Up Survey of Graduates of Avery Institute, Charleston, South Carolina, For Years 1930-1940." University of Michigan, 1941.

House, Christopher C. "A Study of the Relationship Between the Variable Factors of Home Background, Environment and Achievement Among Freshmen and Senior Students in Selected Negro Colleges and Universities." Howard University, 1944.

Howard, Edward Ulysses. "Library Budget of Predominantly Negro Colleges and Universities." Atlanta University, 1963.

Howard, Evelyn M. R. "Rural-Urban Differences in Certain Psychological Traits Manifested by Selected Southern Negro College Students." Atlanta University, 1963.

Howard-Waters, Olessa Ladenia. "Personal Problems Brought to Counselors at Jarvis Christian College During 1944-1945." Atlanta University, 1946.

Howell, Sara Bertha Mae. "Booker T. Washington Then and Now." New York University, 1942.

Hucles, Henry Boyd. "A Survey of the Physical Education Personnel in Negro Colleges and Universities." Springfield College, 1949.

Hutton, Leonelle. "Library Personnel in Negro Colleges." University of Chicago, 1948.

Israel, Isaiah. "The Attitude and Interests of Negroes Toward Required Physical Education at West Virginia State College." University of Michigan, 1938.

Jackson, Inez Louise. "The Evolution of State Supported Teacher College Education for Negroes in Pennsylvania." Howard University, 1949.

Jackson, Willie, Jr. "Levels of Identification of First and Second Year Students in the Atlanta University School of Social Work." Atlanta University, 1958.

James, Felix. "A Study of Selected Factors Associated With College Attendance of Negro High School Seniors." Fisk University, 1954.

Jarrett, Corrie Johnson. "Practices in Purchasing Certain Textile and Clothing of Home Economics Students in the Four Negro Colleges in Arkansas." Iowa State College, 1948.

Jefferson, Mary Alice. "Status of Libraries in Negro Degree Granting Colleges." Virginia State College, 1946.

Jellins, Miriam Harris. "Analysis of Reading Research at Atlanta University From 1933 Through 1959." Atlanta University, 1961.

Jenkins, Martin D. "Personnel Work in Twenty-Two Negro Institutions of Higher Learning." Northwestern University, 1933.

Johnson, Arthur Lee. "The Social Theories of W. E. B. Du Bois." Atlanta University, 1949.

Johnson, Bernice D. "A Comparative Study of the Levels of Emotional Maturity of Freshmen and Senior Women at Virginia State College." Virginia State College, 1949.

Johnson, Blanche E. "An Analysis of Inservice Teacher Traits Preferred by Students' Parents and Students Teachers of the Prairie View University Training School, Year 1945-1946." Prairie View University, 1946.

Johnson, Carrie Williams. "An Item Analysis of English Literature; Test Scores for Five Selected Years of the Academic Meet at State Teachers College." State Teachers College, 1944. [Montgomery, Alabama]

Johnson, Freddie George. "A Study of the School Library Experiences of a Selected Group of College Freshmen at Texas Southern University, Houston, Texas." Atlanta University, 1965.

Johnson, Gladys. "A Study of the Music Schools and Departments of the A and B Class Colleges for the Negro." Northwestern University, 1928.

Johnson, K. L. "Teacher Training Programs of Physical Education in Colleges and Universities for Negroes." Springfield College, 1940.

Johnson, Minerva Hatcher. "Evaluation of Entrance Examinations Given at Fisk University as Predictive Measures of Collegiate Success." Fisk University, 1940.

Johnson, Roger H. "A Survey of Music in Colleges for Negroes Rated Class "A" by the Southern Association of Colleges and Secondary Schools." Virginia State College, 1943.

Johnson, Rose Mary. "The Relationship of College Aptitude and Achievement to Admission to Medical Professional Schools." Fisk University, 1957.

Johnson, Victoria Louise. [See Sugg].

Johnson, Virginia Lee. "A Study to Determine an Adequate Program in Business Administration and in Business Education at Tennessee Agricultural and Industrial State College." University of Tennessee, 1944.

Johnston, W. C. "The Relationship Between Vocabulary and Scholastic Achievement of a Group of Prairie View State College Students." Prairie View State College, 1945.

Jones, Franklin S. "Courtship Patterns and Practices of Married Veterans in College." Atlanta University, 1949.

Jones, Jacqueline Butler. "A Study of Segregated Negro Colleges in a Bi-Racial Situation." Tennessee, 1951. [Tennessee A. & I. State College, 1951].

Jones, Lee A. "The Influence of Tuskegee Institute on the Education of Negroes in Macon County, Alabama, 1881-1946." Tuskegee Institute, 1947.

Jones, Lelia Belle. "The Relationship Between Performance on Selected Entrance Examinations and Other Factors to the Graduation of College Students." Fisk University, 1952.

Jones, Martha Crosby. "Some Cognitive and Noncognitive Characteristics of Counselor Education Students." Atlanta University, 1965.

Jones, Robert Fulton. "A Study of the Account Classification of 14 State Colleges and 14 Members of the United Negro College Fund." Atlanta University, 1953.

Jones, Roy Lee, Jr. "Adjustments of Early Admission Students at a Southern College." Atlanta University, 1962.

Jordan, Casper Leroy. "A Content Analysis and Cumulative Index Annotated of Phylon Quarterly, 1940-49." Atlanta University, 1951.

Jordan, Mary E. C. "Proposed Revisions of the Activity Program at Lincoln University Laboratory High School." Hampton Institute, 1947.

Keith, Ethel Hannah. "The Home and Social Background of the Women Students at Samuel Huston College for Negroes During 1937-1938." Kansas State College, 1938.

Kelly, John Forrest. "Personal Problems Brought to the Dean of Dormitory Life of Morehouse College, 1947-1948." Atlanta University, 1948.

Kennedy, Elizabeth Carolyn. "The Development of Higher Education in Tennessee for Negroes From 1865 to 1900." Fisk University, 1950.

Kenyon, Harr C. "The Relation Between Intelligence Quotient and Teachers' Marks: A Study of Freshmen at Prairie View University." Prairie View University, 1946.

Kerr, Victor E., Jr. "A Study of the Educational Background, Experience, and Evaluation of Football and Basketball Officials of the Colored Intercollegiate Athletic Association." Boston University, 1950.

Kincaide, John C. "A Comparison of Facilities for Higher Education for Negro and White Students at the University of Missouri and at Lincoln University." Drake University, 1951.

Kinchelow, Howard J. "Employment Trends of Negro Graduates From Land-Grant Colleges." Colorado State College of Agriculture and Mechanic Arts, 1947.

King, Eugene. "An Evaluation of the Biology Collection of the Trevor Arnett Library of Atlanta University, Atlanta, Georgia." Atlanta University, 1963.

King, Letitia Johnson. "A Comparative Study of Nursery School Feeding at Lane College and Spelman College With Proposals for Improved Nursery School Feeding at Lane College." Atlanta University, 1948.

King, William Judson. "The Effects of Certain Developments in Public Education in the South Upon the Recent Educational Policies and Practices of the American Missionary Association." Fisk University, 1953.

Kitchen, G. H. "The Status of Physical Education in Colleges for Negroes Sponsored by the American Missionary Association." University of Michigan, 1940.

Knowlen, Marvin John Henry. "A Survey of the Speech Curricula in the Negro Teachers College and High Schools of Saint Louis, Missouri." Saint Louis University, 1950.

Koo, Suen-Yow. "A Study of the Ability of the Freshmen Students of Morehouse College to Use the Card Catalog of the Trevor Arnett Library at Atlanta University." Atlanta University, 1963.

Lane, Cecelia Scott. "The Place of Home Economics in the Curriculum for Women of Houston College for Negroes." Iowa State College, 1937. [See also-Scott, Lane Cecelia]

Lane, Josephine Berry. "A Study of the Leisure Time and Recreational Activities of the Students of Atlanta University." Atlanta University, 1942.

Lanier, Raphael O'Hara. "The History of Negro Education in Florida." Stanford University, 1928.

Larkins, John R. "A Study of the Employment of Negroes in Social Work Based Upon a Study of the Present Employment of Graduates of the Atlanta University School of Social Work From 1930 to 1940." Atlanta University, 1941.

Lash, Harry E. "A Study of the Graduates of the Division of Engineering and Industrial Education of Tennessee A. & I. State College From 1930-1947." Tennessee Agricultural and Industrial State College, 1948.

Lawless, Oscar Godfrey. "A Statistical Analysis of the Achievement of the Atlanta University College Students Who Took the Thurstone Psychological Examination for the Years 1924-1928." Atlanta University, 1932.

Laws, Melzetta Peterson. "An Index to the _Bulletin of Atlanta University_ for the Period January, 1897, Through December, 1900." Atlanta University, 1962.

Lee, Elizabeth Cora. "Use of the Card Catalog by Spelman Students in the Spelman and Trevor Arnett Libraries." Atlanta University, 1952.

Lee, Jeane Ann. "Some Factors Influencing the Choice of Intimate Intra and Intersexual Companions Among a Group of Negro College Students." Howard University, 1941.

Lee, Owen Griffin. "Sex Differences in Performance of College Freshmen on Intelligence and Achievement Examinations for the Years 1945-1947." Fisk University, 1950.

Lee, Robert Henry. "An Evaluation of the Physical Education Curricula of the Negro Colleges of Tennessee." Ohio State University, 1940.

Lee, Wister M. "An Evaluation of the Physical Education Program at Prairie View University." Prairie View University, 1946.

Lehmann, Allan B. "A Consumer Survey of the Services at the Atlanta University National Defense Educational Act Guidance and Counseling Center, 1962-1963." Atlanta University, 1963.

Leigh, Louisa Flossie. "A Follow-Up Study of One Hundred Graduates of Atlanta University Who Obtained the Master of Arts Degree in Education Between 1932 and 1949." Atlanta University, 1950.

Lemons, James. "An Evaluation of the Physical Facilities of Negro Vocational Agricultural Departments in Tennessee." Tennessee A. & I. State College, 1950.

Leonard, Katherine Estelle. "A Study of the Negro Collection of the Trevor Arnett Library of Atlanta University." Atlanta University, 1951.

Lett, Phyllis. "A Comparison of Two Scholastic Tests for Predicting Academic Achievement of College Students." Fisk University, 1962.

Lewis, Cecil T. "A Study of the Present Status of Alumni Programs in Thirty-Six Negro Colleges." Hampton Institute, 1943.

Lewis, Clarence Osceola. "How Does the Use of Negative Grade Points Affect Probation at Howard University?" Howard University, 1935.

Lewis, Gaston Frederick. "A Health Instruction Program for College Freshmen at Wilberforce University." Ohio State University, 1938.

Lillard, Helen Maxine. "The Adjustment of Negro American College Students, as Measured by the Bell Inventory." Fisk University, 1961.

Littman, Harry. "The Negro Physician, His Training and Status." New York University, 1949.

Locke, Charlie E. "A Comparative Follow-Up Study of 2 Groups of College Graduates From a State and a Privately Supported College in Georgia." Atlanta University, 1960.

Long, Wylma G. "Characteristics of Science Educators and Their Training Program in the United States of America." Atlanta University, 1963.

Lyells, Ruby E. Stutts. "The Library in Negro Land-Grant Colleges." University of Chicago, 1942.

McAlpin, Ruth Duvall. "An Analysis of the Introductory Literature Course in Twenty-Two Representative Negro Colleges." Tennessee Agricultural and Industrial State College, 1947.

McCain, Virgil Bowden. "Private Philanthropy in Negro Education in Alabama, 1939." University of Alabama, 1939.

McCants, Alice Jane F. "A Study of the MMPI Profiles of Highly Rated Counselor Trainees at Atlanta University in 1962-63." Atlanta University, 1963.

McCombs, Mabel Frances. "A Follow-Up Study of the Graduates of Allen University, 1942-1957." Atlanta University, 1960.

McDonald, Fannie Ruth. "Preparation and In-Service Training Opportunities of Negro School Teachers in Alabama."

DePaul University, 1944. [Chicago, Illinois]

McDonald, Jack Arthur. "Higher Education for Negroes in Texas." University of Southern California, 1947.

McDowell, Ruth Doris Angel. "Beliefs About Sex Among College Women and the Sources of Their Information." Atlanta University, 1949.

McGinty, Willetta. "The Nursery-Kindergarten School of the State Teachers College, Montgomery, Alabama." The State Teachers College, 1947. [Montgomery, Alabama]

McIntosh, Eranell Irene. "The Relationship of Selected Background Factors to Scholastic Aptitude and Achievement of College Students." Fisk University, 1962.

McIver, Annie Mae Rainey. "A Socio-Econometric Study of Inter-Personal Relations Among the Sixth and Seventh Grade Pupils at Atlanta University Laboratory School." Atlanta University, 1949.

McLauren, Phyllis Cardeza. "Religious Beliefs of College Students." Howard University, 1938.

McLean, Margaret Grace. "An Evaluation of the Reference Book Collection of the Trevor Arnett Library." Atlanta University, 1951.

McLemore, Erma Deloris. "An Evaluation of the Fiction Collections in the Libraries of the Atlanta University Center." Atlanta University, 1952.

McMahon, William Otis. "The Litigation of the National Association for the Advancement of Colored People, 1910-1942." Howard University, 1942.

McMurdock, Bertha J. "The Development of Higher Education for Negroes in Missouri." Howard University, 1939.

McShann, Frances Carpenter. "A Study of the Training Needed by Teachers Supervising Home Management Houses in Negro Colleges." Kansas State Teachers College, 1937.

Mackay, Sarah Edith. "The Performance of the 1945 Fisk Freshmen Women on the Entrance Achievement Examination by Regions and Socio-Economic Status." Fisk University, 1949.

Mackey, Sarah Edith. "Socio-Economic Status and the Performance on Entrance Achievement Tests of Freshmen Women From the North and South." Fisk University, 1950.

Mackintosh, Barry. "The Carver Myth." University of Maryland, 1974.

Marion, Claud Collier. "A Qualitative Study of the

Effectiveness of Instructional Programs in Technical Agriculture in Negro Land-Grant Colleges." Cornell University, 1948.

Martin, Eva Samuel. "A Study of Certain Aspects of the Personnel Services to Women in Selected Institutions of Higher Learning in Georgia." Atlanta University, 1953.

Martin, Marcella Wallace. "Industrial Arts in the Elementary Education Programs at Wilberforce University." Ohio State University, 1937.

Matter, Sister M. E. "A Study of the Food Practices of One-Hundred Freshmen Students at Xavier University of Louisiana." Louisiana State University, 1946.

Mayo, Beatrice Adelaide. "Content and Scope of Accounting Courses Being Offered in Negro Colleges in the United States 1945-1946." Catholic University of America, 1948.

Menard, W. M. "A Comparative Study of White and Negro Land-Grant and Private Colleges and Universities." Pennsylvania State College, 1933.

Merriwether, Mary Olivia. Sociology in Negro Institutions of Higher Learning in the United States." State University of Iowa, 1940.

Middleton, Agnes B. "Mental Hygiene in Negro Colleges of the United States." University of Michigan, 1942.

Midgette, Lillian Avon. "A Bio-Bibliography of Alain Leroy Locke." Atlanta University, 1963.

Miles, Esmie E. "Amory D. Mayo, Northern Promoter of Southern Education." Howard University, 1955.

Miller, Carroll Lee. "The Aims and Objectives of Graduate Instruction in Education With Special Reference to the Masters Degree." Howard University, 1930.

Mitchell, Eva C. "Integrating Student Teaching and Related Courses in Education in the Education of Elementary Teachers at Hampton Institute." Columbia University, 1942.

Mitchell, Lila May Barnett. "History Courses in Colored Colleges and Universities." University of Chicago, 1936.

Mobley, Eva Erlene. "A Study of the Extent to Which Special Types of Material are Catalogued in a Selected Number of Negro College and University Libraries." Atlanta University, 1953.

Montgomery, William H. "The Status of Intramural Sports in Negro Colleges and Universities." Springfield College, 1950.

Moon, Clyde Lee. "The Development of Higher Education for Negroes in the State of Florida." University of Florida, 1941.

Moone, Ruby T. R. "Student Personnel Services in Eight Selected Undergraduate Colleges in Georgia." Atlanta University, 1965.

Moore, Charles Davis. "A Background Study of 100 Enrollees in Literacy Classes at Fisk University Social Center." Fisk University, 1950.

Morgan, Geraldine Cecelia. "The Organization and Administration of the Catalog Department in Three Negro College Libraries." Atlanta University, 1950.

Morris, Alverta Nevels. "A Bio-Bibliography of E. Franklin Frazier." Atlanta University, 1962.

Morris, Harold White. "A History of Indian Education in the United States." Oregon State, 1954.

Morris, Talitha Long. "A Determination of Freshmen Guidance Needs at Wiley College." Cornell University, 1937.

Moses, Louise Jane. "An Evaluation of the Morris College Library, Sumter, South Carolina." Atlanta University, 1952.

Mosley, Ellis Greenlee. "The History of Higher Education for Negroes in Arkansas." University of Texas, 1949.

Mumford, Arnett William. "Present Status of Health and Physical Education in Negro Senior Colleges." University of Southern California, 1947.

Mundy, Nina Scurlock. "The Effect of Remedial Training in Reading Upon Predicted and Probable Failures Among Howard University Freshmen." Howard University, 1940.

Neal, Audrey De Conge. "A Study of the Family Background, the Personality Development, and College Experiences of Three Hundred and Six College Students." Atlanta University, 1942.

Neel, Virginia Poyne. "Race Attitudes of College Women." Fisk University and Southern Y.M.C.A. Graduate School, 1934.

Neilson, H. N. "Evaluation of the Physical Education of Negro Professional Schools." Springfield College, 1936.

Nicholas, Josephine. "A Comparative Study of Grades of Home Economics Graduates of Prairie View College, 1939-1944." Prairie View State University, 1945.

Nichols, Rudolph Van. "A Job History of the Atlanta University School of Library Service Graduates, 1942-1947." Atlanta University, 1951.

Norris, Hubert Webster. "The Theory of College Accounting and Criteria for an Efficient Accounting System for a Private College." Atlanta University, 1935.

Norwood, Edwin F. "An Examination of the Extension Program at Florida A. & M. College." Florida A. & M. University, 1951.

Oak, Vishu. "Commercial Education in Negro Colleges." State University of Iowa, 1932.

Officer, Arizona M. "A Comparison of Employed and Unemployed Students at Tennessee Agricultural and Industrial College, Fall Quarter, 1946." A. & I. State College, 1946.

Oldham, Milton B. "Building a Business Curriculum in the Negro College." New York University, 1939.

O'Neal, Edmund J. "The Rise and Development of State Teacher Training for Negro Elementary Teachers in Alabama." University of Cincinnati, 1939.

Owens, Dorothy Elizabeth. "W. E. Burghardt Du Bois: A Case Study of a Marginal Man." Fisk University, 1944.

Pace, William Max. "Currents of Opinion in Regard to the Ideas of Booker T. Washington." Ohio State University, 1947.

Parker, E. R. "An Analysis of the Trends and Practices in Teacher Education as it Relates to the Home Economics Curricula of Twenty-Two Colleges and Universities for Negroes." Virginia State College, 1940.

Parker, Erva Jean. "The Difference in Relationships of Intelligence, General Reading Ability, and Achievement in Communications Among College Freshmen and Higher Level and Lower Level Critical Reading Abilities." Atlanta University, 1964.

Parris, Evelyn Lauretta. "An Evaluation of Food Selection by Freshmen Students at Howard University." Howard University, 1954.

Patterson, E. H. "The Work of the Methodist Episcopal Church in Establishing and Maintaining Schools in the South for Negroes, 1866-1892." University of Chicago, 1940.

Pearman, Reginald Aubra. "A Survey of Student Health Service in Negro Colleges." Boston University, 1950.

Perry, Benjamin Luther. "Present Status of the Agricultural Departments in 17 Negro Land-Grant Colleges." Iowa State College, 1935.

Perry, Grace Naomi. "The Educational Work of the African Methodist Episcopal Church Prior to 1900." Howard University, 1948.

Perry, Marie Evangeline. "The Development of the Education of the Negro in the District of Columbia, 1807-1864." Howard University, 1937.

Peters, Wilk S. "Library Budgets in Negro Colleges." Columbia University, 1941.

Petrof, Barbara Jean Gainey. "A Study of the Use Made of the Subject Approach to Library Materials of the Trevor Arnett Library." Atlanta University, 1962.

Pharr, Julia M. "The Activities of the Society of Friends in Behalf of Negro Education." Howard University, 1937.

Phillips, Laura Pinn. "The Development of Education for Negroes in West Virginia." Howard University, 1937.

Phillips, Mable V. "The Characteristics of Superior Negro College Students." Howard University, 1947.

Phillips, Myrtle Redmond. "The Development of Public Education for Negroes in the State of Kentucky." University of Chicago, 1931.

Phillips, Ollie Reynolds. "Higher Education for Negro Women in Alabama." Fisk University, 1939.

Pickens, James D. "The Significance of the John F. Slater Fund in the Development of Public Education in Alabama." Alabama State College, 1953.

Pierce, Juanita Hortense. "The Organization and Administration of Health, Physical Education, and Recreation in the Atlanta University Center." New York University, 1946.

Pilgrim, Helen. "An Evaluation of the Program for Treating Tuberculosis in Negro Colleges and Universities Through Health Service." Howard University, 1940.

Pinkett, Maude Moore. "A Bibliography of Works on Africa in the Trevor Arnett Library of Atlanta University Published Before 1900." Atlanta University, 1962.

Pinter, Jean Burnette. "The Stated Aims of Representative Negro Colleges in the South." Baylor University, 1950.

Pipes, William Harrison. "Sources of Booker T. Washington's Effectiveness as a Public Speaker." Atlanta University, 1937.

Plummer, Sallie B. "A Follow-Up Study of the Counselor

Enrollees Who Attended the Counseling and Guidance Training Institutes at Atlanta University, Atlanta, Georgia, 1959-1962." Atlanta University, 1963.

Plunkett, Gene Raymond. "The Prediction of Academic Achievement Over a Four Year Period From College Placement Tests." Fisk University, 1960.

Porter, D. B. "The Health and Physical Education Programs of 53 Colleges and Universities for Negroes." Indiana State Teachers College, 1934.

Porter, David Wilborn. "A Brief History of the Julius Rosenwald Fund School Building Program With Special Reference to Arkansas." Fisk University, 1951.

Porter, Dorothy B. "Howard University Masters' Theses, 1918-1945." Howard University, 1946.

Porter, Ruth Metella. "The Health Program for Women Students in Southern Colleges." University of Colorado, 1937.

Porter, William Henry. "A Study of the Needs for an Individual Physical Education Program in Negro Colleges, and a Consideration of the Principles and Procedures Involved in Conducting Such a Program." Ohio State University, 1946.

Pouncy, Mitchell Louis. "A Annotated Cumulative Index to Phylon From 1950 Through 1959." Atlanta University, 1961.

Powell, Jerry. "An Intensive Study of the Personal and Social Adjustments of Four Pupils of the Sixth and Seventh Grades, Atlanta University Laboratory School, Atlanta, Georgia." Atlanta University, 1949.

Pritchett, Willie W. "An Analysis of Grades Made by Greek-Letter and Non-Greek-Letter Members of the Fisk University Senior Class of 1949-1950." Fisk University, 1950.

Puryear, Bryte H. "An Analysis of Personal Adjustment Problems of the Freshmen at Prairie View College." Prairie View State College, 1945.

Quarterman, Mildred Victoria Wilson. "An Analysis of the Atlanta University Center Internship Program for Prospective Public School Teachers." Atlanta University, 1964.

Quick, Helen J. "A Job Analysis of Group Work Positions Held by the Graduates of the Atlanta School of Social Work From 1930 to 1940." Atlanta University, 1941.

Quivers, Evelyn Seace. "A Study of the School Library Experiences of a Selected Group of College Freshmen." Atlanta University, 1952.

Randolph, Eugene Christopher. "Self-Concepts, Values,

Attitudes, and Scholastic Achievement of Negro College Males." Atlanta University, 1964.

Ray, Lillian Beatrice. "A Study of the Socio-Economic, Intellectual, and Cultural Status of Negro College Students." University of Colorado, 1939.

Reed, Ernest Ellsworth. "The Educational Philosophy of Booker T. Washington." University of Cincinnati, 1928.

Reese, LaVerne. "Food Service in the Negro Colleges of Texas." Iowa State College, 1947.

Regulus, Homie. "An Evaluation of the Savannah State College Library, Savannah, Georgia." Atlanta University, 1953.

Rhambo, Ernest L. "An Occupational Survey as a Basis for the Establishment of Terminal Education at Wharton County Junior College (1949)." Prairie View A. & M. College, 1949.

Rice, Robert Aaron. "A Follow-Up Study of the Graduates of the Electrical Department of Hampton Institute From 1933-1951." Hampton Institute, 1951.

Richards, Essye D. "A Study of the Effects of Part-Time Employment Upon the Scholastic Achievement of Home Economics Students at Prairie View State College, 1926-1940." Prairie View State College, 1942.

Richardson, Fannie Ruth. "A Dietary Survey of Food Habits of Students at Alcorn Agricultural and Mechanical College, Alcorn, Mississippi." Tuskegee Institute, 1951.

Riley, Louise Elise. "A Study of the Performance on a Library Orientation Test in Relation to the Academic Achievement and Scholastic Aptitude of a Selected Group of Freshmen College Students at Tuskegee Institute." Atlanta University, 1963.

Roberts, H. C. "The Attitude of Congress Toward the Education of Negroes, 1860-1890." Fisk University, 1933.

Robertson, Edith L. "A Survey of Deficiencies in Mechanics and Affectiveness of Expression of Twenty-Five Freshmen at Hampton Institute as Revealed by the Cooperative English Test." Hampton Institute, 1943.

Robinson, E. U. "The Intelligence of Virginia State College Freshmen Class." Virginia State College, 1940.

Robinson, Florence Ann. "A Study of the Occupational Choices of the Negro Women of the Senior Classes in Atlanta Colleges, 1940-1941, in Relation to Possible Employment." Atlanta University, 1941.

Robinson, James McKinley, Sr. "Relation of the Degree of Ego-Involvement to the Character of the Stereotype "Negro" Held by Negro College Students." Howard University, 1950.

Robinson, Jimmie Lee. "A Study of Samples of Composition of Alabama State College Freshmen as an Indication of Their High School English Training." Alabama State College, 1954.

Rooks, Alberta Rosetta. "Socio-Economic Status and Performance on the A.C.E. of Freshmen Women Students, 'North and South'." Fisk University, 1946.

Roquemore, Pauline Frances. "A Study of Negro College Libraries as Presented in Their College Catalogs." Atlanta University, 1964.

Ross, Addie Kate. "Development of Vocational Home Economics Program for Negroes in Mississippi." Iowa State College, 1932.

Russell, E. C. "The Status of Practice Teaching in Negro Teacher Training Institutions." University of Michigan, 1932.

Russell, Ulysses W. "James Solomon Russell: Priest, Educator, Humanitarian." Virginia State College, 1962.

Rust, L. "The Home and Social Background of the Women Students at Samuel Huston College for Negroes During 1937-1938." Kansas State College, 1938.

Ryan, Cecil M. "A Study of the Airage Education Program at Tennessee A. & I. State College, Period 1946-1949." Tennessee A. & I. State College, 1949.

Saine, Matilda Lynette. "A Comparison of the Effectiveness of Drills and Guided Free Readings as Methods for Improving the Reading Abilities of Twenty-Eight Spelman College Freshmen." Atlanta University, 1942.

Sampson, Robert L. "A Comparison of NSF Participants of Atlanta University Before and After Their Participation in Atlanta University National Science Foundation Institutes." Atlanta University, 1965.

Sanders, Oliver Wendell. "Environmental and Occupational Adjustments of Alcorn College Students." Iowa State College of Agriculture and Mechanic Arts, 1943.

Saunders, Florence Therese. "Predicting Scholastic Success in Home Economics and Industries at Virginia State College." Virginia State College, 1954.

Saundle, H. P. "The Preparation and Professional Training of the Negro High-School Teachers in West Virginia." University of Cincinnati, 1928.

Scott, Lane Cecelia. "The Place of Home Economics in the Curriculum for Women of Houston College for Negroes." Iowa State, 1937. [See also-Lane, Cecelia Scott]

Scott, Lenora Mae. "A Comparative Study of Students Who Were Active, Apathetic, and Non-Active in Sit-In Demonstrations." Fisk University, 1961.

Seldon, Inez Isabel. "The Use of Z-Scores in the Prediction of Academic Achievement of College Freshmen." Howard University, 1942.

Sellers, James Benson. "A History of Negro Education in Alabama." University of Chicago, 1925.

Shannon, Magnolia Edmonia. "A Study of the Predictive Value of High School Grades." Fisk University, 1941.

Shields, Adella R. "The Influence of Tuskegee Institute on the Health, Educational, Economic and Political Aspects of the Negro Population of Macon County, Alabama." Tuskegee Institute, 1961.

Sibley, Ellen Corine. "A Survey of a Selected Number of Negro Junior Colleges and Their Libraries." Atlanta University, 1962.

Simmons, Rosemary T. "An Index to the Bulletin of Atlanta University for the Period January, 1904, Through December, 1907." Atlanta University, 1963.

Smith, Lamar F. "A Personnel Study of the Directors of Physical Education in Negro Colleges in the United States." Iowa, 1936.

Smith, Lucy. "The Life, Work, and Influence of George Washington Carver." University of Cincinnati, 1943.

Smith, Rosine T. "An Analysis of Inquiries Made at the Reference Desk in the Trevor Arnett Library." Atlanta University, 1963.

Smith, Samuel Lee. "A Study of Tested Differences, if any, in Intelligence and Achievement Between College Freshmen From Accredited High Schools in Georgia and College Freshmen From Non-Accredited High Schools in Georgia." Atlanta University, 1953.

Smith, Shirley Temple. "A Study of the Graduate Record Examination Performances of Students Enrolled at Atlanta University During the Period 1957-1962." Atlanta University, 1964.

Smothers, James Roy. "Socio-Economic Status and Academic Achievement of College Women, 'North and South'." Fisk University, 1947.

Sorrell, Florence Beatrice Stevens. "A Survey of the Relation of Negro Business Requirements to Courses Offered in Negro Institutions." Hampton, 1940.

Sowers, Joseph Cullen. "Some Phases of State Control of State-Supported Institutions of Higher Education in Texas, With Particular Reference to the State." University of Texas, 1949.

Spearman, Fannie Louise. "A Catalogue of the Curricula Offerings of the Negro Land-Grant Colleges in the Field of Home Economics Education." Atlanta University, 1943.

Spencer, Glen Thomas. "Correlation Between English Placement Test From X-2 Scores and Freshmen English Course Averages for One Hundred and Eighty-Eight Freshmen of the Agricultural and Technical College of North Carolina." A. & T. College of [Greensboro] North Carolina, 1949.

Stafford, Joseph Thomas. "A Comparative Study of Selected Religious Attitudes of Freshmen and Senior College Students." Fisk University, 1952.

Staley, F. M. "Suggestions for Curriculum-Making in Agriculture for the Negro Agricultural and Technical College of North Carolina and Experiences of Teachers of Agriculture." Cornell University, 1929.

Stanley, Curtis Emory. "A Comparative Study of the Performance of Fisk Freshmen on the ACE Test 'North and South' for Five Selected Years From 1936 Through 1946." Fisk University, 1949.

Stephens, Ryburn Glover. "An Analysis of Theses Written in the Field of Education at Atlanta University From 1941-1951." Atlanta University, 1953.

Sturgis, Gladys Marie. "A Study of Masters' Theses Submitted by Students of the Atlanta University School of Library Service in Partial Fulfillment of the Requirements of the Degree of Master of Science in Library Service, 1955 Through 1959." Atlanta University, 1964.

Sugg, Vera Louise. "An Analysis and Evaluation of the Spelman-Morehouse Reading Program for the Year 1943-1944." Atlanta University, 1944.

Summersette, John Fred. "An Analysis of the English Placement Test Given at the North Carolina College for Negroes During 1940-41." North Carolina College for Negroes, 1946.

Sumner, Frances. "The Mental Health of White and Negro College Students." Howard University, 1932.

Sumter, Richard S. "A Follow-Up Study of the Proposed Plans in the Master's Investigations Written at Atlanta University, Atlanta, Georgia, 1944-1947." Atlanta University, 1949.

Swift, Leroy R. "A Survey of Health Facilities in the Negro College and a Proposed Health Education Program for the North Carolina College." University of Michigan, 1942.

Swinton, Toney Vance. "Career of Booker T. Washington." Indiana University, 1936.

Talbert, Charles A. "The Methodist Episcopal Church and the Negro During the Reconstruction Period 1865-1885." Northwestern University, 1932.

Tanksley, Hassell. "A Survey of the Health and Physical Education Program in the Negro Colleges and Universities of Texas." Prairie View A. & M. College, 1950.

Tarrow, Willie A. "A University for Negroes of Texas-A Promise Unfulfilled." Prairie View University, 1946.

Taylor, Carol R. "The Use of Trevor Arnett Library by Atlanta University Faculty Members, 1960-1961." Atlanta University, 1963.

Taylor, William S. "Intramural Athletics for Men in Negro Colleges." University of Michigan, 1937.

Thomas, Edith Dalton. "The Orientation Program for New Students at Clark College, Atlanta, Georgia." Atlanta University, 1963.

Thomas, Mamie Jackson. "A Study of the Requirements for Admission to One Hundred and Fifty State-Controlled Colleges and Universities." Atlanta University, 1960.

Thomas, Samuel S. "A Survey of Guidance Services Presently Functioning in the Schools Represented by the Twenty-Five Members of the Atlanta University First Academic Year Guidance and Counseling Institute, 1962." Atlanta University, 1964.

Thompson, Dorothy P. "An Index to the _Bulletin of Atlanta University_, for the Period January, 1892, Through December, 1896." Atlanta University, 1963.

Thornton, David Howard. "Establishment of Land-Grant Colleges for Negroes." University of Wisconsin, 1936.

Tomlinson, John Henry. "Growth and Development of Federal Credit Unions of Atlanta University, Morehouse, and Spelman; University Homes and Atlanta Teachers." Atlanta University, 1949.

Tooks, Kelly Tollolah. "Neurotic Tendency of Negro Women of Low Socio-Economic Status Compared With Neurotic

Tendency of Socio-Economic Status of Negro College Women." Howard University, 1950.

Totten, Herman L. "A Survey of the Use of the Carnegie Library of Wiley College Students, 1964." University of Oklahoma, 1964.

Trawick, Henrietta Bernice. "A Comparative Study of the Vocabularies of Ten Four-Year Old Boys and Girls, and Ten Three and One-Half Year Old Boys and Girls in the Nursery School of Spelman College, Atlanta, Georgia." Atlanta University, 1935.

Trolinger, Sara Ruth. "A Survey of the Education Books and Periodicals in the Trevor Arnett Library." Atlanta University, 1960.

Tuggle, Dewey Highgate. "A Study of the Deans of Negro Colleges." Fisk University, 1936.

Tukes, Sarah Adams. "A Follow-Up of the Graduates of Clark College, Atlanta, Georgia, for the Period 1953 Through 1957." Atlanta University, 1964.

Turner, John A. "Dental Health Conditions in Negro Colleges." New York University, 1940.

Tyler, Homer Duke. "The Relationship Between the Scholastic Averages of Athletes and Non-Athletes Enrolled at Fisk From 1936-1939." Fisk University, 1941.

Tyms, Brittie Ann Martin. "Problems of Adjustment Among Students Within the Morehouse College Community." Atlanta University, 1949.

Ume, Kalu Egwuonwu. "Analysis of Reading Difficulties of Fifty Freshmen of Morehouse College Who Enrolled in Reading in September, 1962." Atlanta University, 1964.

Urguhart, George Richard. "The Status of Secondary and Higher Education of Negroes in Texas." University of Texas, 1931.

Van-Arkadie, Lena Frederica. "A Study of Art Education in the Negro Colleges Approved as Class 'A' by the Association of Colleges and Secondary Schools of the Southern States." Virginia State College, 1941.

Vowell, Raymond Woodrow. "The Need and Suggested Areas for the Location of Public Junior Colleges for Negroes in the State of Texas." University of Texas, 1948.

Wadlowe, Emory Alvin. "A Study of the Religious Program of Five Church - Related Colleges." Oberlin College, 1945.

Walker, Gwendolyn L. "A Study of Student Assistants in

a Selected Group of Negro Colleges: Their Selection, Training and Duties." Atlanta University, 1958.

Walker, Joseph Wesley. "A Study of the Educational Adjustment of Fifty Negro Veterans of World War II in the Atlanta University Center of Atlanta, Georgia." Atlanta University, 1946.

Walker, Marjorie Elizabeth. "An Evaluative Study of the Dormitory Recreation Program Based on the Needs of Students at the Florida Agricultural and Mechanical College, 1951-1952." Atlanta University, 1952.

Waller, James E. "Emmett Jay Scott: The Public Life of a Private Secretary." University of Maryland, 1971.

Walls, William Jacob. "Joseph Charles Price, Pioneer Negro Educator and Race Leader." University of Chicago, 1942.

Ward, Ruth Leflore. "An Index to the _Bulletin of Atlanta University_, for the Period January, 1901, Through December, 1903." Atlanta University, 1963.

Ware, Ardella Clark. "Food Habits of Three Hundred Twenty Howard University Freshmen." Howard University, 1943.

Washington, E. M. "A Study of the Nursery School at Virginia State College and Its Relation to the Home Economics Education." Virginia State College, 1940.

Washington, Samuel N. "The Land-Grant Colleges for Negroes, 1914-1945: A Study in Higher Education." Prairie View A. & M. College, 1949.

Webb, Elaine Lockhart. "Reading and Library Use by Student Leaders of Alabama Agricultural and Mechanical College, Normal, Alabama, 1959-1960." Atlanta University, 1964.

Weddington, Rachel Thomas. "The Potential Effect of Selective College Admission at Howard University." Howard University, 1940.

Westbrooks, Johnnie Mae. "The Sweatt Case: A Study in Minority Strategy in Texas." Prairie View A. & M. College, 1953.

Wheeler, Martha Williams. "A Study of Selected Abilities of First Quarter Freshmen Majoring in Business at Agricultural and Industrial State College." Tennessee Agricultural and Industrial State College, 1944.

White, Delbert Wayman. "A Study of Intramural Programs in Negro Colleges." State University of Iowa, 1938.

White, Eleanor Shirley. "A Study of the Ability of Graduate Students of Atlanta University to Use the Trevor Arnett Library." Atlanta University, 1952.

White, Johnnie E. "The Environmental Forces in the Behavior and Development of 411 Freshmen Enrolled at Prairie View 1947-1948." Prairie View A. & M. College, 1950.

White, Zula Patterson. "The Relationship of Hampton Institute to the Beginning and Operation of the Jeanes Fund." Hampton Institute, 1943.

Whitehurst, Keturah Elizabeth. "A Statistical Investigation of Desire: With Special Reference to Sex and College." Howard University, 1934.

Whitten, Benjamin C. "Certification, Training and Employment of Industrial Arts Graduates of Negro Teacher Training Institutions in Ten Selected States." The Pennsylvania State College, 1948.

Wilcox, Berry Octavious. "A Graphical Study of the Relationship Between Scholastic Achievement and Performance on ACE and Other Selected Entrance Examinations for College Freshmen." Fisk University, 1950.

Wilder, Jennie Taylor. "Efficiency of Predicting College Achievement on Basis of High-School Grades." Howard University, 1940.

Wilkinson, Lulu L. "The Present Status of Physical Education for Women in Negro Colleges and Universities." New York University, 1932.

Williams, Avery White. "Survey of State College Libraries for Negroes in Mississippi." Atlanta University, 1951.

Williams, Billye Jewel Suber. "Content Analyses of Five Short Stories Preferred by a Group of College Freshmen." Atlanta University, 1961.

Williams, Earl. "The Influence of the Okolona College Food Processing Plant Activities Upon Food Production and Preservation of One Hundred Negro Farm Families of East Chickasaw County, Mississippi." Tuskegee Institute, 1951.

Williams, Edward Pendleton. "The Religious Concepts of Fisk Freshmen and Seniors Compared With Themselves and With the Freshmen and Seniors at Bethany College." Fisk University, 1943.

Williams, Elveta Leona. "A Study of Speech Needs of Freshmen at Fisk University." Fisk University, 1947.

Williams, Gwendolyn Carter. "A Survey of the Periodicals Collections and General Problems Relating to the Use of Periodicals in the Libraries of the Atlanta University Center." Atlanta University, 1953.

Williams, Helen Holt. "A Study of the Attitudes of 105

Graduates of Atlanta School of Social Work Toward the Training They Have Received." Atlanta University, 1947.

Williams, Juanita Lee. "Federal Legislation in Relation to Negro Land-Grant Colleges." Howard University, 1933.

Williams, Leonora Patton. "The Possible Contribution of Home Economics to the Development of Men and Women Students in the Negro Junior College of Little Rock, Arkansas." Iowa State College, 1938.

Williams, Ola E. "How Much General Education is Included in the Home Economics Teaching Curricula of a Representative Group of Colleges?" Howard University, 1948.

Williams, Robert Earl. "An Analysis of Certain Supreme Court Decisions Affecting Opportunities in Higher Education for Negroes Since the Gaines Decision." Fisk University, 1952.

Williams, Roger Kenton. "An Exploratory Study of the Adjustment of 49 Male Negro College Students at One Segregated and Two Mixed Colleges." Pennsylvania State University, 1940.

Willie, Charles Vert. "A Study of Courtship Patterns of College Men." Atlanta University, 1944.

Wilson, Henry A. "Development of Smith-Hughes Agriculture for Negroes in Arkansas." Ohio State University, 1929.

Wilson, Hulda A. "An Evaluation of the Materials Collection of the Spelman College Library." Atlanta University, 1963.

Wilson, James C. "Heights and Weights of Negro College Men and Women." Springfield College, 1948.

Winston, Daisy. "Reading as an Approach to the Deficiencies in English of the Freshmen at Miles College, Birmingham, Alabama." Atlanta University, 1946.

Wise, Robertta Morse. "The Educational Significance of the General Aptitude Test Battery for Howard University School of Pharmacy." Howard University, 1954.

Wisner, Genevieve McVey. "A Comparative Study of the Qualifications of Teachers of Music in Negro and White Colleges." University of Colorado, 1944.

Woods, Clara Williams. "The Effect of Course Work in Consumer Buying With Especial Emphasis on the Hosiery Buying Practices of Negro Students of Rust College." Iowa State, 1937.

Wright, Giles O. "The Administration and Control of

Intercollegiate Athletics in Negro Colleges." University of Michigan, 1935.

Wright, Stephen Junius. "The Use of Socio-Economic Factors and Intelligence Test Scores in the Prediction of Academic Achievement of Negro College Students." Howard University, 1939.

Yerby, Frank Garvin. "The Little Theatre in the Negro College." Fisk University, 1938.

Young, Sister Mary David. "A History of the Development of Catholic Education for the Negro in Louisiana." Louisiana State University, 1944.

SELECTED BOOKS AND GENERAL REFERENCES 5

Abajian, James de T. Compiler. Blacks and Their Contribution to the American West; A Bibliography and Union List of Library Holdings Through 1970. Boston: G. K. Hall and Company, 1974.

Ames, Mary. From a New England Woman's Diary in Dixie in 1865. Norwood, Mass.: The Plimpton Press, 1906.

Anderson, Lewis F. History of Manual and Industrial School Education. New York: D. Appleton and Company, 1926.

Anderson, Matthew. Presbyterianism in its Relation to the Negro. Philadelphia: McGill, White & Company, 1897.

Armstrong, Byron K. Factors in the Formulation of Collegiate Programs for Negroes. Ann Arbor, Michigan: Edwards Brothers, 1939.

Armstrong, Samuel Chapman. Ideas on Education Expressed by Samuel Chapman Armstrong. Hampton, Va.: Hampton Institute Press, 1908.

_____. Normal School Work Among the Freedmen. Boston: The Author, 1872.

Arnett, Ethel Stephens. Greensboro, North Carolina. Chapel Hill: The University of North Carolina Press, 1955.

Atlanta University, Trevor Arnett Library. Guide to Manuscripts and Archives in the Negro Collection of Trevor Arnett Library. Atlanta: Atlanta University, Trevor Arnett Library, 1971.

Barksdale, Gaynelle. Compiler. Graduate Theses of Atlanta University, 1931-1942. Atlanta, Ga.: The Library, Atlanta University, 1944.

Barnes, E. A. How the Problem is Solved at Talladega College. New York: American Missionary Association, 1903.

Beall, Noble Y. Northern Baptists in Higher Education of

Negroes During 1865-1875. New York: Board of Education of the Northern Baptist Convention, 1944.

Beam, Lura. He Called Them by the Lightning: A Teacher's Odyssey in the Negro South, 1908-1909. Indianapolis: Bobbs-Merrill, 1967.

Beard, Augustus F. A Crusade of Brotherhood: A History of the American Missionary Association. Boston: The Pilgrim Press, 1909.

Bede, Brother [Rouse, Michael Francis]. A Study of the Development of Negro Education Under Catholic Auspices in Maryland and the District of Columbia. Baltimore: Johns Hopkins University Press, 1935.

Beer, G. Pitt. Ministers to Turbulent America: A History of the American Baptist Home Mission Society Covering Its Fifth Quarter Century, 1952-1957. Philadelphia: The Judson Press, 1957.

Bender, Richard N. The Church-Related College Today: Anachronism or Opportunity. Nashville, Tennessee: The General Board of Education, The United Methodist Church, 1971.

Board of Freedmen's Missions of the United Presbyterian Church. Our Work Among the Freedmen. Cincinnati, Ohio: 1911.

Bond, Horace Mann. The Education of the Negro in the American Social Order. Englewood Cliffs, N. J.: Prentice-Hall, 1934. (New York: Octagon, 1966)

Bond, Horace Mann. "A Century of Negro Higher Education," in William Brickman and Stanley Leher, eds., A Century of Higher Education. New York: Society for the Advancement of Education, 1962.

_____. Black American Scholars, A Study of Their Beginnings. Detroit: Balamp Publishing, 1972.

_____. A Statistical Study of State and Federal Appropriations to Institutions Offering Higher Education in Seventeen Southern States by Race, 1899-1900 to 1931-1932. Chicago: Associated Negro Press, 1937.

_____. "The Negro Scholar and Professional in America," in The America Negro Reference Book. John P. Davis, ed. Englewood Cliffs, N. J.: Prentice-Hall, 1966.

_____. Negro Education in Alabama: A Study in Cotton and Steel. Washington, D. C.: The Associated Publishers, 1939.

Boone, Richard Gouse. A History of Education in Indiana. New York: D. Appleton & Co., 1892.

Bortune, Elizabeth Hyde. First Days Amongst the Contrabands. Boston: Lee & Shepard, 1893.

Bowles, Frank, and DeCosta, Frank A. Between Two Worlds: A Profile of Negro Higher Education. New York: McGraw-Hill Book Company, 1971.

Boyer, Alan E., and Boruch, Robert F. The Black Student in American Colleges. Washington, D. C.: American Council on Education, March 1969.

Bragg, George F. History of the Afro-American Group of the Episcopal Church. Baltimore: Church Advocate Press, 1922.

Branson, Herman R. "The Negro Scientist: His Sociological Background, His Record of Achievement and His Potential," in Julius H. Taylor, ed. The Negro in Science. Baltimore: Morgan State College Press, 1955.

Brawley, Benjamin. A Short History of the American Negro. New York: The Macmillan Company, 1913.

_____. A Social History of the Negro. New York: The Macmillan Company, 1921.

Brawley, James P. Two Centuries of Methodist Concern: Bondage, Freedom and Education of Black People. New York: Vantage Press, Inc., 1974.

Broderick, Francis L., and Meier, August, eds. Negro Protest Thought in the Twentieth Century. New York: Bobbs-Merrill Company, Inc., 1966.

Brown, Hugh Victor. A History of the Education of Negroes in North Carolina. Raleigh: Irving Swain Press, 1961.

_____. E-Quality Education in North Carolina Among Negroes. Raleigh, North Carolina: Irving-Swain Press, Inc., 1964.

Brown, Ina Corinna. The Story of the American Negro. New York: Friendship Press, 1936.

Brown, William Henry. The Education and Economic Development of the Negro in Virginia. Charlottesville, Virginia: Surber-Arundale Company, Inc., 1923.

Brownlee, Frederick Leslie. New Day Ascending. Boston: The Pilgrim Press, 1946.

Bryant, J. A. A Survey of Black American Doctorates. New York: Ford Foundation, 1969, 1970.

Bullock, Henry Allen. A History of Negro Education in the South From 1619 to the Present. Cambridge, Massachusetts: Harvard University Press, 1967.

Bumstead, Horace. Secondary and Higher Education in the South for Whites and Negroes. Publication of the National Association for the Advancement of Colored People, 1910.

_____. Higher Education of the Negro--Its Practical Value. Atlanta, Ga.: Atlanta University Press, 1870.

Caliver, Ambrose. Freshman Orientation. Fisk University Bulletin, 1927.

Carnegie Commission on Higher Education. From Isolation to Mainstream: Problems of the Colleges Founded for Negroes. New York: McGraw-Hill, 1971.

Church, J. W. The Halifax Plan for the Practical Education of the Negro. Hampton, Va.: Hampton Institute Press, 1910.

Clark, J. S. The Work of the Negro Land-Grant College. Baton Rouge, Louisiana: Southern University Press, 1929.

Clayton, Victoria V. White and Black Under the Old Regime. Milwaukee: Young Churchman Co., 1899.

Clift, Virgil A.; Anderson, Archibald W.; and Hullfish, H. Gordon, eds. Negro Education in America, Its Adequacy, Problems and Needs. New York: Harper and Row, 1962.

_____. "Educating the American Negro," in American Negro Reference Book, John P. Davis, ed. Englewood Cliffs, N. J.: Prentice-Hall, 1966.

Cobb, W. Montague. The First Negro Medical Society; A History of the Medico-Chirurgical Society of the District of Columbia, 1884-1939. Washington, D. C.: Associated Publishers, 1939.

Commission on Colleges. Black Colleges in the South. Atlanta, Ga.: Southern Association of Colleges and Schools, 1971.

Commission on Higher Education in the South. The Negro and Higher Education in the South. Atlanta: Southern Regional Education Board, 1967.

Cooley, Rossa B. Homes of the Freed. New York: New Republic, Inc., 1926.

Cooper, James Wesley. The American Missionary Association in Alabama. New York: American Missionary Association, 1900.

Cromwell, John. The Negro in American History. Washington, D. C.: The American Negro Academy, 1914.

Cromwell, Otelia. Readings From Negro Authors, for

Schools and Colleges, With a Bibliography of Negro Literature. New York: Harcourt, Brace and Company, 1931.

Crowin, E. H. L., and Sturges, G. E. Opportunities for the Medical Education of Negroes. New York: C. Scribner's Sons, 1936.

Cruse, Harold. The Crisis of the Negro Intellectual. New York: William Marrow and Company, 1967.

Cummings, A. W. The Early Schools of Methodism. [Part 4; Central Tennessee College, Clark University, Baker Institute, and Claflin University] Cincinnati: Phillips and Hunt, 1886.

Curnock, Nehemiah, ed. The Journal of the Rev. John Wesley, A.M. Vols. I and IV. London: Epworth Press, 1938.

Curtis, James L. Blacks, Medical Schools, and Society. Ann Arbor: University of Michigan Press, 1971.

Cuthbert, Marion Vera. Education and Marginality. New York: American Book, Stratford Press, 1942.

Dabney, Charles William. Universal Education in the South. 2 Vols. Chapel Hill: University of Carolina Press, 1936.

Dabney, Charles W. The Education of Negro Ministers, Based Upon a Survey of Theological School for Negroes in the United States. New York: George H. Doran Company, 1925.

Dabney, Lillian G. The History of Schools for Negroes in the District of Columbia, 1807-1947. Washington, D. C.: Catholic University of America Press, 1949.

Daedalus. The Future of the Black Colleges. Issued as Vol. 100, No. 3, of the Proceedings of the American Academy of Arts and Sciences, Summer, 1971.

Daniels, John. In Freedom's Birthplace: A Study of the Boston Negroes. Boston, New York: Houghton Mifflin Co., 1914.

Davis, John P., ed. The American Negro Reference Book. Englewood Cliffs, N. J.: Prentice-Hall, 1966.

Davis, John W. Problems in the Collegiate Education of Negroes. Department of Education, Study No. 8. Institute, West Virginia: West Virginia State College, 1937.

DeBow, J. D. B. Statistical View of the United States. Washington, A. O. P.: Nicholson, Public Printer, 1854.

Derbigny, Irving Anthony. General Education in the Negro College. Stanford, California: Stanford University Press, 1947.

Diggs, Margaret Agneta. Catholic Negro Education in the United States. Washington, D. C., 1936.

Douglass, Harlan Paul. Christian Reconstruction in the South. Boston: Pilgrim Press, 1909.

Dreer, Herman. The History of the Omega Psi Phi Fraternity, A Brotherhood of Negro College Men, 1911 to 1939. Washington: The Fraternity, 1940.

Du Bois, W. E. Burghardt. The Negro Common School. Atlanta University Publications, No. 6. Atlanta: Atlanta University Press, 1901.

_____, ed. The College-Bred Negro. Atlanta University Publications, 5. Atlanta, Ga.: Atlanta University Press, 1900.

_____. The Education of Black People: Ten Critiques, 1906-1960. Edited by Herbert Aptheker. Amherst: University of Massachusetts Press, 1973.

_____. The College-Bred Negro American. Atlanta University Publications, 15. Atlanta, Ga.: Atlanta University Press, 1910.

_____, and Dill, Augustus G., eds. The Common School and the Negro American. Atlanta University Publications, 16. Atlanta, Ga.: Atlanta University Press, 1912.

Du Bois, W. E. B. Encyclopedia of the Negro: Preparatory Volume. New York: The Phelps-Stokes Fund, 1945. Revised edition in 1946.

_____. The Gift of Black Folk. Boston: Stratford Co., 1924.

_____. "The Talented Tenth," in Washington, Booker T. et al. The Negro Problem. New York: James Pott & Co., 1903.

_____. Black Reconstruction. New York: Harcourt, Brace & Co., 1935.

_____. The Souls of Black Folk. Chicago: A. C. McClug & Company, 1904.

_____. The Negro Artisan. Atlanta, Georgia: Atlanta University Publications, 1902.

_____. Dusk of Dawn: An Essay Toward an Autobiography of a Race Concept. New York: Harcourt, Brace & World, Inc., 1940.

Dummett, Clifton Orrin, ed. The Growth and Development of the Negro in Dentistry in the United States. Chicago: National Dental Association, 1952.

Dunlap, Mollie Ernestine. Institutions of Higher Learning Among Negroes in the United States of America: A Compendium. Wilberforce University, 1947.

_____. A Partial Bibliography of the Publications of the Faculty of the College of Education and Industrial Arts, Wilberforce, Ohio. Yellow Springs, Ohio: Antioch Press, 1949.

Eaton, John, Jr. Colored Schools in Mississippi, Arkansas and Tennessee, April, 1865. Memphis: 1865.

_____. Grant, Lincoln and the Freedmen. New York: Longmans, Green and Co., 1907.

_____. Report of General Superintendent of Freedmen, Tennessee and Arkansas, 1864. Memphis: 1864.

Eddy, Edward Danforth, Jr. Colleges for Our Time: The Land-Grant Idea in American Education. New York: Harper, 1956, 1957.

Egerton, John. State Universities and Black Americans; An Inquiry into Desegregation and Equity--for Negroes in 100 Public Institutions. Atlanta, Southern Education Foundation, 1969.

_____. Higher Education for "High Risk" Students. Atlanta: Southern Education Foundation, 1968.

_____. The Public Black College Fact Book. Nashville, Tennessee, Race Relation Information Center, 1971.

Embree, Edwin R. Julius Rosenwald Fund (Review of Two Decades), 1917-1936. Chicago: Rosenwald Fund, 1936.

_____. The Julius Rosenwald Fund. Chicago, Illinois: The Julius Rosenwald Fund, 1933.

_____. A Review for the Two-Year Period, 1933-1935. Chicago, Illinois: The Julius Rosenwald Fund, 1935.

_____. Brown America. New York: The Viking Press, 1932, 1936.

Fairchild, James H. Oberlin, the Colony and the College. Oberlin: E. J. Goodrich, 1883.

Fisk University Library. Fisk University Theses, 1917-1939. Nashville: Fisk University Library, 1940. Ibid., 1940 Supplement, March, 1940.

Fleming, Walter L. Documentary History of Reconstruction: Political, Military, Social, Religious, Educational, and Industrial, 1865 to the Present Time. 2 vols. Cleveland: Arthur H. Clark Company, 1906 and 1907.

_____. Civil War and Reconstruction in Alabama. New York: Columbia University Press, 1905.

Fletcher, Robert Samuel. A History of Oberlin College. 2 vols. Oberlin, Ohio: Oberlin College, 1943.

Floyd, Arthur. Current Practices and Trends in Vocational Education. Tuskegee Institute, Alabama, 1934.

Foley, Albert S., S. J. God's Men of Color. New York: Farrar, Strauss, & Co., 1955.

Forten, Charlotte L. The Journal of Charlotte Forten, A Free Negro in the Slave Era. New York: Dryden Press, 1953, 1967.

Franklin, John Hope. Reconstruction: After the Civil War. University of Chicago Press, 1961.

_____. From Slavery to Freedom: A History of Negro Americans. New York: Knopf, 1967, 1969.

Frazier, Edward Franklin. The Negro in the United States. New York: The Macmillan Company, 1949, 1957.

_____. "The Role of the Social Scientist in the Negro College," in Robert E. Martin, ed. The Civil War in Perspective: Papers Contributed to the Twenty-Fourth Annual Conference of the Division of the Social Sciences. Howard University, 1961.

_____. Black Bourgeoisie. New York: Free Press, 1957.

French, Mrs. A. M. Slavery in South Carolina and the Ex-Slaves, of the Port Royal Mission. New York: William French, 1862.

From Servitude to Service, Being the Old South Lectures on the History and Work of Southern Institutions for the Education of the Negro. Boston: American Unitarian Association, 1905. Reprinted, American Education Its Men, Ideas and Institutions. Lawrence A. Cremin and Frederick A. P. Barnard, editors. New York: Arno Press, 1969.

Gallagher, Buell G. American Caste and the Negro College. New York: Columbia University Press, 1938. [N. Y.: Gordian Press, 1966]

Gallagher, Buell G. College and the Black Student. New York: National Association for the Advancement of Colored People, 1971.

Garner, James Wilford. Reconstruction in Mississippi. New York: Macmillan Co., 1901.

Geier, Woodrow. Campus Unrest and the Church-Related

College. Nashville, Tennessee: Board of Higher Education, The United Methodist Church, 1970.

Gillard, J. The Catholic Church and the American Negro. Baltimore: St. Joseph's Society Press, 1929.

Gore, George William. In-Service Professional Improvement of Negro Public School Teachers in Tennessee. New York: Teachers College, 1940.

Gray, William Herbert. Administrative Provisions for Guidance in Negro Colleges and Universities. Madison, Wis.: Journal of Educational Research, 1942.

Greene, Harry Washington. An Adventure in Experimental Cooperative Teaching; A General Account of Recent Work in Progressive Education. Institute, W. Va., 1938.

_____. Efforts to Improve a Teacher-Education Program Through Studies in Intergroup Relations, 1945-1948. Institute, West Virginia: West Virginia State College, 1949.

_____. Holders of Doctorates Among American Negroes; An Educational and Social Study of Negroes Who Have Earned Doctoral Degrees in Course, 1876-1943. Boston: Meador Publishing Company, 1946.

Griffin, M. I. J. Petition of the Catholic People of Color in Philadelphia, 1817. Philadelphia, American Catholic Historical Researches, VII, 1890.

Gurin, Patricia, and Katz, Daniel. Motivation and Aspiration in the Negro College. Ann Arbor: Institute for Social Research, University of Michigan, 1966. [Eric No. ED 010 537.]

Guzman, Jessie Parkhurst. "George Washington Carver: A Classified Bibliography." Bulletin of Bibliography, 21 : 1 (May-August, 1953), 13-16. Ibid., 21 (September-December, 1953), 34-38.

Hampton Negro Conference (Report of 3rd Conference). Hampton University: The Conference, 1898.

Hampton Institute. What Hampton Graduates Are Doing, 1878-1904. Hampton, Va.: Hampton Institute Press, 1904.

Hampton Institute. Acts of Incorporation, Laws of the State of Virginia, By-Laws, etc. Hampton, Va.: Hampton Institute Press, 1883.

_____. Annual Reports of Hampton Institute, 1868-1939. Hampton, Va.: Hampton Institute Press, 1868-1939.

_____. A History of the Negro in Virginia From 1619 to the Present Day. [1940] Compiled by workers of the Writer's Program of the Works Projects Administration in the State of

Virginia, sponsored by the Hampton Institute. New York: Hastings House, 1940.

Harlan, Louis R. Booker T. Washington: The Making of a Black Leader, 1856-1901. New York: Oxford University Press, 1972.

_____. The Booker T. Washington Papers. 4 Vols. Urbana: University of Illinois Press, Vols. 1 & 2, 1972; Vol. 3, 1974; and Vol. 4, 1975.

Harrison, W. P. The Gospel Among Slaves, A Short Account of Missionary Operations Among the African Slaves of the Southern States. Nashville, Tennessee: Publishing House of the Methodist Episcopal Church, South, 1893.

Hartshorn, William Newton. An Era of Progress and Promise, 1863-1910. Boston: Priscilla Publishing Co., 1910.

Hartshorne, Hugh. From School to College. New Haven: Yale University Press, 1939.

_____. Standards and Trends in Religious Education. New Haven: Yale University Press, 1933.

Hawkins, Hugh, ed. Booker T. Washington and His Critics. Lexington, Mass.: D. C. Heath and Company, 1962.

Hennings, Lloyd. The American Missionary Association, A Christian Anti-Slavery Society. Oberlin, Ohio: Oberlin College, 1933.

_____. History of the American Missionary Association. New York: American Missionary Association, 1875.

_____. History of the American Missionary Association With Illustrative Facts and Anecdotes. New York: American Missionary Association, 1891.

Hill, Johnny R. A Study of the Public Assisted Black College Presidency. New York: The Carlton Press, Inc., 1974.

Holland, Rupert Sargent, ed. Letters and Diary of Laura M. Towne, Written From the Sea Islands of South Carolina, 1862-1884. Cambridge: The Riverside Press, 1912.

Holmes, Dwight Oliver Wendell. The Evolution of the Negro College. New York City: Teachers College, Columbia University, 1934, [Reprinted New York, 1969].

Hood, James Walker. One Hundred Years of the African Methodist Episcopal Zion Church. New York: African Methodist Episcopal Zion Book Concern, 1895.

_____. Sketch of the Early History of the A. M. E. Zion Church, with Jubilee Souvenir and Appendix, 1914.

Industrial Training at Talladega College--Many Departments. New York: American Missionary Association, n. d.

Industrial Training in the Institutions of the American Missionary Association on the Prairie--In the South. New York: American Missionary Association, n. d.

Jaffe, Abram J., et al. _Negro Higher Education in the 1960's_. New York: Frederick A. Praeger Co., 1968.

Jay, J. M. _Negroes in Science: Natural Science Doctorates, 1876-1969_. Detroit: Balamp Publishing, 1971.

Jencks, Christopher, and Reisman, David. _The Academic Revolution_. New York: Doubleday and Company, 1968.

Johnson, Charles Spurgeon. _The Negro College Graduate_. Chapel Hill: University of North Carolina Press, 1938. (McGrath 1969). [Reprinted, West Port, Conn., 1970]

_____. _The Negro in American Civilization_. New York: Henry Holt & Company, 1930.

_____. _The Negro Population of the Tennessee Valley Area_. Fisk University, 1934.

Johnson, Roosevelt. _Black Scholars on Higher Education in the 70's_. Columbus, Ohio: ECCA Publication, Inc., 1974.

Jolly, David. _Hampton Institute Master's Theses, 1932-1945; An Annotated List_. Hampton, Va.: Collis P. Huntington Library, 1946.

Jones, Ann. _Uncle Tom's Campus_. New York: Praeger Publishers, 1973.

Jones, L. G. E. _The Jeanes Teacher in the United States, 1908-33; An Account of Twenty-Five Years' Experience in the Supervision of Negro Rural Schools_. Chapel Hill: University of North Carolina Press, 1937.

_____. _Negro Schools in the Southern States_. Oxford, England: Clarendon Press, 1928.

Jones, Thomas Jesse. _Social Studies in the Hampton Curriculum_. Hampton, Va.: Hampton Institute Press, 1908.

Jordan, Lewis G. _Negro Baptist History, 1875-1930_. Nashville: The Secondary School Publishing Board, National Baptist Convention, 1931.

Kelley, Robert. _The American College and the Social Order_. New York: Macmillan, 1940.

Kent, C. F. _Undergraduate Courses in Religion at the Tax-Supported Colleges and Universities of America_. New York: The National Council on Religion in Higher Education, 1924.

Kent, Raymond A. Higher Education in America. Boston and New York: Ginn and Company, 1930.

Knight, Edgar W. Education in the United States. Boston: Ginn and Company, 1929.

_____. Public Education in the South. Boston: Ginn and Company, 1922.

_____. The Influence of Reconstruction on Education in the South. New York: Teachers College, Columbia University, 1913.

Knight, Edgar Wallace. A Study of Hampton Institute. Chapel Hill, N. C.: The Author, 1937. [3 Vols. Mimeographed]

_____. Public School Education in North Carolina. Boston: Houghton Mifflin Co., 1916.

Knoll, Dorothy M. Black Student Potential. New York: American Association of Junior Colleges, 1970.

Lander, Earnest McPherson, Jr. A History of South Carolina, 1865-1960. Chapel Hill: The University of North Carolina Press, 1960.

LeMelle, Tilden J., and LeMelle, Wilbert J. The Black College: A Strategy for Achieving Relevancy. New York: Frederick A. Praeger, 1969.

Leonard, Robert Josselyn. Survey of Higher Education for the United Lutheran Church in America. New York: Teachers College, Columbia University, 1929.

Lewinski-Corwin, E. H., and Sturges, G. E. Opportunities for the Medical Education of Negroes. New York: Scribner, 1936.

Lewinson, Paul. Race, Class and Party; A History of Negro Suffrage and White Politics in the South. London and New York: Oxford University Press, 1933.

Logan, Rayford W. The Negro in the United States, Vol. I, A History to 1945--From Slavery to Second-Class Citizenship. New York: Van Nostrand Reinhold Co., 1970.

Long, Hollis Moody. Public Secondary Education for Negroes in North Carolina. New York: Teachers College, Columbia University, 1932.

Lovinger, Warren. General Education in Teachers Colleges. Oneonta, New York: American Association of Colleges for Teacher Education, 1948.

Low, W. A. "The Education of Negroes Viewed Historically." Negro Education in America: Its Adequacy, Problems, and Needs. Virgil A. Clift and others, editors. New York: Harper and Row, 1962.

McCuistion, Fred. Graduate and Professional Education for Negroes in the South. George Peabody College for Teachers Press, 1939.

_____. Financing Schools in the South. Nashville: Julius Rosenwald Fund, 1930.

_____. The South's Negro Teaching Force. Nashville: Julius Rosenwald Fund, 1931.

_____. Higher Education of Negroes. Nashville: Southern Association of Colleges and Secondary Schools, 1933.

McElreath, Walter. A Treatise on the Constitution of Georgia. Atlanta: The Harrison Company, 1912.

McFeely, William S. Yankee Stepfather: General O. O. Howard and the Freedmen. New Haven: Yale University Press, 1968.

McGrath, Earl J. The Predominantly Negro Colleges and Universities in Transition. New York: Bureau of Publications. Teachers College, Columbia University, 1965.

McKinney, Richard I. Religion in Higher Education Among Negroes. New Haven: Yale University Press, 1945.

McKinney, Theophilus Elisha. Higher Education Among Negroes. Charlotte: Johnson C. Smith University, 1932.

McMillan, Lewis K. Negro Higher Education in the State of South Carolina. Orangeburg, S. C.: The Author, 1952. Ibid., South Carolina State A. & M. College, 1962.

McPherson, James M., et al. Blacks in America Bibliographical Essays. Garden City, New York: Doubleday and Company, Inc., 1971.

MacLean, Malcolm S. Higher Education and the Negro. New York: Committee for Democracy and Intellectual Freedom, 1941.

Mann, Peter B. The Negro and Higher Education in the South. Atlanta: Southern Regional Education Board, 1967.

Mayo, Amory D. The Work of Certain Northern Churches in the Education of the Freedmen, 1861-1900. 1903.

Mays, B. E. The Occupational Outlook of 1,714 Negro College Students. New York: National Council of the Y.M.C.A., 1930.

_____, and Nicholson, J. W. The Negro's Church. New York: Institute of Social and Religious Research, 1933.

Mays, Edward. History of Education in Mississippi. Washington, D. C.: N.P., 1899.

Mazyck, Walter H. George Washington and the Negro. Washington, D. C.: The Associated Publishers, Inc., 1932.

Meier, August. Negro Thought in America, 1880-1915: Racial Ideologies in the Age of Booker T. Washington. Ann Arbor: University of Michigan Press, 1963.

Melchor, Beulah H. The Land Possessions of Howard University. Washington, D. C.: The Author, 1945.

Meriwether, C. History of Higher Education in South Carolina, With a Sketch of the Free School System. Washington, D. C.: N.P., 1889.

Miller, Elizabeth W. Compiler. The Negro in America A Bibliography. Cambridge: Harvard University Press, 1966, 1970.

Miller, Helen Sullivan. The History of Chi Eta Phi Sorority, Inc., 1932-1967. Washington, D. C.: Association for the Study of Negro Life and History, 1968.

_____. Out of the House of Bondage. New York: The Neale Publishing Company, 1914.

_____. "Howard: The National Negro University," in Alain Locke, ed. The New Negro: An Interpretation. New York: Albert and Charles Boni, 1925.

Mixon, Winfield Henry. History of the African Methodist Episcopal Church in Alabama. Nashville: A. M. E. Church Sunday School Union, 1902.

Montgomery, Winfield S. Historical Sketch of Education for the Colored Race in the District of Columbia, 1807-1905. Washington, D. C.: Smith Brothers, 1907.

Moore, J. J. History of the African Methodist Episcopal Zion Church. York, Pennsylvania: 1884.

Morais, Herbert M. The History of the Negro in Medicine. New York and Washington: Publishers Inc., 1967, 1969.

Morehouse, Henry Lyman. Baptist Home Missions in North America. New York: Baptist Home Mission Rooms, 1883.

Morgan, B. S., and Cork, J. F. History of Education in West Virginia. Charleston: Moses W. Donnally, Public Printer, 1893.

Morgan, John William. The Origin and Distribution of the Graduates of the Negro Colleges of Georgia. Milledgeville: Privately Printed, 1940.

Mumford, Frederick B. The Land-Grant College Movement. Columbia, Missouri: University of Missouri [Press], 1940.

Murray, Andrew E. Presbyterians and the Negro. Philadelphia: Presbyterian Historical Society, 1966.

Murry, Florence. Compiler. The Negro Handbook. New York: Wendell Malliett & Company, 1942.

Newbold, N. C., ed. Five North Carolina Negro Educators. Chapel Hill: University of North Carolina Press, 1939.

Newby, I. A. Black Carolinians. A History of Blacks in South Carolina From 1895 to 1968. Columbia, S. C.: University of South Carolina Press, 1973.

Noble, Jeanne L. The Negro Woman's College Education. New York: Bureau of Publications, Teachers College, Columbia University, 1956.

Noble, Stuart Grayson. Forty Years of the Public Schools in Mississippi. New York: Columbia University Press, 1918.

Olmsted, Frederick Law. A Journey in the Back Country. New York: 1863.

_____. A Journey in the Seaboard Slave States. New York: Dix & Edwards, 1856.

Orson, Claire, and Osborne, William. "Perceptions of White Faculty and Students on Historically Black College and University Campuses," in Research in Humanities and Social Sciences. George Breathett and Ewa U. Eko, eds. Greensboro, N. C.: Consortium on Research Training, [1977].

Orum, Anthony M. Black Students in Protest: A Study of the Origin of the Black Student Movement. Washington: American Sociological Association, 1972.

Parker, Marjorie H. Alpha Kappa Alpha: A History. Chicago: Bankers Press, 1958.

_____. Alpha Kappa Alpha Sorority, A History 1908-1958. Chicago: Alpha Kappa Alpha Sorority, Inc., 1966.

Payne, Daniel A. History of the African Methodist Episcopal Church. Nashville, Tennessee: A. M. E. Sunday School Union, 1891.

Phelan, James. History of Tennessee, the Making of a State. Boston and New York: Houghton Mifflin Co., 1869.

Pike, Gustavus D. The Singing Campaign for Ten Thousand Pounds, or the Jubilee Singers in Great Britain. New York: American Missionary Association, 1875.

Porter, Dorothy B. Compiler. Howard University Masters' Theses. Washington, D. C.: The Graduate School, Howard University, 1946.

_____, ed. A Working Bibliography on the Negro in the United States. Ann Arbor: University Microfilms, 1969.

_____, and Lanier, Betty Jo. Compilers. Howard University: A Selected List of References. Washington, D. C.: Howard University Library, 1965.

Public Higher Education in South Carolina. Nashville: Division of Field Services, Peabody College for Teachers, 1946.

Range, Willard. The Rise and Progress of Negro Colleges in Georgia 1865-1949. Athens: The University of Georgia Press, 1951.

Redcay, Edward Edgeworth. County Training Schools and Public Secondary Education for Negroes in the South. Washington: John F. Slater Fund, 1935.

Reitzes, Dietrich C. Negroes and Medicine. Cambridge: Harvard University Press, 1955.

Reynolds, John S. Reconstruction in South Carolina, 1865-1877. Columbia: The State Company, 1905.

Richings, G. F. Evidences of Progress Among Colored People. Philadelphia: G. S. Ferguson, 1896.

Riley, B. F. History of the Baptists in the Southern States East of the Mississippi. Philadelphia: American Baptist Publishing Society, 1898.

Robinson, Vivian U. "Contributions of the Christian Methodist Episcopal Church Through Its Educational Institutions," in Research in Humanities and Social Sciences. George Breathett and Ewa U. Eko, eds. Greensboro, N. C.: Consortium on Research Training, [1977].

Roche, Richard J. Catholic Colleges and the Negro Student. Washington, D. C.: Catholic University, 1950.

Rountree, Louise M. Compiler. An Annotated Bibliography on Livingstone College Including the Presidents and College-Church History. Salisbury, North Carolina: Livingstone College, Carnegie Library, 1963.

Rouse, Michael Francis. A Study of the Development of Negro Education Under Catholic Auspices in Maryland and the District of Columbia. Baltimore: The John Hopkins Press, 1935.

Rubin, Louis D., Jr., ed. Teach the Freeman: The Correspondence of Rutherford B. Hayes and the Slater Fund for

Negro Education. Two Volumes. Baton Rouge: Louisiana State University Press, 1959.

Rudwick, Elliott M. W. E. B. Du Bois: A Study in Minority Group Leadership. Philadelphia: University of Pennsylvania Press, 1960.

Rudwick, Elliott M. W. E. B. Du Bois Propagandist of the Negro Protest. New York: Atheneum, 1968.

Rust, R. S. The Freedmen's Aid Society of the Methodist Episcopal Church. New York: Tract Department, 1880.

Saunders, Doris E., ed. The Negro Handbook. Chicago: Johnson Publishing Company, 1966.

Scott, Emmett Jay. Negro Migration During the War. New York: Oxford University Press, 1920.

_____. The American Negro in the World War. Washington, D. C.: Associated Publishers, 1919.

Scott, John Irving E. Negro Students and Their Colleges. Boston: Meador Publishing Company, 1949.

_____. The Education of Black People in Florida. Philadelphia: Dorrance Publishing Company, 1974.

Searles, Herbert L. State Constitutional and Legislative Provisions and Supreme Court Decisions Relating to Sectarian Religious Influence on Tax-Supported Universities, Colleges and Public Schools. New York: The National Council on Religion in Higher Education, Bulletin V, 1924.

Shea, John Gilmary. History of the Catholic Church in the United States. 4 Vols. Akron, Ohio: D. H. McBride & Co., 1886.

Sherwood, Grace H. The Oblates' Hundred and One Years. New York: Macmillan, 1931.

Simkins, Francis B., and Woody, Robert H. South Carolina During Reconstruction. Chapel Hill: University of North Carolina, 1932.

Simmons, William J. Men of Mark: Eminent, Progressive, and Rising. Cleveland: George M. Rewell & Co., 1887.

Simpson, Matthew. A Hundred Years of Methodism. New York: Methodist Book Concern, 1885.

Slaughter, Linda W. The Freedmen of the South. Cincinnati: Elm Street Publishing Company, 1869.

Smith, Dwight L., ed. Afro-American History A Bibliography. Santa Barbara: A. B. C. Clio, Inc., 1974.

Smith, Samuel Leonard. Builders of Goodwill: The Story of the State Agents of Negro Education in the South. Nashville: Tennessee Book, 1950.

Sowell, Thomas. Black Education: Myths and Tragedies. New York: David McKay Co., 1973.

Spencer, Samuel Reid, Jr. Booker T. Washington and the Negro's Place in American Life. Boston: Little, Brown and Company, 1955.

Stampp, Kenneth M. The Era of Reconstruction, 1865-1877. New York: Alfred A. Knopf, 1965.

Stowell, Samuel J. Methodist Adventures in Negro Education. New York: The Methodist Book Concern, 1922.

Sumner, F. A. Talladega College, Talladega, Alabama. New York: American Missionary Association, n. d.

Swanson, Ernest W., and Friffin, John A., eds. Public Education in the South, Today and Tomorrow; A Statistical Survey. Chapel Hill: University of North Carolina Press, 1955.

Swint, Henry Lee. The Northern Teacher in the South, 1862-1870. Nashville: Vanderbilt University Press, 1941. [Reprinted New York: Octagon Books, 1967.]

Talladega College. New York: American Missionary Association, n. d.

Talladega College. New York: American Missionary Association, 1927.

Talladega College Alumni Are Making Good: Our Graduates in Educational Work. Talladega: The College Press, n. d.

Talladega College Alumni Are Making Good Pastors. Talladega: The College Press, 1921.

Talladega College: Catalog and Announcements, 100th Anniversary Issue. March, 1967.

Talladega College. The Graduates of Talladega College and What They Are Doing. Talladega: Press of Our Mountain Home, 1900.

Tanner, Benjamin T. An Apology for African Methodism. Baltimore: 1867.

Taylor, Alrutheus A. The Negro in South Carolina During Reconstruction. Washington, D. C.: Association for the Study of Negro Life and History, 1924.

_____. The Negro in the Reconstruction of Virginia.

Washington, D. C.: The Association for the Study of Negro Life and History, 1926.

Taylor, Harold. "The Philosophical Foundations of General Education." _General Education_, Part 1. Edited by Nelson Henry. _Yearbook of the National Society for the Study of Education_. Chicago: University of Chicago Press, 1952.

_____. _Education and Freedom_. New York: Abelard-Schuman, 1954.

Taylor, Julius H., ed. _The Negro in Science_. Baltimore: Morgan State College Press, 1955.

Tewksbury, Donald G. _The Founding of American Colleges and Universities Before the Civil War_. New York: Teachers College, Columbia University, 1932.

Thirkield, Wilbur Patterson. _The Training of Physicians and Ministers for the Negro Race_. Washington: Howard University Press, 1909.

Thompson, Daniel C. _Private Black Colleges at the Crossroads_. Westport, Conn.: Greenwood Press, Inc., 1973.

Tindall, George B. _South Carolina Negroes, 1877-1900_. Columbia, S. C.: University of South Carolina Press, 1952.

Trenholm, H. Councill. _Some Background and Status of Higher Education for Negroes in Alabama_. Montgomery: State Teachers College, 1949.

Vroman, Mary Elizabeth. _Shaped to Its Purpose: Delta Sigma Theta--The First Fifty Years_. New York: Random House, 1965.

Walker, Anne Kendrick. _Tuskegee and the Black Belt_. Richmond, Va.: The Dietz Press, Inc., 1944.

Washington, B. T., Wood, N. B., and Williams, F. B. _A New Negro For a New Century_. Chicago: American Publishing House, 1900-1901.

Washington, Booker T. _My Larger Education: Being Chapters From My Experiences_. Doubleday, Page & Co., 1911.

_____. _The Future of the American Negro_. Boston: Small, Maynard & Co., 1902.

_____. "Industrial Education for the Negro," _The Negro Problem, A Series of Articles by Representative American Negroes of Today_. W. E. B. Du Bois, Paul Lawrence Dunbar, Charles W. Chestnutt, et al. New York: James Pott & Co., 1903.

Washington, Booker Taliaferro, 1856-1915. _Black-belt Diamonds; Gems From the Speeches, Addresses, and Talks to Stu-_

dents of Booker T. Washington. New York: Fortune & Scott, 1898.

_____. Daily Resolves. New York: E. P. Dutton & Company, 1896.

_____., ed. Tuskegee and Its People; Ideals and Achievements. New York: D. Appleton and Company, 1906. [Reprinted, New York: Negro University Press, 1969.

_____. Character Building: Being the Addresses Delivered on Sunday Evenings to the Students of Tuskegee Institute. New York: Doubleday, Page and Company, 1902.

Washington, Booker T., and Du Bois, W. E. Burghardt. The Negro in the South, His Economic Progress in Relation to His Moral and Religious Development: Being the William Levi Bull Lectures for the Year 1907. Philadelphia: George W. Jacobs and Company, 1907.

Washington, E. Davidson. Quotations of Booker T. Washington. Tuskegee, Ala.: Tuskegee Institute Press, 1938.

Washington, E. Davidson, ed. Selected Speeches of Booker T. Washington. Garden City: Doubleday, Doran & Co., Inc., 1936, 1932.

Weinberg, Meyer. W. E. B. Du Bois: A Reader. New York: Harper and Row, 1970.

_____. The Education of the Minority Child: A Comprehensive Bibliography of 10,000 Selected Entries. Chicago: Integrated Education Associates, 1970.

Welsch, Erwin K. The Negro in the United States: A Research Guide. Bloomington, Indiana University Press, 1964.

Werner, M. R. Julius Rosenwald. New York: Harper and Brothers Publishers, 1939.

Wesley, Charles H. Negro Labor in the United States. New York: Vanguard Press, 1927.

_____. History of Sigma Pi Phi, First of the Negro-American Greek-Letter Fraternities. Washington, D. C.: Association for the Study of Negro Life and History, 1954.

_____. The History of Alpha Phi Alpha: A Development in Negro College Life. Washington, D. C.: Howard University Press, 1929. Ibid., Washington: Foundation Publishers, 1953.

West, Anson. Methodism in Alabama. Nashville: Southern Methodist Publishing Co., 1893.

West, Earle H. Compiler. A Bibliography of Doctoral Research on the Negro 1933-1966. Ann Arbor, Michigan: University Microfilm, 1969.

Wharton, Vernon Lane. The Negro in Mississippi, 1865-1890. Chapel Hill: University of North Carolina Press, 1947.

White, Charles L. A Century of Faith. Philadelphia: The Judson Press, 1932.

Whitehead, A. R. History of Education in West Virginia. Washington: Government Printing Office, 1902.

Whiting, Joseph Livingston. Shop and Class at Tuskegee; A Definitive Story of the Tuskegee Correlation Technique, 1910-1930. Boston: Chapman & Grimes, 1940.

Wickersham, J. P. A History of Education in Pennsylvania, Private and Public, Elementary and Higher, From the Time the Swedes Settled on the Delaware to the Present Day. Lancaster, Pennsylvania: The Author, 1886.

Wiggins, Samuel Paul. Higher Education in the South. Berkeley, Calif.: McCutchan, 1966.

_____. The Desegregation Era in Higher Education. Berkeley, Calif.: McCutchan Pub. Co., 1966.

Wilkinson, R. S. The Negro Colleges of South Carolina. Orangeburg: State Agricultural and Mechanical College, 1928.

Williams, Daniel T. Compiler. Eight Negro Bibliographies. New York: Kraus Reprint Co., 1970. [See No. 6, "The Awesome Thunder of Booker T. Washington: A Bio-Bibliographical Listing.]

Williams, G. W. History of the Negro Race in America, 1619-1880. 2 Vols. New York: G. P. Putnam's Sons, 1883.

Wilson, Charles H., Sr. Education for Negroes in Mississippi Since 1910. Boston: Meador Publishing Company, 1947.

Wolters, Raymond. The New Negro on Campus: Black College Rebellions of the 1920's. Princeton: Princeton University Press, 1975.

Woodson, C. G. The Negro Professional Man and the Community With Special Emphasis on the Physician and Lawyer. Washington: Association for the Study of Negro Life and History, 1934. [Reprinted Westport, Conn: Greenwood Press, 1970.]

_____. The Education of the Negro Prior to 1861: A History of the Education of the Colored People of the United States From the Beginning of Slavery to the Civil War. Washington: Association for the Study of Negro Life and History, 1919. [Reprinted New York: Arno Press, 1968.]

_____. The Mis-Education of the Negro. Washington, D. C.: Associated Publishers, Inc., 1933.

_____. The Negro in Our History. Washington, D. C.: The Associated Publishers, Inc., 1927.

_____. History of Early Negro Education in West Virginia. Institute: West Virginia Collegiate Institute, 1921.

Woody, Thomas. A History of Women's Education in the United States. 2 Vols. New York: The Science Press, 1929.

Woofter, Thomas Jackson. In His Black Yeomanry: Life on St. Helena Island. New York: Henry Holt and Company, Inc., 1930.

Work, Monroe N. A Bibliography of the Negro in Africa and America. New York: H. W. Wilson, 1928. [Reprinted New York: Octagon Books, Inc., 1965.]

Work, Monroe N., ed. Negro Year Book, Annual Encyclopedia. Nashville: Sunday School Union Printers, 1912, 1913, 1914-1915, 1916-1917, 1918-1919, 1921-1922, 1925-1926, 1931-1932.

Work, Monroe N. Industrial Work of Tuskegee Graduates and Former Students During the Year 1910. Tuskegee: Tuskegee Institute Press, 1911.

Wright, Arthur D. The Negro Rural School Fund, Inc., 1907-1933. Washington: Negro Rural School Fund, Inc., 1933.

Wright, Nathan, Jr., ed. What Black Educators are Saying. New York: Hawthorne Books, 1970.

Wright, Richard Robert, Sr. A Brief Historical Sketch of Negro Education in Georgia. Savannah, Ga.: Robinson Print. House, 1894.

Young, Donald R. America's Minority Peoples. Harper's, New York, 1932.

MISCELLANEOUS ______________ 6

AUTOBIOGRAPHIES—BIOGRAPHIES

Abbott, Layman. "Hollis Burke Frissell." The Outlook, 116 (August 15, 1917), 576-578.

"Alain LeRoy Locke." Journal of Negro History, 39 (October, 1954), 332-334.

Alderman, Edwin A., and Gordon, Armstead Churchill. J. L. M. Curry: A Biography. New York: Macmillan Company, 1911.

Alexander, Will W. "Phylon Profile, IX; John Hope." Phylon, 8 (1st Quarter, 1947), 4-13.

Armstrong, Samuel Chapman. Leader of Freemen, A Life Story of Samuel Chapman Armstrong for U. S. Soldiers and Sailors. Edited by Evertt T., and Paul G. Tomlinson. Philadelphia: American Sunday School Union, 1917.

_____. Twenty-Two Year's Work of Hampton Institute. Hampton, Virginia: Normal School Press, 1893.

"Andrew Carnegie." Negro History Bulletin, 1 (November, 1937), 5.

Aptheker, Herbert. "W. E. B. Du Bois: The First Eighty Years." Phylon, 9 (1st Quarter, 1948), 59-62.

Atlanta University. "Charles Spurgeon Johnson: Social Scientist, Editor and Education Statesman." Phylon, 17 (4th Quarter, 1957), 317-325.

Baker, Ray Stannard. "A Statesman of the Negro Problem." (An Appreciation of the Late Dr. Hollis B. Frissell, of Hampton Institute) World's Work, 35 (January, 1918), 306-311. Ibid., Photograph, p. 232.

Bardolph, Richard. The Negro Vanguard. New York: Rinehart, 1959. Reprinted New York: Vintage Books, 1961.

Barlow, Leila Mae. *Across the Years: Memoirs*. Montgomery, Ala.: Paragon Press, 1959.

"Benjamin Quarles: Biographical Sketch." *Negro History Bulletin*, 26 (January, 1963), 134, 154.

Bethune, Mary M. "The Torch is Ours." [Carter G. Woodson] *Journal of Negro History*, 36 (January, 1951), 9-11.

_____. "Stepping Aside . . . at Seventy-Four." *Women United*, October, 1949, 14-15.

Braithwaite, William Stanley. "John Hope." *Negro History Bulletin*, 5 : 6 (March, 1942), 142-143.

_____. "A Tribute to W. E. Burghardt Du Bois First Editor of Phylon." *Phylon*, 10 (4th Quarter, 1949), 302-306.

Brawley, Benjamin G. *Dr. Dillard of the Jeanes Fund*. New York: Fleming H. Revell Company, 1930.

Breaux, Elwyn E., and Perry, Thelma. "Inman E. Page, Outstanding Educator." *Negro History Bulletin*, 32 (May, 1969), 8-12.

Brewer, William M. "William Pickens (1881-1954)." *Journal of Negro History*, 39 (July, 1954), 242-244.

Broderick, Francis L. "The Academic Training of W. E. B. Du Bois." *Journal of Negro Education*, 27 (Summer, 1958), 10-16.

_____. "German Influence on the Scholarship of W. E. B. Du Bois." *Phylon*, 19 (4th Quarter, Winter, 1958), 367-371.

_____. *W. E. B. Du Bois: Negro Leadership in a Time of Crisis*. Stanford: Stanford University Press, 1959.

Brooks, Albert. "N. D. H. Councill Trenholm: Martyr on Alabama Racial Tightrope." *Negro History Bulletin*, 26 (May, 1963), 231-232.

Brown, Hallie Q. *Pen Pictures of the Pioneers of Wilberforce*. Wilberforce, Ohio: Aldine Publishing Company, 1937.

Browne, Rose Butler, and English, James. *Love My Children: An Autobiography*. New York: Meredith Press, 1969. (Virginia State College; Bluefield State College; West Virginia State College)

Bunche, Ralph J. "The World Significance of the Carver Story." *A. M. E. Review*, 72 (October-December, 1956), 35-39.

Carnegie, Andrew. *Autobiography*. New York: Garden City Press, 1933.

Carr, George B., and Finney, William P. _John Miller Dickey, His Life and Times_. Philadelphia: Westminster Press, 1929.

"Charles S. Johnson." _Interracial Review_, 29 (November, 1956), 183-184.

"Charles Spurgeon Johnson--1893-1956, President, Fisk University, 1946-1956." _Quarterly Review of Higher Education Among Negroes_, 24 (October, 1956), 171-173.

Clement, Rufus E. "Richard Robert Wright." _Pulse_, 9 (1st Quarter, 1948), 62-65.

_____. "Jackson Davis." _Phylon_, 8 (2nd Quarter, 1947), 177-178.

Coan, J. R. _Daniel Alexander Payne, Christian Educator_. Philadelphia: A. M. E. Book Concern, 1935.

Cobb, William Montague. "Dr. Charles Victor Roman (1864-1934) Biography." _Journal of the National Medical Association_, 45 (July, 1953), 301-305.

_____. "Charles Richard Drew--1904-1950." _Negro History Bulletin_, 13 (June, 1950), 203-204.

Cornely, Paul B. "Charles R. Drew (1904-1950) An Appreciation." _Phylon_, 11 (2nd Quarter, 1950), 176-177.

Curry, Jabez Lamar Monroe. _A Brief Sketch of George Peabody, and a History of the Peabody Education Fund Through Thirty Years_. Cambridge, Mass.: University Press, 1898. (Reprinted Westport, Conn.: 1970.)

"Daniel A. Payne." _Negro History Bulletin_, 1 (February, 1938), 5-6.

Davenport, Roy K. "E. Franklin Frazier (1894-1962): A Profile." _Journal of Negro Education_, 31 (Summer, 1962), 429-435.

Dedmond, Frederick H. "The Educator--D. O. W. Holmes." _Crisis_, 60 (January, 1953), 9-14.

Dempsey, Elam F. _Atticus Green Haygood_. Nashville: Parthenon Press, 1939.

Denison, J. H. "Samuel Chapman Armstrong." _Atlantic Monthly_, 73 (January, 1894), 90-98.

_____. "The Spirit of Armstrong." _Southern Workman_, 54 (March, 1925), 97-108.

"Dr. Irving Anthony Derbigney, 1899-1957." _Quarterly Review of Higher Education Among Negroes_, 26 (January, 1958), 47-49.

Drinker, Frederick E. Booker T. Washington; The Master Mind of a Child of Slavery. Philadelphia: National Publishing Company, 1915.

DuBois, Shirley Graham. His Day is Marching On: A Memior of W. E. B. Du Bois. Philadelphia: J. B. Lippincott, 1971.

Du Bois, William Burghardt. The Autobiography of W. E. B. Du Bois: A Soliloquy on Viewing My Life From the Last Decade of its First Century. New York: International Publishers, 1968.

Du Bois, W. E. B. "Moton of Hampton and Tuskegee." Phylon, 1 (4th Quarter, 1940), 344-350.

_____. "A Portrait of Carter G. Woodson." Masses and Mainstream, 3 (June, 1950), 19-25.

"Ebony Hall of Fame; Readers Select Charles S. Johnson." Ebony, 12 (February, 1957), 24.

E. Franklin Frazier (1894-1962)." Sociology and Social Research, 46 (July, 1962), 479.

Embree, Edwin R., and Waxman, Julia. Phylon Profile XVII: Julius R. Rosenwald: Philanthropist." Phylon, 9 (3rd Quarter, 1948).

"Ernest Evertt Just." Negro History Bulletin, 2 : 8 (May, 1939), 68-69.

Everett, Syble Ethel Byrd. Adventures With Life: An Autobiography of a Distinguished Negro Citizen. Boston: Meador Publishing Company, 1945.

Fee, John G. Autobiography. Chicago: National Christian Association, 1891.

Floyd, Silas Xavier. A Sketch of Rev. C. T. Walker, D. D. Augusta, Ga.: Sentinal Publishing Company, 1892.

_____. Life of Charles T. Walker, D. D. Nashville: National Baptist Publishing Board, 1902.

Forman, James. Sammy Younge, Jr. The First Black College Student to Die in the Black Liberation Movement. New York, N. Y.: Grove, 1968.

"From Louisiana--President J. S. Clark." Negro History Bulletin, 3 : 2 (November, 1939), 32.

Gavins, Raymond. "Gordon Hancock: An Appraisal." New South, 25 (Fall, 1970), 36-43. [Seneca Junior College and Virginia Union Univ.]

Gibbs, Warmouth T. _President Matthew W. Dogan of Wiley College. A Biography_. Marshall, Texas: Wiley College, 1940.

_____. "Hiram Revels and His Times." _Quarterly Review of Higher Education Among Negroes_, 8 (January, 1940), 25-37.

Guzman, Jessie P. "Monroe Nathan Work and His Contributions." _Journal of Negro History_, 34 (October, 1949), 428-461.

Hamilton, Virginia. _W. E. B. Du Bois: A Biography_. New York: Thomas Y. Crowell, 1972.

Hand, Daniel. _A Sketch of the Life of Daniel Hand, and of His Benefaction to the American Missionary Association for the Education of the Colored People in the Southern States of America_. New York: The Association, 1889.

"Hardy Liston--1889-1956; President Johnson C. Smith University--1947-1956." _Quarterly Review of Higher Education Among Negroes_, 24 (October, 1956), 170-171.

Hastie, William H. "Charles Hamilton Houston." _Negro History Bulletin_, 13 (June, 1950), 207-213.

Hathaway, Isaac Scott. "Isaac Scott Hathaway Artist and Teacher." _Negro History Bulletin_, 21 (January, 1958), 74, 78-81.

Haynes, Elizabeth Ross. _The Black Boy of Atlanta. Life of Richard Robert Wright, 1885-1947_. Boston: House of Edinboro, 1952.

Herrick, Genevieve Forbes. "Queen Mary: Champion of Negro Women." [Bethune] _Negro Digest_, 9 (December, 1950), 32-39.

Hill, Jane. "Fannie Jackson Coppin." _Negro History Bulletin_, 5 (December, 1941), 66-67.

"Hiram Revels." _Negro History Bulletin_, 1 (February, 1938), 6.

Holly, Joseph Winthrop. _You Can't Build a Chimney From the Top: The South Through the Life of a Negro Educator_. New York: William-Frederick Press, 1948.

Holmes, Eugene C. "Alain LeRoy Locke: A Sketch." _Phylon_, 20 (1st Quarter, 1959), 82-89.

Holt, Rackham. _George Washington Carver: An American Biography_. Garden City, N. Y.: Doubleday and Company, Inc., 1946.

_____. _Mary McLeod Bethune, A Biography_. Garden City, N. Y.: Doubleday and Company, 1964.

_____. The Wizard of Tuskegee, George Washington Carver: An American Biography. New York: Doubleday, Dorn and Company, 1943.

Holtzclaw, William Henry. The Black Man's Burden. New York: Neale Publishing Company, 1915.

Holtzclaw, W. H. "A Negro's Life Story." World's Work, 12 (September, 1906), 7989-7993.

Hopkins, Alphonso A. The Life of Clinton Bowen Fisk. New York: Funk and Wagnalls, 1890.

Howard, Oliver Otis. Autobiography. 2 Vols. New York: Baker and Taylor Company, 1907.

Howe, S. H. A Brief Memoir of the Life of John F. Slater. Slater Fund Occasional Papers, Number 2. Charlottesville, Va.: The Fund, 1894.

Hudson, Charles F. "Life of Dr. James E. Shepard." [Durham, N.C.] Morning Herald, April 14, 1940.

Hughes, William Hardin, and Patterson, Frederick D., eds. Robert Russa Moton of Hampton and Tuskegee. Chapel Hill: University of North Carolina Press, 1956.

James, Milton. "M. Leslie Pinckney Hill." Negro History Bulletin, 24 : 6 (1961), 135-138.

"John Mercer Langston." Negro History Bulletin, 5 (January, 1942), 93. Ibid., 1 : 3 (December, 1937), 5.

Johnson, James Weldon, 1871-1938. Along This Way: The Autobiography of James Weldon Johnson. New York: Viking Press, 1933, and 1938. [Reprinted, New York: Penguin Books, 1941; New York: Compass Book - Viking Press, 1968.]

Johnston, J. H. "Luther Porter Jackson, 1892-1950." Negro History Bulletin, 13 : 9 (June, 1950), 195-197.

"Joseph Charles Price." Negro History Bulletin, 1 : 5 (February, 1938), 6. Ibid., (February, 1942), 110.

Karpman, Ben. "Earnest Everett Just, A Reprint." Phylon, 4 (2nd Quarter, 1943), 159-163.

Lacy, Leslie. The Life of W. E. B. Du Bois: Cheer the Lonesome Traveler. New York: The Dial Press, 1970.

Lane, Isaac, 1834-1937. Autobiography of Bishop Isaac Lane, L.L.D.; With a Short History of the C. M. E. Church in America and of Methodism. Nashville: M. E. Church South, 1916.

Langston, John Mercer, 1829-1897. From the Virginia Plantation to the National Capitol; Or the First and Only

Negro Representative in Congress From the Old Dominion. Hartford, Conn.: American Publishing Co., 1894. [Reprinted New York: Arno Press; Bergman Pub.; Kraus Reprint Co. 1969.]

Lillie, Frank R. "Earnest Everett Just." Science, 95 (January 2, 1942), 10.

Locke, Zelma G. "The Geni of Tuskegee." [George W. Carver] Negro Digest, 9 (May, 1951), 85-89.

Logan, Rayford W. W. E. B. Du Bois: A Profile. New York: Hill and Wang, 1971.

Lynk, Miles Vandahurst. Sixty Years of Medicine; Or, the Life and Times of Dr. Miles V. Lynk: An Autobiography. Memphis: Twentieth Century Press, 1951. [Univ. of West Tenn. and Meharry.]

McFeely, William S. Yankee Stepfather: General O. O. Howard and the Freedmen. New Haven: Yale University Press, 1968.

McGill, Ralph. "W. E. B. Du Bois." Atlantic, 216 (November, 1965), 78-81.

McKenzie, L. L. "Byrd Prillerman." Negro History Bulletin, 5 : 4 (January, 1942), 94-95.

McKinney, T. E. "Ferdinand D. Bluford, President of A. & T. College." Quarterly Review of Higher Education Among Negroes, 24 (January, 1956), 39.

McKinney, Theophilus Elisha, 1899- . Higher Education Among Negroes: Addresses Delivered in Celebration of the Twenty-fifth Anniversary of the Presidency of Dr. Henry Lawrence McCrory of Johnson C. Smith University. Charlotte, North Carolina: Johnson C. Smith University, 1932.

_____. "David Dallas Jones, President of Bennett College." Quarterly Review of Higher Education Among Negroes, 24 (January, 1956), 39-40.

McKinney, Theophilus Elisha. "In Memoriam: Henry Lawrence McCrory, 1863-1951." Quarterly Review of Higher Education Among Negroes, 19 (October, 1951), 171-173.

Maloney, Arnold Hamilton. Amber Gold: An Adventure in Autobiography. Boston: Meador Publishing Co., 1946. [Howard Univ.] [Lincoln U., Penna.]

"Man With a Mission--Mordecai Wyatt Johnson." Negro History Bulletin, 20 (November, 1956), 26, 37-38.

Marshall, Albert P. "Winston-Salem Teachers College and Its President." Wilberforce Quarterly, 3 (April, 1942), 44-46.

"Mary McLeod Bethune." Journal of Negro History, 40 (October, 1955), 393-395.

Mason, H. J. "M. W. Dogan, Pioneer in Education." The Oracle, 19 (June, 1940), 52-53.

Mathews, Basil Booker T. Washington: Educator and Interracial Interpreter. Cambridge: Harvard University Press, 1948.

Mays, Benjamin E. Born to Rebel: An Autobiography. New York: Charles Scribner's Sons, 1971.

Merritt, R. H. From Captivity to Fame--The Life of George Washington Carver. Boston: Meador Publishing Company, 1936.

Molohon, Bernard. "The Quiet Leader." [Ambrose Caliver] Negro Digest, 12 (April, 1963), 33-38.

Moreland, Marc. "Samuel Howard Archer: Portrait of a Teacher." Phylon, 10 (4th Quarter, 1949), 351-355.

Moss, W. Wade. "The Wizard of Tuskegee." Opportunity, 14 (December, 1936), 362-365, 382.

Moton, Robert Russa. "A Negro's Uphill Climb." World's Work, 13 (April, 1907), 8739-8743. Ibid., 14 (May, 1907), 8915-8918; 14 (August, 1907), 9198-9201.

Moton, Robert Russa. Finding a Way Out; An Autobiography. Garden City, N. Y.: Doubleday, Page, 1920.

Nabrit, S. Milton. "Phylon Profile, VIII: Earnest E. Just." Phylon, 9 (3rd Quarter, 1946), 121-125.

"Negro Leader." [William Pickens] Wilson Library Bulletin, 28 (June, 1954), 828.

Nelson, B. H. "Dr. William H. Crogman." Negro History Bulletin, 5 : 6 (March, 1942), 130, 142.

Nettleton, Tully. "Fisk's First Negro President." [Charles S. Johnson] Negro Digest, 7 (May, 1949), 32-34.

"New Boss for Fisk." [Charles Spurgeon Johnson] Our World, 3 (March, 1948), 10-17.

Oak, Vishnu V. "Dr. W. E. B. Du Bois at 72." Wilberforce University Quarterly, 1 (October, 1940), 18-22.

O'Connor, Ellen M., ed. Myrtilla Miner, A Memoir. Boston: Houghton Mifflin and Company, 1885.

O'Connor, John. "Dr. Charles Richard Drew: Pioneer in Blood Plasma." Interracial Review, 22 (March, 1949), 37-40.

Ogden, Robert C. In Memory of Robert Curtis Ogden. Winston-Salem, N. C.: Privately Printed by H. E. Fries, 1916.

Ogden, Robert C. Samuel Chapman Armstrong. A Sketch. New York: Fleming H. Revell Company, 1894.

_____. A Life Well Lived. Hampton, Va.: Hampton Institute, 1914.

Parker, Franklin. George Peabody: A Biography. Nashville: Vanderbilt University Press, 1956, 1971.

Parker, John W. "Benjamin Brawley and the American Cultural Tradition." Phylon, 16 (2nd Quarter, 1955), 183-194.

_____. "Phylon Profile 19: Benjamin Brawley-Teacher and Scholar." Phylon, 10 (1st Quarter, 1949), 15-24.

Parker, John W. "Benjamin Brawley." Crisis, 46 (May, 1939), 144.

Payne, Daniel A. Recollections of Seventy Years. Nashville: Publishing House of the A. M. E. Sunday School Union, 1888.

Peare, Catherine Owens. Mary [Jane] McLeod Bethune. New York: Vanguard Press, Inc., 1951.

Pickens, William, 1881-1954. The Heir of Slaves: An Autobiography. Boston: Pilgrim Press, 1911.

_____. Bursting Bonds, an Autobiography. Boston: Jordan and Mare Press, 1923. [Talladega College]

"Pickens, William." Journal of Negro History, 39 (July, 1954), 242-244.

Ponton, M. M. Life and Times of Henry M. Turner. Atlanta: A. B. Caldwell Publishing Company, n. d.

Porter, Dorothy. "Phylon Profile, XIV: Edward Christopher Williams." Phylon, 8 (4th Quarter, 1947), 315-321.

Reddick, L. D. "As I Remember Woodson." Crisis, 60 (February, 1953), 75-80.

_____. "Carter G. Woodson (1875-1950) An Appreciation." Phylon, 11 (2nd Quarter, 1950), 177-179.

Reid, Ira De A. "Three Negro Teachers." Phylon, 2 (2nd Quarter, 1941), 137-143.

Riley, Benjamin Franklin. The Life and Times of Booker T. Washington. New York: Fleming H. Revell Company, 1916.

Savage, Horace C. *Life and Times of Bishop Isaac Lane*. Nashville: National Publishing Company, 1958.

Savage, W. Sherman. "Lincoln University Dedicates Library to Memory of Inman Page--Pioneer Educator." *New Dawn*, 3 (January, 1951), 11-12.

Scott, C. Waldo. "Biography of a Surgeon." [Charles Drew] *Crisis*, 58 (October, 1951), 501-506, 555.

Scott, Emmett Jay, and Stowe, Layman Beecher. *Booker T. Washington: Builder of a Civilization*. Garden City, N. Y.: Doubleday, Page, 1916.

Shaw, G. S. *John Chavis, 1763-1838*. Binghamton, N. Y.: Vail Ballou Press, Inc., 1931.

Shea, John Gilmary. *The Life and Times of the Most Rev. John Carroll*. Philadelphia: John J. McVey, 1888.

Sheeler, J. Reuben. "The Nabrit Family." *Negro History Bulletin*, 20 (October, 1956), 3-9.

Sheeler, J. Reuben. "James Madison Nabrit." *Negro History Bulletin*, 24 (January, 1961), 75-76.

_____. "George Washington Trenholm." *Negro History Bulletin*, 9 (October, 1945), 17-20.

Sherer, Robert G., Jr. "John Williams Beverly: Alabama's First Negro Historian." *The Alabama Review*, 26 : 3 (July, 1973), 194-208.

Simmons, William J. *Men of Mark*. Cleveland: G. M. Revell and Company, 1887.

Singleton, George Arnett, 1896-1970. *The Autobiography of George A. Singleton*. Boston: Forum Publishing Co., 1964. [Paul Quinn, Shorter, Morris Brown.]

Spellman, C. L. *Rough Steps on My Stairway, the Life History of a Negro Educator*. New York: Exposition Press, 1953.

Starks, John Jacob, 1876-1944. *Lo These Many Years: An Autobiographical Sketch*. Columbia, S. C.: State Co., 1941. [Morehouse College, Seneca Institute and Benedict College.]

Starushenko, G. B., et al., eds. *William Du Bois: Scholar, Humanitarian, Freedom Fighter*. Moscow, Novasti Press Agency Publishing House, 1971.

St. Clair, Sadie Daniel. "Myrtilla Miner: Pioneer in Teacher Education for Negro Women." *Journal of Negro History*, 34 (January, 1949), 30-45.

Sterne, Emma (Gelders). Mary McLeod Bethune. New York: Knopf, 1957.

_____. His Was the Voice: The Life of W. E. B. Du Bois. New York: Crowell-Collier Press, 1971.

Stewart, D. "Dr. Carver and the South's New Deal." Southern Workman, 63 : 2 (September, 1934), 259-264.

Still, James. Early Recollections and Life of Dr. Still. Philadelphia: J. B. Lippincott and Company, 1877.

Stokes, Anson Phelps. A Brief Biography of Booker Washington. Hampton: Hampton Institute Press, 1936.

Strange, Douglas C. "Bishop Daniel A. Payne and the Lutheran Church." Lutheran Quarterly, 16 : 4 (1964), 354-359.

Talbot, Edith A. Samuel Chapman Armstrong: A Biographical Study. New York: Doubleday, Page and Company, 1901. [1904]

"Taylor, Alrutheus Ambush." Journal of Negro History, 39 (July, 1954), 240-242.

Terrell, Mary Eliza Church, 1863-1954. A Colored Woman in a White World. Washington: Ransdell, 1940. [Wilberforce]

"The Passing of Alain Le Roy Locke." Phylon, 15 (3rd Quarter, 1954), 243-252.

Thomas, Jessie O. My Story in Black and White...Autobiography. New York: Exposition Press, 1967. [Voorhees]

Thompson, Aretha. "Mary Bethune." Digest and Story, 6 (November-December, 1948), 10-13.

Thorpe, Earl E. "Frederick Douglass, W. E. B. Du Bois and Booker T. Washington." Negro History Bulletin, 20 (November, 1956), 39-42.

_____. "William Hooper Councill." Negro History Bulletin, 19 (January, 1956), 85-86, 89.

"Thurgood Marshall." Negro History Bulletin, 19 (November, 1955), 26, 39.

Torrence, R. The Story of John Hope. New York: Macmillan Company, 1948.

Towns, George A. "Phylon Profile, 16: Horace Bumstead, Atlanta University President, 1888-1907." Phylon, 9 (2nd Quarter, 1948), 109-114.

Troy, Robert. "W. E. B. Du Bois in Retrospect." New South, 25 (Fall, 1970), 27-35.

Turner, Bridges Alfred. From a Plow to a Doctorate--So What! Hampton, Va.: The Author, 1945. [Hampton]

Ulansky, Gene. "The Integrated Careers of Alain Locke, Philosopher of the New Negro." Negro History Bulletin, 26 (May, 1963), 241-243.

Walls, William Jacob. Joseph Charles Price, Educator and Race Leader. Boston: The Christopher Publishing House, 1943.

Ware, Edward Twitchell. "Sketch of the Life of Edmund Asa Ware." MS., Atlanta University Library.

Washington, Booker T. The Story of My Life and Work: An Autobiography. Naperville, Illinois: J. L. Nichols and Company, 1900. [Ibid., Atlanta, Ga.: 1901.]

_____. Up From Slavery: An Autobiography. Garden City, N. Y.: Doubleday, Page and Company, 1900. [1947]

_____. Working With the Hands: Being a Sequel to "Up From Slavery" Covering the Author's Experiences in Industrial Training at Tuskegee. New York: Doubleday, Page and Company, 1904.

Wayman, Alexander W. The Life of Rev. James Alexander Shorter. Baltimore: J. Lanahen, 1890.

Weisenburger, Francis P. "William Sanders Scarborough: Scholarship, The Negro, Religion, and Politics. Ohio History, 72 (January, 1963), 25-50.

Wesley, Charles H. "Carter G. Woodson--As a Scholar." Journal of Negro History, 36 (January, 1951), 12-24.

_____. "W. E. B. Du Bois: The Historian." Journal of Negro History, 50 (July, 1965), 147-162.

Wilkerson, Doxey A. "W. E. B. Du Bois: In Battle for Peace." Masses and Mainstream, 5 (October, 1952), 34-43.

"William Hooper Councill." Negro History Bulletin, 5 : 6 (March, 1942), 134, 143.

"William J. Simmons." Negro History Bulletin, 5 : 4 (January, 1942), 91-92.

Williams, Rose Berthenia Clay. Black and White Orange: An Autobiography. New York: Vantage Press, 1961. [FAMC]

Woodson, Carter G. "Thomas Jesse Jones." Journal of Negro History, 35 (January, 1950), 107-109.

_____. "The Record of the Clements." Negro History Bulletin, 9 (June, 1946), 197-200.

Wright, Clarence W. "Negro Pioneers in Chemistry." School and Society, 65 (February 1, 1947), 86-88.

Wright, Richard Robert J., 1878-1967. Years Behind the Black Curtain: An Autobiography. Philadelphia: Rare Book Co., 1965. [Wilberforce]

PROCEEDINGS

American Baptist Home Mission Society. Baptist Home Missions in North America, Including a Full Report of the Proceedings and Addresses of the Jubilee Meeting, and a Historical Sketch of the American Baptist Home Mission Society, 1832-1882. New York: Baptist Home Mission Society, 1883.

Armstrong, S. C. "Normal School Work Among the Freedmen." Journal of Proceedings and Addresses of the National Educational Association, Boston, Massachusetts, 1872, 12 : 174-181.

Association of Colleges and Secondary Schools for Negroes. Annual Proceedings. 1933-1953. On File, Executive Secretary's Office, Concord, North Carolina.

Atwood, R. B. "The Cooperative Negro College Study." Proceedings of the Annual Conference of Presidents of Negro Land Grant Colleges, Nov. 11, 12, 13, 1941. Wabash Ave., Y. M. C. A., Chicago, Ill. pp. 57-60.

Banks, H. R. "Some Persistent Problems in the Negro Land Grant College Complex of Significance to the Cooperative Extension Service." Proceedings of the Nineteenth Annual Conference of Presidents of Negro Land Grant Colleges, Nov. 11, 12, 13, 1941. Wabash Ave., Y. M. C. A., Chicago, Ill., pp. 38-42.

Beitell, A. D. "Knocking at the Door," A Plea for Negro Membership Before the Southern Association of Colleges and Secondary Schools, Houston, Texas, 1949. Proceedings of the Southern Association of Colleges and Secondary Schools, 1949.

Bryan, E. A. "The Spirit of Land-Grant Institutions." Proceedings of the Forty-Fifth Congress of Land-Grant Colleges and Universities, 1931, pp. 91-93.

[Corson, Oscar Taylor.] "Booker T. Washington--An Appreciation." National Education Association of the United States. Journal of Proceedings and Addresses, 1916, pp. 983-988.

Daniel, V. E. "Some Implications of the Problem of Graduate Studies in Colleges for Negroes." Proceedings of National Association of Collegiate Deans and Registrars in Negro Schools. 1930, pp. 21-26.

Davis, John W. "The Most Important Contribution of the

Negro Land-Grant Colleges." _Proceedings of the 41st Annual Convention of Land-Grant Colleges and Universities_, pp. 35-38.

Du Bois, W. E. B., ed. _Report of the First Conference of Negro Land-Grant Colleges for Co-ordinating a Program of Cooperative Social Studies_. Atlanta University Publication No. 22, Atlanta, Ga., 1943.

Du Bois, W. E. B. "A Program for Negro Land-Grant Colleges." _Proceedings 19th Annual Conference. Presidents of Negro Land Grant Colleges_. November, 1941. Chicago, 1941, pp. 42-57.

Favrot, Leo M. "Negro Education in the South, an Abstract." _Addresses and Proceedings of the National Education Association_. LVIII, 1920, pp. 291-296.

Fisher, Isaac. "Ten Years of the Conference of Presidents of Negro Land-Grant College 1923-1933." _Proceeding of the Annual Conferences of the Presidents of Negro Land-Grant College for 1932-33 and 1935-38_.

Johnson, Campbell C. "Implications of Selective Service Facts to Leaders in the Field of Education." _Proceedings of the Nineteenth Annual Conference of the Presidents of Negro Land-Grant Colleges, Nov. 11, 12, 13, 1941_. Wabash Ave., Y. M. C. A., Chicago, Ill., pp. 16-22.

Jordan, Mildred N. "Significant Services Which College Departments of Home Economics May Render in College Operations," in _Conference of Presidents of Negro Land-Grant Colleges 1955_, No. 9.

Kerr, W. J. "The Spirit of Land-Grant Institutions." _Proceedings of the 45th Annual Convention of the Association of Land-Grant Colleges and Universities_, 1931, pp. 98-104.

McPheeters, A. A. "Transition in Higher Education." _Proceedings of the National Association of Collegiate Deans and Registrars_, 1952.

Peabody Education Fund. _Proceedings of the Trustees_. 6 Vols. Boston: John Wilson and Son, 1916.

Peabody Fund. _Proceedings of the Trustees of the Peabody Education Fund_, 1867-1874. Boston: Press of John Wilson and Son, 1875.

Proceedings of the Tenth Annual Convention of the Conference of Presidents of Negro Land Grant Colleges, Whitelaw Hotel, Washington, D. C., November 14-15, 1932.

Proceedings of the Thirteenth Annual Conference of the Presidents of Negro Land Grant Colleges, Washington, D. C., November 18-20, 1935.

Proceedings of the Fourteenth Annual Conference of the Presidents of Negro Land Grant Colleges, Petersburg, Virginia, November 10-11, 1936.

Proceedings of the Fifteenth Annual Conference of the Presidents of Negro Land Grant Colleges, Howard University, Washington, D. C., November 15, 16, 17, 1937.

Proceedings of the Sixteenth Annual Conference of the Presidents of Negro Land Grant Colleges, University of Chicago, International House, Chicago, Illinois, November 14, 15, 16, 1938.

Proceedings of the Seventeenth Annual Conference of the Presidents of Negro Land Grant Colleges, Howard University, Washington, D. C., November 13, 14, 15, 1939.

Proceedings of the Eighteenth Annual Conference of the Presidents of Negro Land Grant Colleges, Metropolitan Community Center, Chicago, Illinois, November 12, 13, 14, 1940.

Proceedings of the Nineteenth Annual Conference of the Presidents of Negro Land Grant Colleges, Wabash Avenue, Y. M. C. A., Chicago, Illinois, November 11, 12, 13, 1941.

Proceedings of the Twenty-Second Annual Conference of the Presidents of Negro Land Grant Colleges, Wabash Avenue, Y. M. C. A., Chicago, Illinois, October 24-26, 1944.

Proceedings of the Twenty-Third Annual Conference of the Presidents of Negro Land Grant Colleges, Wabash Avenue, Y. M. C. A., Chicago, Illinois, October 23-25, 1945.

Proceedings and Reports of the John F. Slater Fund, 1882-1936. New York: John F. Slater Fund.

Report of the Proceedings of the Conference of Presidents of Negro Land Grant Colleges, Held at the Wabash Avenue Branch of the Y. M. C. A., Chicago, Illinois, November 13-15, 1933.

Rogers, Lydie Jetton. "Some Facts and Figures About Home Economics in Land-Grant Colleges," in *Conference of Presidents of Negro Land-Grant Colleges*, 1955, (No. 9).

Thompson, Charles H. "Improvement of the Negro College Faculty." *Proceedings-Conference of Presidents of Negro Land-Grant Colleges, 24th Annual Session*, 1946.

REPORTS

"A Task Force Report: Special Needs of Traditionally Negro Colleges." Institute for Higher Education Opportunity, Southern Regional Education Board, Atlanta, Georgia, 1969.

Agricultural College Land Script: Letters of S. C. Armstrong and R. W. Hughes, in Behalf of the Hampton Normal and Agricultural Institute at Hampton, Virginia. Richmond: State Journal Printing House, 1870.

Bacon, Alice M. "The Negro and the Atlanta Exposition," in _Slater Fund Occasional Papers_, No. 7. Baltimore, 1896.

Bayer, Alan E., and Boruch, Robert F. _The Black Student in American Colleges_. Washington, D. C.: American Council on Education, 1969.

Bi-Racial Commission of Texas. _Report Recommending Establishment of a University for Negroes_. Submitted to Governor Coke Stevenson, December 17, 1946. On File, Texas State Library, Austin.

Boulware, Marcus Hanna. _Jive and Slang of Students in Negro Colleges_. Hampton, Va., 1947, 8 p.

Bumstead, Horace. _Secondary and Higher Education in the South for Whites and Negroes_. Publication of the National Association for the Advancement of Colored People. No. 2, 1910.

Campbell, Robert F. "Negro Colleges Have a Job." _Southern Education Report_, November, 1967.

Commission on Colleges. _Black Colleges in the South_, Atlanta, Ga.: Southern Association of Colleges and Schools, 1971.

Commission on Higher Educational Opportunity in the South. _The Negro and Higher Education in the South_. August, 1967. Southern Regional Education Board, 130 Sixth Street, N.W., Atlanta, Georgia 30313.

Congressional Land Script, Hampton Normal and Agricultural Institute: Letters of R. W. Hughes, a Trustee, and Gen. S. C. Armstrong, Superintendent of the Hampton Institute. Richmond: B. W. Gillis, Printer, 1872.

Cross, Addie F. _Faculty Publications_ [Hampton Institute] Hampton, Va.: Hampton Library, 1959.

Curry, J. L. M. _Education of the Negroes Since 1860_. Trustees of the John F. Slater Fund, Occasional Paper No. 3. Baltimore: Trustees of the John F. Slater Fund, 1894. 32 pp.

Curry, J. L. M. "Difficulties, Complications, and Limitations Connected With the Education of the Negro," in _Slater Fund Occasional Papers_, No. 5. Baltimore, 1895.

Dillard University. "Preliminary Report the Dillard University Self Study Project. Prepared by the Dillard Self-Study Committee. September 8, 1953. Joseph T. Taylor (Chairman - Dillard's Self-Study Committee).

Directory of Negro Colleges and Universities, March, 1967. Plans for Progress, 1800 G Street, N.W.: Washington, D. C. 20006.

Directory of Predominantly Negro Colleges and Universities in the United States of America (Four-Year Institutions Only). January, 1969. Plans for Progress, 1800 G Street, N.W., Suite 703, Washington, D. C. 20006.

Du Bois, W. E. B. "Careers Open to College Bred Negroes." _Pamphlet_, Nashville, Tennessee: Fisk University Press, 1898.

Du Bois, W. E. B. "The Significance of Henry Hunt," in _Founder's and Annual Report Number_, Fort Valley State College Bulletin, October, 1940.

Expanding Opportunities. Case Studies of Interinstitutional Cooperation, 1969. Atlanta, Ga.: Southern Regional Education Board, 1969 [Cooperation between and among Negro colleges and/or white colleges in the South.]

Flexner, Abraham. "Medical Education in the United States and Canada." (Carnegie Foundation for the Advancement of Teaching, Bulletin no. 4), New York, 1910.

Galloway, Oscar F. _Higher Education for Negroes in Kentucky_. Bulletin of the Bureau of School Service, 5 : 1 (September, 1932). University of Kentucky, 1932.

Gannett, Henry. "Statistics of the Negroes in the United States," in _Slater Fund Occasional Papers_, No. 4. Baltimore, 1894.

General Education Board. _Annual Report of the General Education Board_, 1914-1936. New York: General Education Board, 1936.

General Education Board. _The General Education Board, An Account of its Activities, 1902-1914_. New York: General Education Board, 1915.

Gurin, Patricia, and Katz, Herman. _Motivation and Aspiration in the Negro College_. Project No. 5-0787. Contract No. OE4-10-095. Ann Arbor: Survey Research Center, Institute for Social Research, University of Michigan, November, 1966.

Haygood, Atticus G. _The Case of the Negro as to Education in the Southern States_. Report to the Board of Trustees of the John F. Slater Fund. Atlanta: Jas. P. Harrison & Company, 1885.

Holmes, William T. _Tougaloo College in Mississippi for Colored Youth_. Mississippi Department of Archives and History, Jackson, Mississippi. n.p. n.d. [Charter of Tougaloo College].

Howard University, Washington, D. C. The Inauguration of J. Stanley Durkee, A. M., Ph.D., as President of Howard University, November 12, 1912, and the Readjustment and Reconstruction Congress, November 13, 1919. Washington, D. C.

Howard University, Washington, D. C. Catalogue of the Officers and Students, 1868-69. Washington, Judd & Detweiler, 1869.

Howe, Harold, II. The Negro American and Higher Education. December 3, 1968. 17 pp. ERIC No. ED 026 036

Husan, Carolyn F., and Schiltz, Michael E. College, Color, and Employment: Racial Differentials in Post Graduate Employment Among 1964 Graduates of Louisiana Colleges. Report No. 116. Chicago: National Opinion Research Center, University of Chicago, July, 1966.

Institute for Higher Educational Opportunity. Special Financial Need of Traditionally Negro Colleges. A Task Force Report. Atlanta, Ga.: Southern Regional Education Board, 1969.

John F. Slater Fund Occasional Papers, Number 1 thru 27 and 29, in Atlanta University Library, Black Culture Collection. Microfilm Roll #376. See Nos. 7, 13, 16, 17, 20, 21, 22.

Joint Committee of the National Education Association and the American Teachers Association. Study of the Status of the Education of Negroes. Montgomery, Alabama: American Teachers Association, 1954.

Jones, Lewis E. The Influence of Student Demonstrations on Southern Negro Colleges: Part II--Crises on the Campus. A Report from the Department of Race Relations of Fisk University to the Field Foundation, Inc. 79 pp.

Lawrence, C. Howard, ed. Black Consciousness and Higher Education, 1968. The Church Society for College Work, 2 Brewer Street, Cambridge, Mass. 02138.

_____. Graduate Education for the "Disadvantaged" and Black-Oriented University Graduates. Washington, D. C.: Council of Graduate Schools in the United States. December 18, 1968. 15 pp. ERIC No. ED 026 022

Littig, Lawrence W. A Study of Certain Personality Correlates of Occupational Aspiration of Negro and White College Students. Final Report. Washington, D. C.: Howard University, ERIC No. ED 022 419

Marshall, A. P. Compiler. A Bibliography of Faculty Members, 1951. Occasional Publication No. 5. Lincoln University of Missouri. Jefferson City, Missouri, 1951.

Mobberley, David G., and Wicke, Myron F. The Deanship of the Liberal Arts College. Nashville, Tennessee: Board of Higher Education, The United Methodist Church, 1962.

Montgomery, T. S. The Senior Colleges for Negroes in Texas. A Study made at the direction of the Bi-Racial Conference on Education for Negroes in Texas. Huntsville, Texas: 1944. 95 pp.

Nabrit, Samuel, and Scott, Julius, Jr. Inventory of Academic Leadership. Atlanta: The Southern Fellowship Fund, 1970.

North Carolina. Study of Institutions of Higher Learning for Negroes. Raleigh, Department of Public Instruction, 1931.

Office for Advancement of Public Negro Colleges. Public Negro Colleges. A Fact Book. July, 1969. Office for Advancement of Public Negro Colleges of the National Association of State Universities and Land-Grant Colleges, 805 Peachtree Street, N.E. Suite 577, Atlanta, GA 30308.

Phelps-Stokes Fund. Jones, Thomas Jesse, ed. Educational Adaptations, Report of Ten Years' Work of the Phelps-Stokes Fund, 1910-1920. New York: Phelps-Stokes Fund, 1920.

Phelps-Stokes Fund. Twenty Year Report, 1911-1931. New York: Phelps-Stokes Fund, 1932. 127 pp.

_____. Negro Status and Race Relations in the United States, Thirty-Five Year Report, 1911-1946. New York: Phelps-Stokes Fund, 1948. 219 pp.

Price, J. St. Clair. Improving the Academic Performance of Negro Students. Washington, D. C.: Research Committee, Association of Colleges and Secondary Schools, 1959.

"Report on Negro Universities and Colleges," in Slater Fund Occasional Papers, No. 21. Baltimore, 1922.

"Report of President Hopkins, of Williams College, Mass., Mr. Hyde, of the Board of Agriculture, Mass., Secretary Northrup, of the Board of Education, Conn., and General Garfield, M.C., upon the Hampton Normal and Agricultural Institute." Reprinted from the American Missionary of August, 1869.

Report and Recommendations of the Commission to Study the Question of Negro Higher Education to the Governor, the Legislative Council, and the General Assembly of Maryland. Baltimore: The Commission, 1950.

Schomburg, Arthur Alfonso. Racial Integrity, A Plea for the Establishment of a Chair of Negro History in Our Schools and Colleges. Yonkers, N. Y.: Negro Society for Historical

Research, Occasional Paper No. 3. August Valentine Bernier, Printer and Publisher, July, 1913. [Source AU, BCC - Roll #382]

Smith, Lucius. The Status of Marking in Negro Colleges. Bluefield, W. Va.: Bluefield State Teachers College, 1935.

Southern Association of Colleges and Secondary Schools. (List of Approved Colleges and Secondary Schools for Negro Youth, 1938-39), North Carolina State Department of Public Instruction, Raleigh, North Carolina, [1939].

Southern Education Foundation. Biennial Reports. 1937-1956.

State of Kansas "Report of the Senate Committee Making a Study and Survey of Conditions at the Industrial Department, Western University, Kansas City, Kansas, 1935.

Task Force on Higher Education. "Black Methodists for Church Renewal." Position Paper, July 25, 1969.

Task Force Report. Special Financial Needs of Traditionally Negro Colleges, Atlanta: Institute for Higher Educational Opportunity, Southern Regional Education Board, 1968.

Texas Legislative Council. Higher Education for Negroes in Texas. Staff Monograph, Texas Legislative Council. Austin: April, 1951. 77 pp.

_____. Public Higher Education in Texas. Staff Research Report, Texas Legislative Council. Austin: November, 1950. xii 178 pp.

The Administration of Admissions and Financial Aid in the United Negro College Fund Colleges. New York, N. Y.: College Entrance Examination Board, 1969.

The Student Protest Movement: A Recapitulation, Atlanta: The Southern Regional Council, September 29, 1961.

Thompson, Charles Henry, 1896- . Revision of the Twenty-Year Plan With Special Reference to the College of Liberal Arts. Washington, D. C.: Howard University, February 20, 1939.

Truman, B. C. "Report to the President, April 9, 1866." Documentary History of Reconstruction: Political, Military, Social, Religious, Educational and Industrial, 1865 to the Present Time, Walter L. Fleming, editor. Cleveland: Arthur H. Clark Company, 1906.

Tuskegee Institute. Publications of the Faculty at Tuskegee Institute, 1953-1959. Tuskegee, Ala.: Frissell Library, 1960.

Tuskegee Normal and Industrial Institute. Opinions of educators regarding the Tuskegee normal and industrial school . . . From members of the Department of Superintendence. Tuskegee Institute press, 1911. 47 p.

West Virginia State College. Publications of the Faculty and Staff of West Virginia State College. West Virginia State College [Library] 1960.

Williams, W. T. B. Report on Negro Universities in the South. New Orleans: Tulane University Press, 1913. 16 p.

UNITED STATES GOVERNMENT PUBLICATIONS

U. S. Department of Agriculture. A History of Agricultural Education in the United States 1875-1925, Publication No. 36. Washington, D. C.: U. S. Government Printing Office, 1929.

U. S. Bureau of the Census. "Characteristics of Students and Their Colleges, October, 1966." Current Population Reports, Series P-20 No. 183. May 22, 1969. Washington, D. C.: Government Printing Office, 1969.

United States Federal Board for Vocational Education. A Study of Home Economics Education in Teacher-Training Institutions for Negroes. Bulletin No. 79. Home Economics Series No. 7. Washington, D. C.: U. S. Government Printing Office, 1923.

_____. Vocational Education in Agriculture for Negroes: Recommendations for the Establishment of Agricultural Schools and Programs for Negroes. Washington, D. C.: U. S. Government Printing Office, 1926.

_____. Project and Other Supervised Practical Work at the Agricultural and Mechanical Colleges, by H. O. Sargent. Mimeographed. U. S. Federal Board for Vocational Education, 1929.

_____. Report of Progress in Vocational Education in Agriculture in Negro Schools of the South for the Year 1928-1929. Circular Misc. 1078. Washington, D. C.: U. S. Government Printing Office, 1929.

U. S. Public Health Service. Graduates of Predominantly Negro Colleges, Class of 1964. By Joseph H. Fichter. Publication No. 1571. Washington, D. C.: U. S. Government Printing Office, 1967.

Report of the United States Commissioner of Education for 1902. "The Work of Certain Northern Churches in the Education of the Freedmen, 1861-1900," by A. D. Mayo. Washington, D. C.: U. S. Government Printing Office, 1903.

Report of the United States Commissioner of Education for 1895. "Higher Education of the Negro," by Samuel C. Mitchell. 2 Vols. Washington, D. C.: U. S. Government Printing Office, 1896. Ibid., "The Slater Fund and the Education of the Negro," Vol. 5, Part 2. pp. 1367-1424.

Report of the United States Commissioner of Education for 1901. "The Education of the Negro," by Kelly Miller. Vol. 1. Washington, D. C.: U. S. Government Printing Office, 1903. Ibid., "Laws Relating to Land-Grant Colleges," Vol. 1. Chapter 3, pp. 195-198.

Report of the United States Commissioner of Education, 1894-1895. Vol. II. "Education of the Negro Since 1860," by J. L. M. Curry. Washington, D. C.: U. S. Government Printing Office, 1894-1895. Ibid., "Difficulties, Complications and Limitations Connected With Education of the Negro," pp. 1367-1374.

U. S. Department of the Interior. Annual Report of the Department of the Interior. Annual Report of the Secretary of the Interior for the Fiscal Year Ending June 30, 1890. Vol. 5, Part 2. "Education of the Colored Race." Washington, D. C.: U. S. Government Printing Office, 1893. pp. 1073-1102.

_____. Report of the Commissioner of Education for the Year, 1890-1891. Vol. 2. "Education of the Colored Race." Washington: Government Printing Office, 1894. pp. 961-980.

_____. U. S. Bureau of Education. Report of the Commissioner of Education for the Year, 1891-1892. Vol. 2. "Education of the Colored Race." Washington: Government Printing Office, 1894. pp. 861-872.

_____. Report of the Commissioner of Education for the Year, 1892-1893. Vol. 2. "The Education of the Negro - Its Character and Facilities." Washington: Government Printing Office, 1895. pp. 1551-1572.

_____. The U. S. Bureau of Education. Report of the Commissioner of Education for the Year 1893-1894. Vol. 1. "Education of the Colored Race." Washington: Government Printing Office, 1896. pp. 1019-1037. Ibid., "Bibliography of the Colored Race." pp. 1038-1061.

Annual Reports of the Department of the Interior. Bureau of Education. Report of the Secretary of the Interior for the Fiscal Year Ending June 30, 1887. Vol. 4. "Education of the Colored Race." Washington: Government Printing Office, 1889. pp. 988-998.

_____. U. S. Bureau of Education. Report of the Commissioner of Education for 1887-1888. "Education of the Colored Race." Washington: Government Printing Office, 1889. pp. 988-998.

______. U. S. Bureau of Education. Report of the Commissioner of Education for the Year, 1888-1889. Vol. 2. "Education of the Colored Race." Washington: Government Printing Office, 1891. pp. 1412-1425.

______. Report of the Commissioner of Education for the Year, 1894-1895. Vol. 2. "Education of the Colored Race." Washington: Government Printing Office, 1896. pp. 1331-1366. Ibid., "The Slater Fund and the Education of the Negro." pp. 1367-1423.

______. Report of the Commissioner of Education for the Year, 1895-1896. Vol. 2. "Education of the Colored Race." Washington: Government Printing Office, 1897. pp. 2081-2115.

______. Annual Reports of the Department of the Interior for the Fiscal Year Ended June 30, 1897. Report of the Commissioner of Education. Vol. 2. "Education of the Colored Race." Washington: Government Printing Office, 1898. pp. 2295-2333.

______. The U. S. Bureau of Education. Report of the Commissioner of Education for the Year 1897-1898. Vol. 2, Part 2. "Education of the Colored Race." Washington: Government Printing Office, 1899. pp. 2479-2507.

______. The U. S. Bureau of Education. Annual Reports of the Department of the Interior for the Fiscal Year Ended June 30, 1899. Report of the Commissioner of Education. Vol. 1. "Address of President McKinley at the Tuskegee Normal and Industrial Institute, December 8, 1898." Washington: Government Printing Office, 1900. pp. 514-516. Ibid., "The Future of the Colored Race," by A. D. Mayo, Address Delivered Before the Agricultural and Mechanical College for Negroes, at Normal, Ala., May 29, 1899. pp. 1227-1246.

______. The U. S. Bureau of Education. Annual Reports of the Department of Interior for the Fiscal Year Ended June 30, 1899. Report of the Commissioner of Education. Vol. 2. "Education of the Colored Race." Washington: Government Printing Office, 1900. pp. 2201-2231.

______. The U. S. Bureau of Education. Report of the Commissioner of Education for the Year, 1899-1900. Vol. 2. "Education of the Colored Race." Washington: Government Printing Office, 1901. pp. 2501-2530. Ibid., "Plea for Higher Education of the Negro." pp. 1420-1421. [Fisk University]

______. The U. S. Bureau of Education. Report of the Commissioner of Education for the Year 1900-1901. Vol. 2. "Education of the Colored Race." Washington: Government Printing Office, 1902. pp. 2299-2331.

______. The U. S. Bureau of Education. Report of the Commissioner of Education for the Year, 1902. Vol. 2. "Education of the Colored Race." Washington: Government Printing Office, 1903. pp. 2063-2095.

______. The U. S. Bureau of Education. Report of the Commissioner of Education for the Year 1903. Vol. 2. "Schools for the Colored Race." Washington: Government Printing Office, 1905. pp. 2253-2285.

______. United States Bureau of Education. Report of the Commissioner of Education for the Year, 1902. Vol. 1. "College-Bred Negro." Washington: Government Printing Office, 1903. pp. 191-229.

______. Bureau of Education. Report of the Commissioner of Education for the Year Ending June 30, 1904. Vol. 2. "Schools for the Colored Race." Washington: Government Printing Office, 1906. pp. 2175-2207.

______. Bureau of Education. Report of the Commissioner of Education for the Year Ended June 30, 1914. Vol. 2. "Statistics of Schools for Negroes." Washington: Government Printing Office, 1915. pp. 491-503.

______. Bureau of Education. Report of the Commissioner of Education for the Year Ended June 30, 1916. Vol. 2. "Statistics of Schools for Negroes." Washington: Government Printing Office, 1917. pp. 585-600.

______. Bureau of Education. Report of the Commissioner of Education for the Year Ended June 30, 1917. Vol. 2. "Statistics of Schools for Negroes." Washington: Government Printing Office, 1927. pp. 611-624.

U. S. Department of the Interior. U. S. Bureau of Education. Agricultural and Mechanical Colleges, 1915-1916, by Benjamin F. Andrews. Washington, D. C.: U. S. Government Printing Office, 1917.

______. The Land-Grant Colleges in Relation to the National Development. Bulletin II. No. 3. Washington, D. C.: U. S. Government Printing Office, 1924.

______. Statistics of Land-Grant Colleges. Bulletin No. 34. Washington, D. C.: U. S. Government Printing Office, 1923.

______. Statistics of Land-Grant Colleges. Bulletin No. 6. Washington, D. C.: U. S. Government Printing Office, 1924.

______. Statistics of Land-Grant Colleges. Bulletin No. 26. 1925. Washington, D. C.: U. S. Government Printing Office, 1926.

______. Land-Grant Colleges. Bulletin No. 44. 1925. Washington, D. C.: U. S. Government Printing Office, 1926.

______. Land-Grant College Education 1910-1920. Bulletin No. 37. Washington, D. C.: U. S. Government Printing Office, 1921.

_____. Statistics of Land-Grant Colleges. Bulletin No. 34. Washington, D. C.: U. S. Government Printing Office, 1921.

_____. Statistics of Land-Grant Colleges. Bulletin No. 6. Washington, D. C.: U. S. Government Printing Office, 1922.

_____. Statistics of Land-Grant Colleges. Bulletin No. 19. Washington, D. C.: U. S. Government Printing Office, 1923.

_____. Statistics of Land-Grant Colleges. Bulletin No. 26. Washington, D. C.: U. S. Government Printing Office, 1924.

_____. Land-Grant Colleges for the Year Ended June 30, 1926. Bulletin No. 37. 1927. Washington, D. C.: U. S. Government Printing Office, 1927.

_____. Land-Grant Colleges and Universities. Bulletin No. 13. Washington, D. C.: U. S. Government Printing Office, 1929.

_____. Land-Grant Colleges and Universities. Bulletin No. 28. Washington, D. C.: U. S. Government Printing Office, 1930.

_____. The Land-Grant College Education. Bulletin No. 30. Washington, D. C.: U. S. Government Printing Office, 1934.

_____. Land-Grant College Education 1910 to 1920. Bulletin, 1925. No. 4. Part III. Washington, D. C.: U. S. Government Printing Office, 1925.

_____. Agricultural and Mechanical Colleges Including Statistics for 1917-1918. Bulletin, 1920. No. 8. Washington, D. C.: U. S. Government Printing Office, 1920.

_____. Philanthropy in the History of American Higher Education. Bulletin No. 26. Washington, D. C.: U. S. Government Printing Office, 1922.

_____. Survey of Negro Colleges and Universities. Bulletin, 1928. No. 7. Washington, D. C.: U. S. Government Printing Office, 1929.

_____. Federal Legislation and Administration Pertaining to Land-Grant Colleges. Bulletin, 1924. No. 20. Washington, D. C.: U. S. Government Printing Office, 1924.

_____. Biennial Survey of Education, 1926-1928. Bulletin No. 16. 1930. Washington, D. C.: U. S. Government Printing Office, 1930.

_____. Biennial Survey of Education, 1928-1930. Bulletin No. 20. 1931. Washington, D. C.: U. S. Government Printing Office, 1931.

_____. Biennial Survey of Education, 1930-1932. Bulletin No. 2. 1933. Washington, D. C.: U. S. Government Printing Office, 1933.

_____. History of Public School Education in Alabama. Bulletin, 1915. No. 12. Whole No. 637. Washington, D. C.: U. S. Government Printing Office, 1915.

_____. Negro Education. A Study of the Private and Higher Schools for Colored People in the United States. Prepared in Cooperation With the Phelps-Stokes Fund. Bulletin, 1916. No. 39. 2 Vols. Washington, D. C.: U. S. Government Printing Office, 1917. [Reprinted in one Volume, New York: Arno Press, 1969.]

_____. Recent Progress in Negro Education. Bulletin, 1919. No. 27. Washington, D. C.: U. S. Government Printing Office, 1919.

_____. A Survey of Agricultural Education in Land-Grant Colleges. Bulletin, 1925. No. 4. Washington, D. C.: U. S. Government Printing Office, 1925.

_____. Statistics of Teachers of the Negro Race. Bulletin 1927-1928. No. 14. Washington, D. C.: U. S. Government Printing Office, 1930.

_____. The Georgia State Industrial College. Report of a Survey, June 15, 1923. Washington, D. C.: U. S. Government Printing Office, 1923.

_____. Statistics of Education of the Negro Race. Bulletin, 1928. No. 19. Washington, D. C.: U. S. Government Printing Office, 1928.

_____. Professional Distribution of College and University Graduates. Bulletin 1912. No. 19. Washington, D. C.: U. S. Government Printing Office, 1912.

_____. Statistics of the Education of Negroes 1935-1936. Bulletin No. 13. Washington, D. C.: U. S. Government Printing Office, 1938.

_____. Biennial Survey of Education in the United States, 1920-1930. Bulletin No. 20. Washington, D. C.: U. S. Government Printing Office, 1931.

_____. National Survey of the Education of Teachers. Bulletin 1933. No. 10. 4 Vols. Washington, D. C.: U. S. Government Printing Office, 1933.

_____. History of Negro Education. Bulletin I. No. 38. Washington, D. C.: U. S. Government Printing Office, 1916.

_____. Educational Boards and Foundations, 1920-1922. Bulletin 1922, No. 38. Washington, D. C.: U. S. Government Printing Office, 1922.

_____. Education in Georgia. Circular of Information 1888, No. 4. Washington, D. C.: U. S. Government Printing Office, 1889.

_____. Survey of Negro Colleges and Universities. Bulletin, No. 7. 1926. Washington, D. C.: U. S. Government Printing Office, 1926.

_____. Survey of Negro Colleges and Universities. Bulletin, 1928. No. 7. Washington, D. C.: U. S. Government Printing Office, 1929.

_____. History of Education in Maryland. Circular No. 2. Washington, D. C.: U. S. Government Printing Office, 1894.

_____. Statistics of Teachers Colleges and Normal Schools. Bulletin, 1929. No. 14. Washington, D. C.: U. S. Government Printing Office, 1929.

_____. History of Education in Texas, by J. J. Lane. Contributions to American Educational History, edited by H. B. Adams. Circular No. 2. 1903. Washington, D. C.: U. S. Government Printing Office, 1903.

_____. History of Higher Education in Kentucky, by Alvan F. Lewis. Washington, D. C.: U. S. Government Printing Office, 1889.

_____. History of Education in Mississippi, by Edward Mayes. Washington, D. C.: U. S. Government Printing Office, 1899.

_____. Southern Women in the Recent Educational Movement in the South. Circular of Information, No. 1. 1891. Washington, D. C.: U. S. Government Printing Office, 1892.

_____. History of Higher Education in South Carolina. Circular of Information 1888, No. 3. Washington, D. C.: U. S. Government Printing Office, 1889.

_____. The Land-Grant Colleges and Educational Values. Bulletin, 1924. No. 30. Washington, D. C.: U. S. Government Printing Office, 1924.

_____. History of Education in Delaware, by Lyman P. Powell. Washington, D. C.: U. S. Government Printing Office, 1893.

_____. Industrial Education. Bulletin, 1925, No. 37. Washington, D. C.: U. S. Government Printing Office, 1926.

_____. The History of Education in North Carolina, by

Charles L. Smith. Circular of Information, 1888. No. 2. Washington, D. C.: U. S. Government Printing Office, 1888.

_____. _Higher Education in Missouri_, by Marshall S. Snow. Washington, D. C.: U. S. Government Printing Office, 1898.

_____. _History of Higher Education in South Carolina_, by Merriwether Colyer. Washington, D. C.: U. S. Government Printing Office, 1889.

U. S. Department of the Interior. U. S. Office of Education. _Statistics of Education of the Negro Race, 1925-1926_. Bulletin, 1928, No. 19. Washington, D. C.: U. S. Government Printing Office, 1928.

_____. _Statistics of the Negro Race, 1927-1928_. Pamphlet No. 14. Washington, D. C.: U. S. Government Printing Office, 1930.

_____. _Statistics of the Education of Negroes, 1929-1930 and 1931-1932_. Bulletin, 1935, No. 13. Washington, D. C.: U. S. Government Printing Office, 1936.

_____. _Statistics of the Education of Negroes_. Bulletin, 1938, No. 13. Washington, D. C.: U. S. Government Printing Office, 1939.

_____. _A Background Study of Negro College Students_. Bulletin, 1933, No. 8. Washington, D. C.: U. S. Government Printing Office, 1933.

_____. _Fundamentals in the Education of Negroes_. Bulletin, 1935, No. 6. Washington, D. C.: U. S. Government Printing Office, 1935.

_____. _Federal Grants for Education_. Leaflet No. 45. Washington, D. C.: U. S. Government Printing Office, 1935.

_____. _Digest of Federal Subsidies for Education_. Bulletin, No. 9. Washington, D. C.: U. S. Government Printing Office, 1930.

_____. _Educational Boards and Foundations_. Bulletin, 1931, No. 20. Washington, D. C.: U. S. Government Printing Office, 1931.

_____. _Federal Laws, Regulations and Rulings Affecting Land-Grant Colleges of Agriculture and Mechanic Arts_. Washington, D. C.: U. S. Government Printing Office, 1911, 1916.

_____. _Land-Grant Colleges and Universities_. Bulletin, 1928, No. 14. Washington, D. C.: U. S. Government Printing Office, 1928.

_____. Land-Grant Colleges and Universities. Bulletin, 1932, No. 21. Washington, D. C.: U. S. Government Printing Office, 1932.

_____. Preliminary Report Land-Grant Colleges and Universities. Circular No. 136. Washington, D. C.: U. S. Government Printing Office, 1934.

_____. Survey of Land-Grant Colleges and Universities. Bulletin No. 9. 1930. Vol. 2, Part I. Washington, D. C.: U. S. Government Printing Office, 1930.

_____. Survey of Land-Grant Colleges and Universities. Bulletin 1930, No. 9. Washington, D. C.: U. S. Government Printing Office, 1930.

_____. Federal Aid to Public Schools. Bulletin, 1922. No. 47. Washington, D. C.: U. S. Government Printing Office, 1923.

_____. Education of Certain Racial Groups in the United States and Its Territories. Bulletin, 1931. No. 20. Vol. 1. Chapter 17. Washington, D. C.: U. S. Government Printing Office, 1931.

_____. National Survey of Higher Education of Negroes. Miscellany Bulletin No. 6. 4 Vols. Vol. 1. Corinnie Brown, "Socio-Economic Approach to Educational Problems." Vol. 2. General Studies of Colleges for Negroes. Vol. 3. Lloyd Black and Martin D. Jenkins, "Intensive Study of Selected Colleges for Negroes." Vol. 4. Ambrose Caliver, "Summary." Washington, D. C.: U. S. Government Printing Office, 1942, 1943.

_____. Education of Negro Leaders. Bulletin, 1948. No. 3. Washington, D. C.: U. S. Government Printing Office, 1948.

_____. Freedmen's Aid Societies. Bulletin 1916, No. 38. Washington, D. C.: U. S. Government Printing Office, 1916.

_____. Statistics of the Education of Negroes. Circular 215. Washington, D. C.: U. S. Government Printing Office 1943.

_____. Bibliography of Research Studies in Education, 1933-1934, Bulletin 1935, No. 5. By Ruth A. Gray. Washington, D. C.: U. S. Government Printing Office, 1935.

_____. Bibliography of Research Studies in Education, 1934-1935, Bulletin 1936, No. 5. By Ruth A. Gray. Washington, D. C.: U. S. Government Printing Office, 1936.

_____. Bibliography of Research Studies in Education, 1935-1936, Bulletin 1937, No. 6. By Ruth A. Gray. Washington, D. C.: U. S. Government Printing Office, 1937.

_____. Bibliography of Research Studies in Education, 1936-1937. Bulletin, 1938, No. 5. By Ruth A. Gray. Washington, D. C.: U. S. Government Printing Office, 1938.

_____. Bibliography of Research Studies in Education, 1937-1938. Bulletin, 1939, No. 5. By Ruth A. Gray. Washington, D. C.: U. S. Government Printing Office, 1940.

_____. Education of Negroes A 5-Year Bibliography. Bulletin 1937, No. 8. By Ambrose Caliver. Washington, D. C.: U. S. Government Printing Office, 1937.

U. S. Federal Security Agency. U. S. Office of Education. Statistics of Land-Grant Colleges and Universities Year Ended June 30, 1948. Bulletin 1949, No. 8. Washington, D. C.: U. S. Government Printing Office, 1949.

_____. Statistics of Land-Grant Colleges and Universities Year Ended June 30, 1949. Bulletin 1950, No. 11. Washington, D. C.: U. S. Government Printing Office, 1950.

_____. Statistics of Land-Grant Colleges and Universities Year Ended June 30, 1947. Bulletin 1948, No. 8. Washington, D. C.: U. S. Government Printing Office, 1948.

_____. Special Problems of Negro Education. Advisory Committee on Education, Staff Study No. 12. Washington, D. C.: U. S. Government Printing Office, 1939.

_____. Statistics of Land-Grant Colleges and Universities. Bulletin No. 14. Washington, D. C.: U. S. Government Printing Office, 1946.

_____. Premedical Education for Negroes; Interpretations and Recommendations Based on a Survey in Fifteen Selected Negro Colleges. Washington, D. C.: U. S. Government Printing Office, 1949.

_____. U. S. Office of Education. Bibliography of Research Studies in the United States, 1939-1940. Bulletin 1941, No. 5. By Ruth A. Gray. Washington, D. C.: U. S. Government Printing Office, 1941.

_____. Bibliography of Research Studies in the United States 1938-1939. Bulletin, 1940, No. 5. By Ruth A. Gray. Washington, D. C.: U. S. Government Printing Office, 1940.

U. S. Department of Health, Education and Welfare. Office of Education. National Survey of the Higher Education of Negroes. Misc. No. 6. Washington, D. C.: U. S. Government Printing Office, 1942.

U. S. Department of Labor. Directory of 1965-1966 Graduates From Predominantly Negro Colleges, 2nd ed. Washington, D. C.: U. S. Government Printing Office, 1966.

United States Supreme Court. "Sweatt vs. Painter, et al." _Supreme Court Reports_ CCCXXXIX, October Term 1949, February 20-June 5, 1950. Washington, D. C.: U. S. Government Printing Office, 1950.

_____. _Memorandum for the United States as Amicus Curiae_, Filed in the Case of Sweatt vs. Painter, et al., by Philip B. Perlman, Solicitor General. February, 1950. Washington, D. C.: U. S. Government Printing Office, 1950.

INDEX

About the Compiler

Frederick Chambers, associate professor of secondary education at Kent State University, Kent, Ohio, specializes in the principles and methods of secondary education. He has had an article published in *Journal of Negro History.*